Canada's Greatest Wartime Muddle
National Selective Service and the Mobilization of Human
Resources during World War II

In this exhaustively researched and carefully documented account, Michael Stevenson argues that National Selective Service (NSS) – the agency responsible for controlling the nation's military and civilian mobilization apparatus – failed in its attempts to regulate Canadian society. He challenges traditional views that Prime Minister Mackenzie King handled the conscription issue by creating a comprehensive, centralized, and efficient human resource mobilization strategy, carefully supervised by government bureaucrats in Ottawa. Stevenson argues instead that a fractured, decentralized, and widely unpopular mobilization program often prevented NSS officials from channelling eligible men into Canada's system of compulsory training for home defence or allocating workers to essential industrial jobs.

To determine the government's commitment to a comprehensive mobilization strategy, Stevenson considers the effect of NSS policies on eight significant sectors of the Canadian population: Native Canadians, university students, war industry workers, coal miners, longshoremen, meatpackers, hospital nurses, and textile workers. These case studies show that mobilization officials achieved only a limited number of their regulatory goals and that Ottawa's attempt to organize and allocate the nation's military and civilian human resources on a rational, orderly, and efficient scale was largely ineffective.

This detailed assessment of the effect of NSS activities on a broad cross-section of Canadian society provides a new perspective on the domestic impact of the Second World War and will appeal to a wide range of readers interested in Canada's economic, military, social, and political history.

MICHAEL D. STEVENSON is a researcher at the Department of Foreign Affairs and International Trade.

Canada's Greatest Wartime Muddle

National Selective Service and the Mobilization of Human Resources during World War II

MICHAEL D. STEVENSON

McGill-Queen's University Press
Montreal & Kingston · London · Ithaca

ISBN 0-7735-2263-8

Legal deposit fourth quarter 2001
Bibliothèque nationale du Québec

Printed in Canada on acid-free paper

This book has been published with the help of a grant
from the Humanities and Social Sciences Federation of
Canada, using funds provided by the Social Sciences
and Humanities Research Council of Canada.

McGill-Queen's University Press acknowledges the
financial support of the Government of Canada
through the Book Publishing Industry Development
Program (BPIDP) for its activities. It also acknowledges
the support of the Canada Council for the Arts for its
publishing program.

**National Library of Canada Cataloguing
in Publication Data**

Stevenson, Michael D., 1967–
   Canada's greatest wartime muddle: National Selective
   Service and the mobilization of human resources during
   World War II
   Includes bibliographical references and index.
   ISBN 0-7735-2263-8
   1. Canada. National Selective Service. 2. Industrial
   mobilization – Canada – History – 20th century.
   3. Draft – Canada. 4. World War, 1939–1945 –
   Manpower – Canada. I. Title.
   FC582.5.S73 2001   940.53'71   C2001-901353-1
   F1034.S73 2001

Typeset in Sabon 10/12
by Caractéra inc., Quebec City

Contents

Tables and Figure

Abbreviations

APC   Army Port Company
CCL   Canadian Congress of Labour
CDA   Central Despatching Agency
CHC   Canadian Hospital Council
CLSC   Coal Labour Survey Committee
CLS   Coal Labour Survey
CNA   Canadian Nurses Association
COTC   Canadian Officers Training Corps
CVT   Canadian Vocational Training
DCC   Dominion Coal Company
DMR   Department of Mines and Resources
DMS   Department of Munitions and Supply
DND   Department of National Defence
DNWS   Department of National War Services
DPNH   Department of Pensions and National Health
DVA   Department of Veterans Affairs
ECPB   Emergency Coal Production Board
HLA   Halifax Longshoremen's Association
ICLC   Inter-departmental Committee on Labour Coordination
IDCCM   Industrial Development Council of Canadian Meat Packers
ILPC   Inter-departmental Labour Priorities Committee
IMSC   Industrial Mobilization Survey Committee
IMSP   Industrial Mobilization Survey Plan
ISRB   Industrial Selection and Release Board
ISRC   Industrial Selection and Release Committee

ISRP   Industrial Selection and Release Plan
LSIC   Labour Supply Investigation Committee
NA   National Archives of Canada
NCCU   National Conference of Canadian Universities
NLSC   National Labour Supply Council
NRMA   National Resources Mobilization Act
NSS   National Selective Service
NWLB   National War Labour Board
PTI   Primary Textiles Institute
TLC   Trades and Labour Congress
UIC   Unemployment Insurance Commission
UMWA   United Mineworkers of America
WBTP   Wartime Bureau of Technical Personnel
WPTB   Wartime Prices and Trade Board

Acknowledgments

This work could not have been undertaken without the assistance of many individuals and organizations. I am truly indebted to Peter Neary for his unwavering support of my research during the past ten years, particularly in his capacity as my dissertation supervisor at the University of Western Ontario. Jim Struthers offered constructive commentaries on successive drafts of this manuscript. Although they bear no responsibility for any errors or omissions, the following individuals are among those who have provided advice and support: Terry Copp, Greg Donaghy, Ben Forster, Erich Hahn, Roger Hall, Margaret Kellow, Jean Matthews, Jon Parmenter, and Jen Read. Anonymous referees from McGill-Queen's University Press and the Aid to Scholarly Publications Program provided searching and helpful critiques of this manuscript. At McGill-Queen's University Press, Philip Cercone skilfully shepherded this work through the lengthy evaluation process, while Brenda Prince and Joan McGilvray were instrumental in taking care of the many administrative tasks involved in seeing it through to publication. My copy editor, Bruce Henry, has greatly improved the clarity and style of this book.

Research funding for this book was provided by the Social Sciences and Humanities Research Council of Canada and the University of Western Ontario.

This book was written under some unusual circumstances. Through all of them, my family has remained supportive. My mother and father have consistently encouraged me to pursue all academic and occupational opportunities that have presented themselves to me. Most importantly, my wife, Robbie, has patiently endured the lengthy absences from home necessitated by my research and work schedules. It is to her that this book is dedicated.

Canada's Greatest Wartime Muddle

Introduction:
The Mobilization Debate

Historians have paid surprisingly little attention to the activities and programs inaugurated under the sweeping mandate of the National Selective Service (NSS). Almost nothing has been written about NSS and other agencies responsible for carrying out civilian and military mobilization policies, despite the prominence of the 1942 and 1944 conscription crises in Canadian historiography.[1] Accounts that refer in passing to NSS conclude that mobilization policies in Canada were comprehensive, centralized, coercive, and compulsory. For example, in their account of conscription in Canada, Granatstein and Hitsman conclude that the government "intervened massively" in the civilian labour market, controlled the lives of "virtually every man and women in the land," and regulated the Canadian workforce to an "unheard of degree." Granatstein and Neary's more recent survey of contemporary and scholarly accounts of Canada's role in World War II concludes that NSS policies in their "full elaboration" meant "regimentation on a scope and scale that Canadian workers had never known before and have never known since."[2]

However, assumptions concerning the comprehensive nature of Canada's civilian and military mobilization effort must be revised once NSS and other Department of Labour documents held in the National Archives of Canada are taken into account. They show that there was little coordination among government departments responsible for the various facets of Canada's war effort; NSS officials often found their concerns marginalized and ignored by other Cabinet ministers with more clout than their own. Far from adopting and implementing a sweeping mobilization agenda, NSS officials presided over a loose and localized administrative structure that largely ignored the technically comprehensive and coercive prescriptions of official government mobilization decrees. NSS confronted strong, organized, and effective opposition from the general population that derailed or diluted many mobilization initiatives in Canada during the Second World War. The wartime mobilization of human resources in Canada under the direction of NSS officials was characterized by gradualism, compromise, conciliation, and decentralization.

Critical Cabinet manpower debates occurred during 1941 and 1942. From the war's outset, Prime Minister Mackenzie King had been bedevilled by the spectre of the level of conscription that would be required to muster armed forces in numbers sufficient to fill the apparently insatiable maw of overseas service. Calamitous events in France during the spring of 1940 strengthened the case of proponents of an expanded Canadian military.[3] In September 1940, military officials submitted proposals for the 1941 army program. Under pressure from Minister of National Defence J.L. Ralston and British officials, the 1941 army program was approved by Cabinet on 28 January 1941. It committed three infantry divisions and one complete armoured division for European service. This did not satisfy demands for increased Canadian participation, however, and Ralston quickly called for the creation of a Canadian overseas army of at least five divisions, two of them armoured, and all necessary ancillary troops. Despite Mackenzie King's bitter opposition to further expansion, Cabinet approved this expanded army program on 6 January 1942. The manpower ceiling for the Canadian overseas army was eventually set at 234,500 troops. The requirements for the air force, the navy, and overseas and home defence army units were substantial and incessant.

After the fall of France, various government committees also identified impending civilian manpower shortages. The most important of these was the Labour Supply Investigation Committee (LSIC), created in the autumn of 1940 to recommend measures to increase the size of the civilian labour force while at the same time freeing eligible men for military service. The exhaustive LSIC report released in October 1941 decried the lack of a comprehensive human resource strategy and condemned the competition among government departments for manpower.[4] The LSIC estimated that 609,000 men were available for military service out of a total manpower pool of 2,124,000 men. To tap this pool, however, would require the widespread recruitment of women for industrial employment and the intensification of military recruitment efforts among industrial workers. The government acted on the LSIC report and in February 1942 announced a tentative plan for a selective service system that hinged on three proposals: agricultural workers would be frozen in their positions; technical workers would be closely managed for use in war industries, and men in specific age groups were to be denied permission to enter non-essential occupations. Spurred by the decision to call 5,000 men per month for home defence duties, Cabinet quickly approved the formation of NSS within the Department of Labour, largely following the proposals of the LSIC report.

Intense manpower debates took place within Cabinet during the summer and autumn of 1942. Industrial and financial concerns, represented by C.D. Howe of the Department of Munitions and Supply and J.L. Ilsley of the Department of Finance, lobbied vociferously against comprehensive and coercive manpower schemes that would drastically re-order Canadian industrial production. Howe, as he attempted to staff essential war industries in the face of increasingly onerous military manpower demands – clashed repeatedly with Ralston. On 11 July 1942, Howe informed Ralston that his department was "at its wit's end" trying to figure out how war-industry payrolls could be maintained, particularly in light of the decision to call single men up to forty years of age for compulsory military duty. Howe claimed that the current system of postponements for essential workers was "wholly inadequate" and that "drastic reductions" in the output of primary industries were inevitable.[5]

Howe's forceful arguments did nothing to alter the beliefs of Ralston, who headed a strong conscription-oriented group within Cabinet that lobbied hard for a large military machine even at the cost of draining manpower from a wide range of Canadian industries. Ralston was the architect of the Big Army scheme, and he firmly believed that the manpower barrel could be tapped for many more recruits. In a detailed memorandum prepared for Ralston in July 1942, Army officials suggested that the October 1941 LSIC estimates of the manpower pool could be revised sharply upwards. First, the LSIC had excluded 97,000 students of military age from consideration. Military planners estimated that 30,000 of these students could be steered into military service. Second, the LSIC report had omitted men from forty to forty-four years of age in its computations of potential military manpower, even though the maximum statutory age for enrolment in the military was forty-four years. Of the estimated 280,000 men in this age bracket, Ralston was informed that 98,000 could be made available for military service. Third, the number of men the LSIC had identified as indispensable to the war economy was open to "serious question" because the entry of the United States into the war against the Axis powers allowed American war industry to supply a greater share of essential goods to the Allies.

A "stricter proportional allocation" across all sectors of the civilian population would allow a minimum of 200,000 men to be added to the manpower stream.[6] In sum, Ralston believed that an additional 328,000 men could be found for military service.

Both Howe and Ralston were able to air their grievances at a special meeting of the Cabinet War Committee held on 17 July 1942 that was also attended by the Minister of Agriculture, Jimmy Gardiner; the Minister of National War Services; J.T. Thorson, the Minister of Labour, Humphrey Mitchell;[7] and the new NSS Director, Elliot Little.[8] Howe emphasized that war plants required 100,000 additional workers to simply maintain current levels of production. Gardiner insisted that no more workers could be stripped from agriculture since male employment in that sector had declined by 12 per cent during 1940 and 1941. Ralston and DND representatives on the War Committee maintained that all three service branches required almost 235,000 recruits prior to 31 March 1943. In Ralston's view, the time had come to drastically curtail non-essential production in the civilian economy to release men for the armed forces. Mitchell conceded that the labour market was drying up, and both he and Little supported the idea of curtailing civilian industry to augment the military manpower pool.

In the weeks following this meeting, government leaders attempted to break the stalemate over how manpower should be allocated by consolidating and streamlining the mobilization administrative structure. The Unemployment Insurance Commission was integrated into the Department of Labour and saw its personnel increased to handle the demands of carrying out NSS civilian mobilization decrees. Furthermore, in September 1942, Cabinet stripped responsibility for the administration of the conscription of men for home defence purposes from the Department of National War Services and transferred it to the Department of Labour. This centralization and consolidation of the administration of Canada's mobilization effort promised increased coordination of military and civilian human resource policies.

Despite these administrative changes, the manpower squeeze immediately became even more pronounced. On 17 September, Little shocked the Cabinet War Committee by announcing that fresh estimates of the potential manpower pool showed only 427,000 men available for military service. More than 200,000 men had disappeared from the reserve of manpower in the previous six months, and many men included in the revised estimate would be physically unsuitable for military service or would be required in essential positions in industry. DND officials continued to berate the inefficiency of the military recruitment system. Ralston produced new manpower estimates calling for almost 240,000 men and women to be inducted into the armed forces between 1 September 1942 and 30 April 1943. Howe submitted his own demands to the War Committee that called for employment in essential war industry to increase from 930,000 workers to 1,080,000 workers by the end of April 1943.[9] In sum, close to 50,000 men and women were required per month during an eight-month period just to maintain the war effort, a 100 per cent increase in the monthly intake forecasts submitted to Cabinet less than one year earlier.[10] Little insisted that the only avenue of escape from the looming manpower catastrophe centred on the massive reorganization of the Canadian industrial environment by curtailing non-essential industry. Cabinet instructed Little to confer with Donald Gordon, chairman of the Wartime Prices and Trade Board, and to formulate proposals to curtail non-essential industries and release men for military service. In August 1942, Mackenzie King had indicated publicly that he supported the curtailment or elimination of non-essential industries.[11] Little quickly tested the practical limits of King's public pronouncements.

At the Cabinet meeting on 23 September 1942, Little astounded many Cabinet members by submitting a draconian proposal that would establish himself as a manpower czar with virtually unchecked authority.[12] Little estimated that 27 per cent of the male labour force in non-essential civilian industries would have to be mobilized to meet a monthly need of almost 50,000 men and women in essential industry and the military. Little proposed four measures to meet this target. First, women needed to be moved *en masse* into industrial employment. Little suggested that firms be required by law to employ a certain percentage of women, and he proposed the expansion of day-care facilities and the compulsory billeting of rural women in urban areas to allow the female labour force to be expanded. Second, men needed to be moved from unproductive or marginal farms to more essential industrial work. Third, the widespread curtailment or outright closure of non-essential industries such as the retailing sector was necessary to allow close to 200,000 men to transfer to more essential jobs. Finally, the promotion of labour efficiency needed to be mandated though the adoption of measures including skill-dilution programs that would see a complex industrial task normally performed by a highly skilled worker broken down into several parts, each of which could be performed by a less experienced or semi-skilled worker. These initiatives, in Little's view, should be carried out under the supervision of a single government agency such as National Selective Service.

Gordon submitted his own report to the War Committee denouncing Little's mobilization scheme.[13] He claimed that only a direct draft could hope to obtain the required 50,000 men and women per month before the end of April 1943. This draft would need to be implemented with virtually no planning and its true impact would only be obvious after irreversible decisions for curtailment were enacted based on the "best guess" of Little. While not impossible, such a plan required a "total disregard" of the potential consequences and the acceptance by the general public of the immediate imposition of "iron rations." Gordon identified many problems with Little's plan, including widespread rationing of all civilian goods, degradation of the quality of civilian goods and services, the adverse impact on large export industries such as newsprint, and inequitable treatment of different firms within an industry that would see smaller firms shut down in favour of large firms located in the major urban centres across the nation. Gordon devoted few words to the development of an alternative plan, but he noted that the required number of men and women could be steered into their proper posts through a WPTB curtailment plan "on a more orderly basis if the pace during the first few months is more gradual and rapidly accelerated during the last few months." Gordon maintained that to fulfill recruitment goals for war industry and the military would require the "utmost ingenuity" of government planners.

In response to both presentations, C.D. Howe criticized curtailment schemes in any form. Curtailment plans would cripple many sectors of the economy and probably not provide immediate relief for essential war industries that were starving for workers. As an example, Howe brought the critical state of the steel industry to the attention of the War Committee. The country's six major steel plants needed more than 2,000 skilled workers. Steel production had declined by more than 15 per cent in recent months, despite a stepped up work-week that saw many workers remaining at their posts for fifty-six hours per week. Howe also attacked the system of deferments that forced men to enlist or enter home defence units once their deferment period expired. J.L. Ilsley noted that the proposal submitted by Little would require "arbitrary, unjust, and drastic decisions" to be taken that would be violently received by the Canadian public. Responding to Howe and Ilsley, Ralston noted that both proposals before the War Committee were, in effect, neither new nor radical and that their adoption would involve only an intensification of controls which had already been instituted. Ralston also vigorously opposed a suggestion offered by Mackenzie King on Howe's behalf that called for the temporary freezing of all men in essential industries to prevent their entry into the military through enlistment or the draft.[14] In the end Donald Gordon received the full support of influential Cabinet members, most notably the Prime Minister, who indicated that Little's "amazing document" advocating a revamped Selective Service scheme would, if implemented, create "chaos in the country." Claiming that Gordon made a "first-rate and sensible" presentation, King sanctioned a path that would dominate NSS mobilization policies for the duration of the war by noting that the "only sensible course was one of gradualness."[15]

After meeting to discuss the manpower problem once again on 29 September, Cabinet directed Little to provide the maximum number of men and women to essential war industry and the military but it refused to provide him with the necessary authority to carry out this nebulous decree. The key to NSS failure during the war was its subservient relationship to the WPTB. Donald Gordon ran an exceptionally business-friendly agency during his tenure at the helm of the Board. Industries were essentially self-regulating in their attempt to comply with limited WPTB production directives, and Gordon steadfastly refused to consider implementing even moderate curtailment schemes that would shut down non-essential civilian industries to allow manpower to be released for other purposes.[16] In a thorough 29 October 1942 memorandum, *Winnipeg Free Press* correspondent Grant Dexter provided a superb account of the prominence of the WPTB in determining the scope of mobilization policies and the corresponding impotence of NSS leaders:

I am surprised to discover that Little well knows that the manpower demands are ridiculous. He was dumbfounded when Cabinet said that the expansion program must stand approved and that he should go ahead – but without wrecking the economy. He has been back twice since then and got the same impossible advice on both occasions ... To this end the concentration of industry and the closing down of non-essential industry are being deliberately hamstrung. As the policy works out, the WPTB concentrates industry and shuts down the non-essential industry, and the manpower thus released flows inevitably into the channels controlled by NSS ... The vital control rests with the WPTB ... [T]he primary task of working out the problem on non-essentials and concentration rests with the industries themselves who are to bat schemes up to Gordon via the administrators. They were asked to go to work last August, but so far not one plan has materialized ... The position occupied by the WPTB is the key to Little's impossible situation ... He is, in fact, debarred. Thus the giving of concentration of industry and the elimination of non-essential industry to the WPTB is, in effect, a withdrawal of all this manpower from the area in which NSS can operate ... Little is left with just about nothing.[17]

Fundamental differences existed, therefore, between Little and the proponents of gradualism within the Cabinet. After two months of inaction, Little resigned his position on 16 November 1942. He then fired off a bitter letter to the *Financial Post* condemning the ineffectual handling of the human resource mobilization question. His exit did not prevent the debate concerning the curtailment of non-essential industries from continuing. WPTB and NSS officials haggled for months in an attempt to institute a modified curtailment scheme that would systematically reduce the use of non-essential human and material resources to the "minimum required for the health, efficiency, and morale of the nation."[18] While many ranking NSS officials felt that curtailment programs were "inevitable and imminent,"[19] no agreement could be reached between NSS and WPTB representatives.

Elliot Little's resignation allowed Associate Deputy Minister of Labour Arthur MacNamara to assume the mantle of NSS Director. Well respected by King and described by Grant Dexter as "easily the coolest-headed and most practical man" in Ottawa,[20] MacNamara left a remarkable imprint in a thirty-five-year civil service career. Entering the Manitoba Department of Labour as an inspector in 1916, he rose through the ranks to become Deputy Minister of Labour and Deputy Minister of Public Works in Manitoba by 1936. His experience dealing with unemployment relief in Manitoba caught the eye of the Dominion government, and Mackenzie King summoned him to Ottawa in 1940 to become chairman of the Dependent's Allowance Board within the Department of National Defence. MacNamara also served as acting chief commissioner of the Unemployment Insurance Commission after the passage of the Unemployment Insurance Act in 1940.

MacNamara proved to be the living embodiment of the concept of gradualness espoused by the King government in the autumn of 1942. Alternately termed the "Great Compromiser," the "Master Conciliator," and the "Man in the Asbestos Suit," MacNamara was an indefatigable negotiator. In 1950 the *Winnipeg Free Press* offered this account of his wartime career and policy outlook:

In [1942] he was named Director of NSS with virtually unlimited powers, which he contrived to use sparingly with characteristic emphasis on consultation and persuasion ... Basic to the MacNamara thinking is the idea that most strikes are unnecessary, that almost anything will yield to compromise, and that labour and management should be left alone to work out agreements – with a little prodding – because it is wrong and undemocratic for government to write labour contracts. Compromise, according to the situation, may be interpreted, and is interpreted, either as wisdom or appeasement.[21]

A strong belief in decentralization and regional authority augmented MacNamara's faith in compromise and conciliation. In the six months following Little's resignation, MacNamara guaranteed that no major initiatives would be undertaken to point NSS on the course advocated by Ralston and those NSS officials who favoured compulsory schemes.

In a May 1943 article, Grant Dexter chronicled the frustration of Major-General H.J. Riley, NSS Associate Director, in the face of MacNamara's refusal to pursue mobilization goals in a more vigorous fashion. According to Dexter, Riley had been turned into a figurehead for public relations purposes and believed that MacNamara was not equal to the task at hand. Four months later, Riley asserted that NSS was in a "state of collapse" under MacNamara's leadership.[22]

MacNamara's personal philosophy came to dominate the entire NSS administrative structure. NSS bureaucrats were drawn primarily from the Unemployment Insurance Commission and the labour movement. The Unemployment Insurance Act, as James Struthers documents, was rooted in the principle of less eligibility. While the Act represented a modest first step in the direction of a comprehensive insurance scheme, few UIC officials ardently supported sweeping regulatory measures. Allan Mitchell, Director of the Unemployment Insurance Commission and the Employment Service, gave a telling response in the summer of 1943 when pressed to allow a work permit policy to be further watered down. Mitchell did not protest that exemptions to established practice would produce chaotic results. Instead, he enthusiastically claimed that "half a loaf is better than no bread"[23] and authorized regulatory retreat. Similarly, many NSS officials recruited from the trade union movement were loath to endorse comprehensive schemes designed to impinge upon the freedom of workers. One of the most influential union recruits was M.M. Maclean, the Director of Industrial Relations within the Department of Labour. A former National Secretary of the Canadian Brotherhood of Railway Employees and an executive member of the Canadian Congress of Labour,[24] Maclean cultivated close ties with MacNamara and occupied a preferred place within the latter's circle of advisors.

The philosophy of MacNamara and senior NSS bureaucrats, therefore, hardly conforms to the traditional notion of committed centralizers and grand planners running much of Canada's mobilization program. According to Mackenzie King, NSS was charged with the "orderly and efficient" mobilization of the Canadian population "in direct furtherance of a total national war effort."[25] In practice, order and efficiency were two qualities manifestly lacking in the NSS administrative structure. MacNamara usually adopted a minimalist position in the daily administration and application of technically thorough and coercive NSS regulations and looked to his subordinates to follow his lead.

THE NATURE OF THIS STUDY

This study details and analyzes the Canadian mobilization structure in an attempt to reshape the historiographic debate about Canada's commitment to the war effort. Historical analysis of the manpower debate has been hampered by the use of a limited number of sources from the highest levels of the political process. Rather than providing another horizontal analysis of Cabinet records and government publications, this study is built on a vertical analysis of records extending from the Cabinet room to the local NSS employment offices.

This book has several aims. First, it will demonstrate that there was no effective coordination among government departments and agencies directly responsible for the efficient mobilization of human resources in Canada during the war. Large departments such as Finance, Munitions and Supply, and Defence, led by powerful and influential ministers, stood first in the manpower pecking order. The Department of Labour and NSS were more often than not left with the scraps from the Cabinet table. The emasculation of NSS at the hands of the WPTB in 1942 is the prime proof of the subservient status of the Department of Labour during the war. Denied the opportunity to manage the country's human resources in a comprehensive fashion from Day One of the agency's inception, NSS officials repeatedly found themselves under assault from all quarters for the remainder of the war. As a result, most NSS initiatives were purely defensive or reactionary and did not constitute the comprehensive, forward-thinking blueprint for managing Canada's manpower resources in a holistic fashion that the situation should have warranted. NSS officials had no influence over other government programs that had a direct bearing on human resource distribution. Restrictive wage control policies enacted by the King administration, for example, were developed with little appreciation for their impact on the distribution of the civilian workforce. Similarly, unrestricted voluntary enlistment in the armed forces – a cornerstone of Canada's war effort – wreaked havoc on NSS attempts to bring a sense of stability and order to the management of the country's human resource problems.

While interdepartmental politics often prevented NSS from implementing a coherent and inclusive manpower policy, Arthur MacNamara also proved myopic in the daily administration of internal NSS affairs over which he had direct and absolute control. Faced with critical labour shortages in virtually every sector of the workforce, MacNamara responded with fragmented and piecemeal initiatives that could never provide stable and long-term solutions to Canada's human resource woes. NSS officials consistently addressed the labour problems of each sector of the economy in isolation, with each sector usually treated as an airtight compartment that had no relation to the others. As a result, solutions for human resource problems in one industry often came at the expense of other industries.

The second goal of this work is to describe critically the administra- tive structure adopted by NSS during the war. In many respects, Mac- Namara's personal outlook was ideally matched to the administrative capacity of the Canadian state during World War II. Canada had a weak record of intervention in the labour market before 1939. Ottawa had not even attempted to control the civilian workforce in a thorough fashion between 1914 and 1918. The Employment Service of Canada created following World War I foundered on the shoals of federal- provincial jurisdictional disputes and starved on a meagre diet of public funding. The public works projects launched in the first years of the Depression were jettisoned by 1932. The relief camp experiment intro- duced in October 1932 ended dismally by 1935. The Dominion- Provincial Youth Training Program, established in 1937 to alleviate youth unemployment, was underfunded, largely ineffective, and admin- istered for the most part by provincial authorities. The Unemployment Insurance Act would not come into force until after the war began.[26]

Canadian officials, therefore, entered uncharted waters in their quest to bring a semblance of order to the Canadian mobilization effort between 1939 and 1945. As a result, effective control of the mobili- zation process often devolved to officials scattered across the country who interpreted NSS policy as they saw fit. This trait was most obvious in the administration of the home defence conscription provisions in effect from 1940 to 1945, but NSS officials charged with mobilizing the civilian labour force also frequently operated without strong guid- ance from senior NSS officials in Ottawa. Arthur MacNamara looked to non-governmental agencies and private organizations to regulate their own affairs and even to dictate the scope of NSS policy affecting a large percentage of the Canadian population. With one or two noticeable exceptions, NSS did not take advantage of the temporary creation of a unitary wartime state under the War Measures Act to impose a national human resource mobilization strategy on the nation. Instead, a decentralized and fragmented administrative structure guar- anteed that NSS would leave a dubious regulatory imprint.

The third aim of this study is to document the lax and permissive regulatory strategy adopted by mobilization administrators during the war. Many Cabinet decrees empowered Ottawa bureaucrats with vir- tually unlimited authority to mobilize the nation's human resources as they saw fit. On few occasions, however, was this authority pressed to full or even partial advantage. In 1943, for example, most Canadian men were legally frozen in their jobs and could not separate from employment without the permission of an NSS officer. In practice, however, these regulations were rarely enforced and tens of thousands of workers regularly migrated from one job to another in a search for the highest possible wage. Similarly, the establishment of a priority system that allowed key industries to lay first claim to scarce workers anchored NSS labour policy during the war. NSS administrators, however, often allowed the coveted highest priority rating to be granted to so many firms as to render the whole scheme unworkable. In sum, NSS refused to make difficult choices and adopt a firm position in the daily administration of its affairs to solve the chronic human resource shortages plaguing Canada during the war.

Finally, the fourth major aim of this book is to demonstrate that Canadians refused to accept unchecked government control of their lives during the war. One of the prime reasons for NSS impotence was the active opposition of individuals and organizations to many NSS mobilization decrees. Thousands of men eligible for compulsory military service avoided complying with mobilization regulations. Business leaders jealously guarded their payrolls from any NSS initiative that would strip them of employees. Canadian workers, conversely, railed against NSS attempts to stabilize essential industrial production by compelling key workers to remain in their posts. NSS policies were also viewed with suspicion and hostility by many sectors of Canadian society based on entrenched historical patterns of mistreatment. Workers in industries plagued with a poisonous history of labour relations were hardly inclined to suddenly march in lockstep with company and government officials who demanded strict obedience to restrictive government mobilization initiatives. Similarly, racial, religious, and linguistic minorities refused to abandon longstanding grievances with the federal government and actively opposed mobilization policies affecting them.

This book is organized into four general sections. First comes a legislative overview of military and civilian mobilization policies adopted by the Canadian government during the war. Canada's scheme for channelling eligible men into home defence units between 1940 and 1945 proved to be dominated by regional mobilization officials and marred by administrative problems that prevented large numbers of men from entering the military. Comprehensive measures to mobilize the civilian labour force were not enacted until 1942, but NSS officials proved unable to wield effective regulatory control over Canadian workers.

Next come three case studies dealing specifically with military mobilization.[27] The first case study chronicles the failed attempt to mobilize the Native Canadian population in an effective or uniform fashion. Faced with the daunting task of mobilizing a scattered Native population largely resistant to the idea of compulsory military service, Ottawa adopted a fractured and irregular regulatory stance that allowed regional mobilization officials to interpret mobilization decrees as they saw fit. In contrast to this, the second case study details the relatively successful attempt to mobilize Canadian university students. As the war progressed, an increasingly strict system of student deferments forced more men out of school and into the military while protecting a vital pool of technical, scientific, and professional students from the draft. The third case study highlights the most ambitious and comprehensive NSS military mobilization initiative. The Industrial Mobilization Survey Plan was designed to remove tens of thousands of eligible Canadian men from non-essential industrial positions and funnel them into military units. This scheme, however, also proved to be the most conspicuous failure of NSS, as bitter inter-departmental disputes and chronic administrative problems effectively destroyed any chance the survey plan could serve its original purpose.

The next four chapters are based on five cases in which NSS attempted to mobilize key sectors of the Canadian labour force. Two case studies deal with the bituminous coal industry in Nova Scotia and the longshore labour force on the Halifax docks. These two groups were subject to maximum and unique NSS regulatory control during the war through, among other strategies, repatriation of ex-coal miners and ex-longshoremen back into their original occupations in the mines or on the docks. These measures were not applied to any other industries across the nation, but the results achieved in these two sectors were markedly different. NSS efforts to stabilize employment and output in the Nova Scotia coal mines were completely ineffective due to the half-hearted application of mobilization decrees and the entrenched opposition of organized labour to government intervention. On the other hand, NSS efforts along the Halifax docks were remarkably successful and stand out as Ottawa's most effective mobilization initiative of the war. Combining tough legislative measures with a conciliatory labour strategy and innovative management policies, NSS completely re-organized the pattern of longshore labour that had prevailed in Halifax for decades and allowed the city to become the most important Canadian port during World War II.

The next three case studies examine NSS attempts to address labour shortages in the meatpacking industry and to funnel women into essential positions in the labour force. The meatpacking case study yields insight into the regulation of a largely seasonal labour force. Faced with massive increases in livestock production during the war, NSS waged a frantic, albeit successful, campaign that relied heavily on agricultural workers and farmers to work in slaughterhouses during the autumn and winter months. The chapter devoted to the employment of women during the war focuses on NSS attempts to provide primary textile firms with unskilled labour and hospitals with qualified nurses. In both instances, the refusal of NSS to adopt any form of compulsion of women or to address longstanding and festering problems of wages and working conditions guaranteed that chronic employment shortfalls would not be dealt with in a satisfactory fashion.

Finally, a concluding chapter recapitulates the key points developed in this study and situates this work within a broader historiographical framework. Evidence of the halting and ineffectual control of Canada's human resource mobilization effort during the war allows an important new perspective to be added to the existing historical material that focuses primarily on the political handling of the conscription problem between 1939 and 1945. This study complements a growing body of academic material that questions the notion that "Canada's War" was managed from Ottawa by a competent band of experts who moved from one success to another in the daily administration of the Canadian wartime unitary state.

In its entirety, therefore, this monograph provides the first complete account of human resource mobilization policies enacted in Canada during World War II. A comprehensive examination of NSS and related mobilization agencies extending beyond an analysis of Mackenzie King and other Cabinet officials provides a fresh and unique perspective on the Canadian war effort. NSS was intimately involved with large segments of the Canadian population, and an investigation of its policies allows for a hybrid analysis combining military and social historical approaches. Placing the history of domestic NSS mobilization strategies within the established chronology of Canada's war effort allows a significant new chapter of Canadian history to be written.

1 The Regulatory Framework of Mobilization

In 1935, after his country had been invaded by Italian forces, Abyssinian Emperor Haile Selassie issued this sweeping mobilization proclamation:

Everyone will now be mobilized and all boys old enough to carry a spear will be sent to Addis Ababa. Married men will take their wives to carry food and to cook. Those without wives will take any women without husbands. Women with small babies need not go. The blind and those who cannot walk or for any reason cannot carry a spear are exempt. Anyone found at home after the receipt of this order will be hanged.[1]

NSS officials might have envied the comprehensive and inclusive nature of Selassie's decree, let alone his dictatorial power to enforce it.

An overview of the procedures adopted and the administrative structures used to realize mobilization goals in an efficient manner reveals structural flaws that virtually guaranteed only limited success in human resource management during World War II. Logistical and structural problems dogged military mobilization initiatives and prevented the drafting of many eligible men into the armed forces. At the same time, the officials responsible for the mobilization of the civilian labour force did not maintain thorough and exhaustive control of men and women in domestic employment. The commonly held view that civilian regulatory measures were sweeping in their scope and application must be revised when mobilization structures are examined in detail. While many statutory regulations for both civilian and military mobilization were comprehensive in theory, key government officials failed to exercise their full powers. The result was a patchwork mobilization system and only limited success.

MILITARY MOBILIZATION IN CANADA, 1940-46

When Canada entered the war against Germany in September 1939, the government anticipated that its primary contribution to the Allied cause would come in the form of economic aid. No comprehensive military mobilization initiatives were undertaken in the first months of the war, and Mackenzie King refused to contemplate the adoption of any policy that would lead in the direction of the conscription of Canadian manpower.

After his sweeping re-election victory of 26 March 1940, however, King was soon faced with the calamitous events of May and June in France. The startling success of German troops against Allied forces eliminated any possibility that Canada could fight a war of limited liability based primarily on the contribution of industrial and agricultural commodities to the British. In addition to the adoption of measures designed to bolster active duty units destined for overseas military service, the prime response of the Canadian government to the defeat of France and the sudden threat to the United Kingdom was to introduce into the House of Commons the bill that eventually became the National Resources Mobilization Act (NRMA). In keeping with his "frequently given" promise not to conscript men for overseas service,[2] King claimed that the time had come to organize a home defence force. The NRMA allowed the government to conscript men to ensure "public safety, the defence of Canada, the maintenance of public order, [and] the efficient prosecution of the war." Men called up under the NRMA would be trained for thirty days. The NRMA became law on 21 June 1940, and on 12 July the Department of National War Services (DNWS) was created to administer it under the direction of Minister of Agriculture James Gardiner. Two issues dominated the administration of conscription legislation for the duration of the war: registration and call-up procedures.

Orders-in-Council PC 3086 and PC 3156 of 9 and 12 July 1941 empowered DNWS officials to undertake a national registration. Under the terms of these regulations, a Registrar and an Assistant Registrar were to be appointed in each federal electoral district across Canada. All residents who had attained the age of sixteen by 1 July 1940 were required to register in person at designated stations or by mail, or, in the case of industrial establishments of a certain size, in the workplace. Separate lists were made of all single men and childless widowers between the ages of nineteen and forty-five as of 15 July 1940. These lists identified 802,458 men who served as the prime pool of military manpower for the duration of the war. Registration questionnaires also contained occupational information so as to identify persons with specialized employment capabilities. The initial national registration was updated as the war progressed to include men who reached military age after 1940.[3]

Once the majority of individual registrations had been processed, action was taken to direct recruits as required. The key regulation in this regard was Order-in-Council PC 4185 of 27 August 1940, known as the National War Services Regulations, 1940 (Recruits). PC 4185 exempted various groups from compulsory military service, including all members of the active military, clergymen, judges, police officers, and penitentiary wardens. All other male British subjects ordinarily resident in Canada as of 1 September 1939 and who were between the ages of twenty-one and forty-five and were single or widowed as of 15 July 1940 were eligible for compulsory military training. PC 4185 also identified various groups who were to be given special consideration by the mobilization authorities, including students, conscientious objectors, and Mennonites. Stiff penalties were provided for any individual found delinquent under the mobilization regulations. A series of proclamations issued following the passage of PC 4185 broadened the group of men covered by the NRMA. PC 4671 of 11 September 1940 designated single men aged twenty-one to twenty-four liable for military service. PC 4238, authorized on 16 June 1944, would extend this designation to married and single men aged eighteen and a half to thirty-one years and single men aged thirty-two to forty-two.[4]

The administrative structure established by the 1940 regulations remained unchanged for the duration of the war. Thirteen Administrative Divisions were established as follows: 1)Division A–London; 2)Division B–Toronto; 3)Division C–Kingston; 4)Division D–Port Arthur; 5)Division E–Montreal; 6)Division F–Quebec City; 7)Division G–Halifax; 8)Division H–Saint John; 9)Division I–Charlottetown; 10)Division J–Winnipeg; 11)Division K–Vancouver; 12)Division M–Regina and 13)Division N–Edmonton. In each Administrative Division, a Divisional Registrar was responsible for using the national registration information to select the men who would be called into military service based on the age groups specified in the mobilization proclamations. In each Administrative District, a National War Services Administration Board was established. Each Board had a minimum of three members, with a Superior Court or provincial judge acting as chair. All decisions concerning postponement of military service based on occupational priority were made by the Boards. The authority of Administration Boards was truly remarkable. All Board decisions were "final and conclusive," and no member of a Board was legally liable for any decision taken since Boards were placed beyond the authority of any judicial body.[5]

In theory, the process of calling up a potential recruit was straightforward. A Divisional Registrar, taking account of age and other national registration information, issued an Order–Medical Examination to each potential recruit to report to civilian physicians approved by the government for medical examination. The examining physician graded each recruit into one of five categories ranging from A (most fit) to E (unfit for military service). The results of the examination would then be forwarded to the Registrar, who could then issue an Order–Military Training to the recruit. All men seeking deferment were required to have the medical examination and then submit their postponement application to the Administration Board in the appropriate Administrative Division.[6]

Eventually, the responsibility of administering the NRMA provisions was transferred from the DNWS. The Canadian government established National Selective Service as a branch of the Department of Labour on 21 March 1942 through the passage of Order-in-Council PC 2254. In his speech introducing the measure to the House of Commons, Prime Minister Mackenzie King outlined three primary objectives for NSS in relation to the mobilization of the civilian labour force: estimating the number of men and women required for various war services; increasing the total human resources available for war purposes; and directing available men and women into the form of wartime service where their contribution would be most beneficial. By the end of 1942, NSS also assumed responsibility for the complex web of regulations governing the compulsory mobilization of military personnel in Canada, because during the summer of 1942 pressing military manpower shortages became evident. Key meetings of the War Cabinet and the Cabinet Manpower Committee in July 1942 revealed that "centralization of ministerial responsibility for manpower policy and administration" was desirable.[7] As a result, through Order-in-Council PC 8800 of 26 September 1942, the control of military mobilization was taken away from the DNWS and placed under the jurisdiction of the Department of Labour. (The DNWS remained in existence and most senior DNWS officials did not transfer to the Department of Labour.) On 1 December 1942, NSS assumed direct responsibility for military mobilization through Order-in-Council PC 10924, the National Selective Service Mobilization Regulations. The administrative structure of Divisional

Registrars and Administrative Boards remained unchanged, with the Boards termed Mobilization Boards under NSS nomenclature.

Following the completion of the first round of national registration efforts in 1940, it became increasingly clear that many men who were eligible for military service were escaping medical examination. The reasons included change of address without notification of Registrars, errors in duplicates of national registration cards on file in Registrars' offices, and outright avoidance of compliance with orders for medical examination. NSS officials addressed this problem by ordering a re-registration as of 15 July 1940 of single men who had been born in the years 1902 to 1922 inclusive. Under Order-in-Council PC 11240 of 11 December 1942 all men who had not previously been served with an Order–Medical Examination were required to complete a form, known as "Schedule C," and return it to the Divisional Registrar. The original expiry date for completing Schedule C was 1 February 1943, but the deadline was subsequently extended first to March 1943 and then to January 1944. More than 146,000 men had re-registered under the Schedule C plan by 10 January 1944.[8]

The medical examination procedure was changed during 1943 to cut down on the problems inherent in allowing large numbers of civilian physicians to examine men issued military training orders and to allow for more consistent measurement of the medical condition of potential recruits. Under Order-in-Council PC 6990 of 7 September 1943, the majority of men requiring medical examination either had to visit medical panels established in DND Army Reception Centres or submit to a medical examination performed by a civilian doctor assigned to a panel of physicians for a specific region. In rural and outlying areas, however, medical examination continued to be done by a civilian physician of the recruit's choice.[9] After a Registrars' meeting in Ottawa on 19 June 1943, steps were taken to introduce the PULHEMS system of medical examination classification to determine the "exact functional capabilities" of each recruit.[10] Each letter of PULHEMS stood for a specific physical capacity: P–Physique; U–Upper Extremities; L–Lower Extremities; H–Ears and Hearing; E–Eyes and Eyesight; M–Mental Capacity; and S–Emotional Stability. Each category was graded on a scale of 1 to 5 in the manner of the old A to E system, but the PULHEMS system allowed a detailed evaluation of the functional capacity of a potential recruit in a much wider range of physical categories. The changes in medical procedure and examination policy were implemented to reduce the loss of recruits through physician error and to facilitate the issuing of medical examination orders to a wider range of men.

Early in 1944, NSS launched another important initiative to identify men contravening mobilization regulations. This took the form of a requirement that employers check the status of all male employees in the age groups subject to military service. By Order-in-Council PC 9919 of 31 December 1943, an employer had to canvass each male employee to determine if the worker possessed an official document such as a discharge certificate or postponement of military training certificate to prove his good standing under regulations. The employer had to fill out a Schedule 9 form for each employee who did not possess official documentation explaining his presence in industry.[11] While the original program was designed to end on 1 May 1944, the Schedule 9 reporting was eventually extended; it became on ongoing check-up and it was not suspended until August 1945. During the life of this program, employers forwarded more than 49,000 Schedule 9 forms to Divisional Registrars. More than 10,000 of the men thus reported on were found to be in contravention of NSS regulations, with close to 49 per cent of the defaulters residing in the province of Quebec.[12]

The administrative effort involved in the mobilization of NRMA personnel was truly impressive. By March 1944 more than 1,800 men and women were involved in mobilization work. Between 1940 and 1945 Registrars issued more than 1.2 million medical examination orders and close to 600,000 orders for military training. During the same period Mobilization Boards heard nearly 750,000 requests for postponement of military service.[13] Part of the effort included government investigations, including the widespread use of civilian reporting agencies,[14] to prevent evasion of the mobilization regulations.

A closer examination of the mobilization structure, however, reveals that Registrars and Mobilization Board officials experienced a great degree of difficulty administering the mobilization regulations. Both groups also actively stood in the way of the efficient call-up of NRMA personnel. Indeed, the authority of the Mobilization Boards proved to be the most significant barrier to a consistent, nationwide policy of military mobilization in Canada during the Second World War.

A scandal in the office of the Montreal Registrar in 1941 almost caused the collapse of the entire mobilization structure in the province of Quebec. In April 1941, it was publicly revealed that a province-wide RCMP probe had been examining cases of fraud involving the issuance of illegal deferment certificates to members of the Syrian-Canadian community.[15] The Syrians allegedly had paid large sums of money to secure either deferment of military training or outright exemption from it. The investigation reached into the offices of the Montreal Divisional Registrar, Pierre Décary, who was arrested along with two other principals in the case, Mike Maloley of the Syrian community, and Jean Tarte, a prominent lawyer with ties to the provincial government. Twelve Syrian-Canadians were arrested as well on charges of evading military service or aiding eligible men to avoid compulsory training. The episode highlighted the sharp differences in attitude in Montreal towards the war. The *Montreal Gazette* trumpeted that the Décary case had "startling repercussions and implications," and painted a "ghastly picture" of the mobilization effort. By contrast, editorials and news coverage in *Le Devoir* tended to avoid criticism of the men involved in the dispute while condemning the coverage of the case by the *Gazette*.

In the end, Maloley and Tarte turned King's evidence and testified against Décary in exchange for eighteen-month prison sentences.[16] DNWS officials in Ottawa were shocked at developments in Montreal, noting that this "most unhappy" episode in Montreal threatened the whole recruitment effort in Quebec.[17] Public opinion of mobilization efforts was hardly improved once Décary took the stand in his own defence in June 1941. Décary flatly denied all charges brought against him, and claimed that Ottawa had told him to treat draft evaders with "white gloves" by not vigorously pursuing 3,000 delinquent cases in the Montreal Administrative Division. Décary chronicled the poor record-keeping procedures and the lack of staff, facts confirmed in the witness box by Acting Montreal Registrar Raymond Ranger. The jury eventually sided with the prosecution but recommended clemency in Décary's sentence. Décary appealed his conviction to the Quebec Court of Appeal. Remarkably, the original conviction was quashed, with the three francophone judges siding with Décary and the two anglophone judges supporting the original conviction. One of the francophone justices noted Décary's personal integrity in the witness box and saw in this the "spontaneous cry of a quiet conscience." Not surprisingly, the *Gazette* castigated the decision to free Décary; "even the man in the street," the paper pronounced, "is aware of the tradition that the judicial power to interfere with the ancient British right of trial by jury should be exercised with the greatest restraint." The Supreme Court of Canada eventually dismissed an appeal in February 1942 on the grounds that the dissent of the two anglophone appeal justices had been based on fact and not law.[18]

While the criminal acts involved in the Décary incident were exceptional, serious logistical problems plagued the Registrar system for the duration of the war. In January 1943 the government released manpower statistics culled from error-riddled DNWS records. In newspaper columns across the country, Grant Dexter ridiculed the inaccuracy of these official mobilization figures: "While the tables are well set up, the whole is all but unintelligible. It is as though the tables were the work of a demented mathematician. No single total agrees with its fellows ... The muddle with respect to the calls for military service is probably unprecedented."[19] In July 1943 Major General H.J. Riley, NSS Associate Director of Mobilization, complained to NSS Director Arthur MacNamara that Registrars were having difficulty securing even "moderately efficient" staff due to a high turnover rate, and that mistakes on registration forms were rampant.[20] Riley complained that the number of postponements and deferments in Quebec was too high, but that NSS had not been given the resources to enforce the mobilization regulations in an effective manner in that province.

Indeed, the biggest administrative problem the Registrars faced was that of keeping their records up to date. Not included in a Registrar's records was the information concerning men who were not on the national registration rolls or who had enlisted in the armed forces. Men who volunteered for active duty were obviously not subject to NRMA conscription, but the DND rarely submitted enlistment data to Registrars to streamline the call-up procedures. Early in 1943, a special effort was made to ensure that Registrars had all of the necessary information on all men in callable age classes. However, approximately 120,000 enlistment notices sent to Registrars by DND officials could not be matched initially with information in their files. While 80,000 of these cases were eventually sorted out, the remaining 40,000 could not be matched with national registration information.[21] Only by the end of the war were the Registrars getting effective control of the vast body of information that had been collected. A 1945 audit by an accounting firm, however, revealed that more than 3 per cent of all information in Registrars' offices was incorrect, with Montreal showing the highest percentage of error at almost 6 per cent.[22]

The problems inherent in managing such a massive registration effort were evident in the hundreds of cases where medical examination and military training orders were sent to servicemen who had been killed in combat. Media support of the mobilization effort was tepid, and many major newspapers sharply criticized the ability of NWS and NSS to secure manpower in an efficient fashion. In October 1942 a sailor was killed in action on the HMCS *Caribou* and his posthumous award for bravery was promptly forwarded to his mother. In December 1942, however, she received a military training order addressed to her son from the Charlottetown Divisional Registrar. Commentary in the *Halifax Chronicle* on this episode echoed sentiments that could be heard in newspapers across the country.

Call it what you will – incompetence, slackness, inefficiency, or downright stupidity – the fact remains that it is absolutely without excuse. NSS, like any other wartime agency, is designed with some regard for the public conscience. In the exercise of its functions it must ever keep before it the chastening observation that it is the servant and not the master of the people. The issue involved goes much deeper than the surface details of this particularly lamentable episode. It goes to the very heart of the manpower problem and the NSS organization. And let us remember that that body can make of our national strength a potent force in the world struggle or an abject farce. One way to insure the latter is to persist in crude incompetence of this order.[23]

While the Department of National Defence was equally to blame in this case for not forwarding enlistment certificates to Divisional Registrars, there can be no doubt that the operations of NWS and NSS were plagued with clerical and administrative difficulties that eroded public confidence and contributed to problems in mobilizing NRMA personnel throughout the war.

Yet another flaw in the system was that a Mobilization Board could take on the personality of its Chair. The case studies in this monograph provide ample illustration of the sticky problems created by Mobilization Boards across the country. Two men in particular tested the patience of NWS and NSS administrators in Ottawa: Justice A.M. Manson of the Vancouver Mobilization Board and Major General and Justice J.F.L. Embury of the Regina Mobilization Board. They vociferously and actively opposed many of the policies devised to mobilize NRMA personnel in an equitable manner.

Embury, a brigadier-general who commanded an infantry brigade during World War I, illustrated his disdain for established procedure by his handling of conscientious objectors in the Regina Administrative Division. The case of Robert Makaroff is typical of the contempt Embury felt for pacifists. Makaroff, the son of Saskatoon lawyer and Doukhobor P.G. Makaroff, applied to the Regina Mobilization Board for a deferment of military service as a medical student. Embury, however, refused to consider his academic qualifications and classified him instead as a conscientious objector.[24] After spending time at an alternative service camp, Makaroff was sent to a rock quarry in British Columbia, where he was required to work for a private contractor in oppressive conditions.[25] When Embury died in late 1943, he was replaced by Justice P.M. Anderson, who immediately set about undoing the harm his predecessor had done. Anderson released Makaroff from his alternative service commitments on the grounds that he had been "singled out for discrimination and persecution." Four members of the Regina Mobilization Board resigned in protest of Anderson's handling of the Makaroff case. Under Anderson's leadership, these men claimed, the Regina operation had degenerated into "petty intrigue, tittle-tattling, and time wasting."[26] The Canadian Legion likewise condemned Anderson for his alleged lenient handling of Makaroff; Embury had been "the honourary president of the Legion, a great soldier, a good citizen, and a kind and sympathetic man."[27]

This was exceptional, but there is abundant evidence that the system established to ensure the efficient mobilization of NRMA personnel was susceptible to procedural and administrative difficulties. The enormous quantity of data that had to be handled and the fluid nature of wartime employment and enlistment patterns overwhelmed the agencies charged with tabulating and organizing the statistical foundation of Canada's domestic military effort. In the end, the bureaucratic structures created to administer mobilization regulations often created barriers to the efficient procurement of men for domestic military service.

On 7 May 1945 the military call-up of eligible men was suspended and all mobilization regulations were gradually relaxed in the months that followed. Finally, on 15 August 1946, all the mobilization and registration regulations were revoked.

CIVILIAN MOBILIZATION IN CANADA,
1940–46

On first examination, it is easy to conclude that the mobilization of civilian human resources in Canada during World War II proceeded with few difficulties. By 1 October 1944, 37 per cent of the Canadian population aged fourteen years and older was gainfully employed in non-agricultural industry. This figure was 25 per cent higher than the level of October 1939. Employment in essential war industries increased from only 121,000 persons in October 1939 to a wartime high of more than 1.1 million in October 1943. The number of men and women gainfully occupied in 1944 had increased by close to 600,000 persons over 1939 employment levels.[28] These are impressive figures. Close examination of the policies adopted to mobilize the labour force, however, reveals that the outward statistical success of the domestic economy belies hidden weaknesses in the regulatory framework. In truth, the officials responsible for the direction and control of the civilian labour force often lacked the powers to respond to serious problems in a wide variety of employment sectors.

Prior to the formation of NSS in March 1942, the government adopted few measures to ensure the efficient mobilization of the civilian workforce. In the first six months of the war only a number of minor initiatives were attempted. In February 1940, for example, a voluntary registration of skilled and semi-skilled workers was undertaken to ascertain the availability of workers for war industry, but fewer than

25,000 men and women responded.[29] Before 1942 two primary pieces of legislation essentially guided the civilian mobilization process. The first was the Unemployment Insurance Act of 7 August 1940. While its most importation function was to devise and administer a contributory insurance scheme, the Unemployment Insurance Commission also launched a Dominion Employment Service with regional and local offices. These offices acted as clearinghouses for vacancies in and applications for employment and from September 1942 they were used by NSS personnel charged with direction of the civilian labour force.[30]

A second body that sought to ensure the smooth operation of civilian industry was the National Labour Supply Council (NLSC), which was established on 19 June 1940 by Order-in-Council PC 2686. The NLSC was initially composed of five representatives each from industry and labour, and its prime function was to adjudicate requests from the DMS concerning the essentiality of particular industrial enterprises. If the NLSC deemed a company essential it would communicate this information to DNWS officials. DNWS Administrative Boards would in turn use this information in judging requests for postponement of military duty from individual employees working in that firm. After the NLSC was disbanded on 24 February 1942, the National War Labour Board (NWLB) administered NLSC functions until early 1943. Over time, more than 500 companies were identified for special consideration under the NLSC worker postponement scheme.[31] At the same time, the Wartime Bureau of Technical Personnel (WBTP) safeguarded the availability of small classes of technical workers and scientific personnel.[32]

By early 1941 it had become clear that this piecemeal approach, which affected but a small percentage of the manpower pool, would not meet the pressing demand for workers. Accordingly, on 25 October 1940, the government established the Inter-departmental Committee on Labour Coordination (ICLC) to recommend measures to deal with the situation. The ICLC quickly commissioned the Labour Supply Investigation Committee (LSIC) to evaluate the mobilization effort and the latter group produced a remarkably complex and detailed report in October 1941 that exposed the extraordinary shortcomings of the existing system. Despite Cabinet opposition to the placing of civilian manpower requirements on the same level as military manpower needs, Mackenzie King responded to the LSIC report by launching National Selective Service operations.

Thirteen Orders-in-Council issued during March 1942 defined the scope of the new agency within the Department of Labour. PC 2250 of 21 March 1942, the Restricted Occupations Order, prevented men between the ages of seventeen and forty-five from entering certain non-essential occupations without the permission of an NSS officer.

Likewise, under the Stabilization of Employment in Agriculture Regulations issued on the same date, persons employed in agriculture at 23 March 1942 could not take employment outside that field without NSS permission. Such persons were, however, permitted to move about freely from one agricultural job to another. Neither of these regulations applied to women. NSS officials were authorized to use the chain of Unemployment Insurance Commission offices across the country to administer these first civilian regulatory measures, and a nationwide registration of unemployed men between the ages of seventeen and sixty-nine was carried out in May 1942. On 17 June 1942, the Control of Employment Regulations revoked the Restricted Occupations Order, and further extended Selective Service control over civilian manpower and employment. These new regulations mandated that every person, male or female, must seek the permission of an NSS officer to enter any employment. Once employment was obtained, an individual had to apply for the permit necessary to begin work. This could be refused by an NSS officer and the worker induced to take some other employment.

All these measures were consolidated by PC 7595 on 26 August 1942. This Order revoked the Stabilization of Employment in Agriculture Regulations and the Control of Employment Regulations. PC 7595 extended and widened NSS control by making it necessary for workers to obtain permits before seeking or entering employment, and by introducing a system of notices of separation. This system required seven days' notice by either employee or employer of intended separation or dismissal. Employers were required to report all employment vacancies to UIC offices and advertising for employment or for employees was prohibited without NSS approval. Administrative difficulties that arose under PC 7595 because of the competing jurisdictions of NSS and the Unemployment Insurance Commission were quickly resolved by PC 7994 on 4 September 1942. This Order placed the UIC structure under NSS control. By February 1944, more than 5,500 NSS personnel worked in UIC offices across the country.[33]

The most critical section of PC 7595 related to priorities in the use of labour across Canada. An embryonic system of priority classifications according to industry had been formulated in June 1941, and the Restricted Occupations Order of March 1942 had begun to formalize the concept of classifying jobs according to essentiality. PC 7595 went much further and inaugurated the priority classification system on a nationwide basis.[34] Labelled by NSS officials as "the key...which guided manpower to its most useful employment during the war,"[35] the priority system used the *Industrial Classification Manual* and a continuously updated series of reports from employers to determine the wartime essentiality of a firm or an industry. Local NSS offices used the priority schedules when referring applicants to employment, with what were rated as highly essential industries receiving priority over less essential industries for available labour.

Under PC 7595, a tiered priority schedule featured nine primary occupational divisions.[36] Within each of these divisions there were a number of major industry groups and within each major group there were sub-groups. The sub-groups were ranked as A, B, C, or D in priority, designations that meant, respectively, very high, high, low, or no essentiality. In the Manufacturing Division, for example, Major Group 22 was classified as Textile Mill Products. Within this industry group there were fourteen sub-groups, each of which was assigned male and female priority ratings. In February 1944, Industry 2211, Cotton Yarn and Broadwoven Goods, had a priority rating of B-A. This rating meant that employment in this sub-group was highly essential for males and very highly essential for females. Individual firms could receive a priority rating different from that of the industry as a whole. In 1942 an Inter-departmental Labour Priorities Committee (ILPC) was formed to establish and update priorities on a continuous basis. This Committee drew its membership from the Department of Labour, the WPTB, and the DMS. The ILPC remained the key NSS regulatory body for the duration of the war, as the complex and changing web of priority ratings anchored the attempt to distribute labour to essential industries in an efficient manner. Sheldon Ross became chair of the ILPC in April 1943, and established a lasting reputation as the miserly guardian of the coveted priority ratings sought by Canadian businesses.

PC 7595 remained in effect for less than five months. For the remainder of the war, Order-in-Council PC 246 of 19 January 1943 formed the regulatory blueprint that would guide NSS control of the civilian workforce. Building on the curtailment debate that had transpired in the months before its passage, this Order, termed the National Selective Service Civilian Regulations (NSSCR), epitomized the flexible and selective approach governing the civilian mobilization effort in Canada. Many of the provisions of PC 7595 were incorporated into PC 246. Seven-day separation notices were still required for an employee to separate from employment or for an employer to terminate an employee. The priority classification system remained intact as the primary lever available to Selective Service officials to direct labour to the most essential use. Strict control of advertising was not only maintained but strengthened. The system of supplementary allowances provided for in PC 7595 was likewise enhanced. This system allowed NSS officials to pay allowances for transportation and accommodation expenses to workers who were directed to or who moved voluntarily to employment deemed essential. A variety of occupation-specific regulations governing, for example, employment in agriculture and technical vocations were also included. A stringent system of labour exit permits increased the ability of Selective Service officials to restrict the movement of workers to the United States.

The most important section of PC 246, however, was the administrative power vested in the office of the Minister of Labour. Section 210 contained two key provisions enabling the direction and control of the labour force in a comprehensive fashion. By the first of these, the Minister had full authority to direct all men in age classes callable for military service to terminate their existing employment on two weeks' notice. Under the second provision, an individual so designated for compulsory transfer was required to report to a local employment office and accept the employment offered to him by NSS. An employee targeted for transfer under Section 210 had the right to appeal to a board of referees established by the Unemployment Insurance Commission in 1940. In some industries – coal mining was the leading example – Orders-in-Council amended Section 210 to grant special considerations or privileges in securing labour. In 1943 a series of formal Compulsory Transfer Orders issued under Section 210 directed men in military age brackets from non-essential employment to more essential employment.

In law, NSS thus possessed three means for the efficient mobilization of the civilian labour force. First, and most important, was the complex web of priorities. This anchored the effort to direct male and female labour to essential military and civilian industries, although it proved incapable of addressing many pressing industrial needs in an effective manner. Second, a small number of industries such as coal mining and longshore work were targeted for special regulatory attention under Section 210 of PC 246. This aspect of the program is detailed in several of the case studies that follow. Finally, Compulsory Transfer Orders issued in 1943 allowed young men to be transferred from occupations deemed non-essential to occupations that were crucial to the war effort. The full authority of these regulations, however, was never utilized because NSS administrators chose to follow tactics of conciliation and compromise.

Other accounts of the period view the NSS compulsory transfer policy as "a clear attempt to get tough with industry and labour,"[37] but an examination of the effect of Compulsory Transfer Orders reveals that Selective Service direction of the workforce was of limited scope. Although the Transfer Orders were designed to comb out men in military age classes from non-essential occupations, only a small percentage of men targeted under them was actually shifted to more essential employment. Compulsory Transfer Order #1 was issued on 4 May 1943. It ordered all callable males employed in occupations such as bartending, sales, barbering, and taxi driving to register at a local Selective Service office, and await direction to other employment. Before November 1943, six more Compulsory Transfer Orders were issued covering a wide range of service and other non-essential industries.[38] More than 104,000 men registered under these Orders, but only 17 per cent of them were placed in more essential employment. Sixty-nine per cent of these men stayed in non-essential employment while the remainder fell into other categories including enlistments in the armed forces and cases in abeyance.[39] An eighth Compulsory Transfer Order was drafted in 1944, but Sheldon Ross, Chairman of the ILPC, noted wryly that it should not be implemented "in view of the fact that a large proportion of those affected by other Compulsory Orders" had not been transferred.[40] Selective Service officials were unwilling to exercise their regulatory powers to the fullest extent.

Perhaps the most significant obstacle facing mobilization planners after the issuance of PC 246 was the matter of separations from employment. Despite the increased supervision of the labour force, tens of thousands of men and women continued to leave essential employment. Between 1 September 1942 and 27 May 1943, there were 1,058,736 separation notices submitted to NSS offices by men and 375,478 by women.[41] NSS officials hesitated during the first eight months of 1943 to use their full powers to direct workers. Pressure to stabilize payrolls and reduce the enormous administrative load on local employment offices, which were struggling with a tidal wave of referrals to and placements in employment, finally forced Arthur MacNamara to step up the pace of control. On 1 September 1943 Order-in-Council PC 6625 classified all firms with a labour priority rating of A or B as "designated establishments." Legally, this meant that workers in these firms, male and female, were frozen in their employment unless given permission to submit a notice of separation. PC 6625 was clearly designed to improve upon what had been happening in relation to separations under PC 7595 and PC 246.

Nonetheless, NSS officials were encouraged to administer the new regulation in a "reasonable and practical manner."[42] In practice, separations from essential employment continued unabated for the duration of the war.[43] Table 1 shows the separation totals for men and women according to essentiality and the corresponding labour demand across Canada.[44] On average, more than 5 per cent of both men and women in the entire Canadian industrial workforce, and close to 10 per cent of persons employed in essential war industry, sought a change in employment every month from mid-1943 to late 1945. Evidence from NSS files

Table 1
Separations and Labour Demand in Canadian Industrial
Establishments, 1943–45

Month	Male A&B*	Male C&D**	Female A&B	Female C&D	Total Separations	Labour Demand
1943						
Aug	101,062	28,177	42,660	17,308	189,207	150,634
Sep	78,301	22,784	37,703	16,203	154,991	145,423
Oct	53,936	14,484	33,522	13,026	114,968	–
Nov	79,587	16,994	39,701	14,482	150,764	143,593
Dec	–	–	–	–	119,079	109,992
1944						
Jan	–	–	–	–	122,977	111,113
Feb	–	–	–	–	–	–
Mar	79,267	15,720	29,317	10,942	135,246	127,473
Apr	77,968	16,293	28,384	10,944	133,589	167,940
May	84,900	21,530	40,235	14,259	160,924	194,972
Jun	–	–	–	–	–	–
Jul	–	–	–	–	–	–
Aug	78,137	26,191	43,048	16,407	163,783	168,249
Sep	67,705	24,612	40,172	16,678	149,167	172,940
Oct	75,321	25,255	42,525	15,336	158,437	154,111
Nov	72,240	19,438	34,197	12,464	138,339	162,633
Dec	64,073	17,266	27,232	13,574	122,145	123,558
1945						
Jan	74,912	24,377	35,523	19,665	154,477	123,224
Feb	66,391	18,772	28,602	12,614	126,379	122,262
Mar	88,824	20,499	28,285	12,361	149,969	134,208
Apr	96,718	31,212	38,052	16,938	182,920	156,847
May	64,947	21,111	32,830	10,823	129,711	147,910
Jun	66,892	24,379	35,162	11,622	138,055	131,910
Jul	–	–	–	–	–	–
Aug	89,570	28,632	38,146	14,557	170,905	129,835
Sep	90,585	36,513	37,443	19,949	184,490	–

Source: Monthly Statistical Reports, NA, RG 27, Volume 984, files 12–15; Volume 985, files 1–4; Volume 1987, files 7–10, and Volume 1988, files 1–11.

* A&B designations refer to workers in very highly essential and highly essential positions or industries, respectively.

** C&D designations refer to workers in less essential and non-essential positions or industries, respectively.

also indicates that thousands of men and women failed to obtain separation notices and permits to seek employment in other industries and were not therefore included in the official employment totals. The labour demand figures indicate that since a sellers' market for labour existed, many workers separated from their existing employment to seek better paid jobs elsewhere. Nor did Selective Service officials necessarily resist the tens of thousands of separated employees streaming into their offices. Acute labour shortages plagued virtually every industry in the country, and job vacancies could be filled temporarily from the constantly revolving pool of labour. There can be no doubt, however, that certain essential industries suffered greatly because of the high separation rate. Despite a flurry of attempts to deal with high turnover, NSS leaders ultimately proved unable to enforce the employment freeze that had been imposed by Order-in-Council.

By the beginning of 1944, therefore, the limited effectiveness of NSS operations had been clearly demonstrated. First, the outcome of the protracted curtailment debate of late 1942 within Cabinet had guaranteed that no significant release of manpower from non-essential industries would take place. Second, limited and non-compulsive legislative measures had targeted only a small section of the workforce for mandatory employment in essential industry. Third, the failure to check the transiency of significant portions of the workforce, in concert with acute labour shortages across the nation, hampered efforts to supply industry with the replacements needed to meet wartime production goals. And, finally, an already decentralized NSS structure in Ottawa was weakened further by Order-in-Council PC 6387 of 10 August 1943. PC 6387 established nine NSS divisions, each of which was placed under the control of an Associate Director. Provision was also made for the appointment of Regional Advisory Boards for the Pacific, Prairie, Ontario, Quebec, and Maritime regions, an arrangement that took effect in January 1944. As a result of these developments, the only consistent NSS operation for the remainder of the war was the labour priority system. In effect, the massive Selective Service bureaucracy (see Figure 1), with local offices in almost every town and city across Canada, was reduced to acting as little more than a giant clearinghouse for labour.

One final attempt to institute a comprehensive management program for the Canadian workforce was launched in May and June of 1944. The initiative for this came from Sheldon Ross, the ILPC Chairman and the most consistent advocate of a re-orientation of NSS policy in the direction favoured by Elliot Little. Ross made the case that WPTB and DMS officials were failing to coordinate their activities in order to conserve precious labour resources. But Arthur MacNamara sided with

Figure 1
Department of Labour Mobilization Structure, 1 February 1944

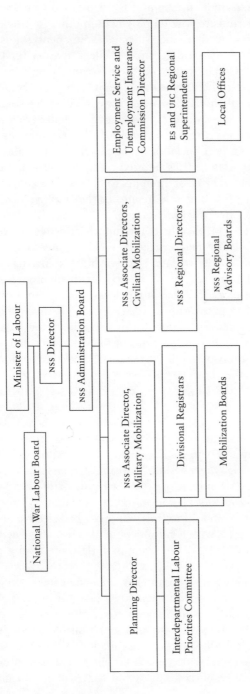

Order-in-Council PC 6387 of 10 August 1943 created the NSS Administration Board as the primary NSS decision making body at the national level. In addition to the NSS Director, members of the Administration Board included the nine NSS Associate Directors, the Planning Director, and the Employment Service and Unemployment Insurance Commission Director. NSS Regional Directors received guidance from Ottawa through the NSS Associate Directors, and they were instructed to work closely with the ES and UIC Regional Superintendents in order to coordinate policy at the local level through Employment Service offices. Each NSS Regional Advisory Board was composed of the NSS Regional Director, the ES and UIC Regional Superintendent, a Chairman of a Mobilization Board or a Divisional Registrar, a representative of the Department of Munitions and Supply, a representative of the Wartime Prices and Trade Board, and a representative of organized labour in a region. Advisory Boards attempted to adapt national mobilization decrees to regional circumstances and the multi-departmental composition of each Board allowed all aspects of human resource mobilization policies in a region to be discussed.

WPTB and DMS administrators; the Department of Labour, he noted, "did not wish to hold down industry in Canada if it can be prevented."[45] In June 1944 Ross returned to the attack. Noting that the labour priority scheme was the "key to the whole system" of human resource control, he lamented the fact that "no one seems to be concerned with production of less essential goods in plentiful supply." Only a vigorous curtailment policy, he concluded, could alleviate pressing shortages:

I realize that plans for curtailment were discarded at the end of 1942 but general conditions have changed considerably since that time. Priorities and the associated compulsory transfers are practically the only methods that have ever been adopted which curtail less essential activities for the direct purpose of improving available labour supply for more essential activities. Priorities can only go so far as a curtailment tool. Actually, thousands of potential workers for war production are engaged in relatively non-essential activities. A great number of these who have never been continuously employed for the last two years have never been directed by Selective Service. These are not touched by priorities, and a very great percentage have not been moved by compulsory transfers. Compulsory transfers must be recognized as not satisfactorily effective in withdrawing men in sufficient numbers from less-essential activities.[46]

No answer to Ross was forthcoming. NSS approached the brink of national curtailment in late 1942, but had opted instead for a flexible, and in most cases ineffective, system of priorities and a limited compulsory transfer scheme that allowed only small numbers of workers to be directed or transferred to essential industries.

Ross's observations concerning the limited scope of the mobilization effort were highlighted by a Canadian Institute for Public Opinion (CIPO) poll taken in November 1944.[47] CIPO officials asked a sample group of Canadians if they had had any contact with an NSS office and, if the answer was yes, how they felt about the service provided. Remarkably, 67 per cent of respondents nationwide reported that they had never dealt with a Selective Service office. On a regional basis, the high in this regard was 73 per cent in the Maritimes and the low 59 per cent in British Columbia. In terms of gender, 60 per cent of men and 74 per cent of women reported no contact. Not surprisingly, younger respondents reported a high use of NSS offices. This was because many men in callable age categories were liable to be interviewed by NSS officers when they were rejected for military service. On a national basis, more than 39 per cent of those reporting contact with an NSS office were dissatisfied with the service they had received. Although public opinion surveys must be viewed with a certain degree of caution, this CIPO poll reveals how much of the Canadian workforce was going about its business unaffected by the operations of NSS.

In the final months of 1944 and the first months of 1945, civilian labour controls were relaxed. Order-in-Council PC 8726, issued on 24 November 1944, allowed war workers to be released from employment in designated establishments without NSS permission and also waived the seven-day waiting period before an employee could enter new employment.[48] Although the employment mobility of women had theoretically been controlled since 1942 through permit requirements, female workers had been separating from employment and entering new jobs with virtual impunity. In 1945 the government acknowledged this reality. Thus, beginning 15 May, women could seek and enter employment without having a permit; employers could interview and hire women who did not have permits; a permit could be obtained after a woman was hired; permits "would be issued automatically without regard to the labour priority rating of the work"; open permits "would be issued freely ... on request," and female job applicants and employers seeking women workers could advertise without NSS permission.[49]

After the end of the war in the Pacific all NSS controls were dismantled, in several stages. On 17 August 1945 Humphrey Mitchell announced that the majority of the regulations adopted under PC 246 and succeeding Orders would be rescinded.[50] On 17 September 1945 the freezing order for men employed in essential A and B industries was lifted. Effective 3 September 1945 all men directed to essential employment were free to return to their old jobs or seek other employment. Advertising restrictions were modified the same day. Local NSS offices were given permission to issue permits to workers to seek out or enter into employment in the United States (they had been withheld since the summer of 1942). Finally, a new priority category was developed to ease the passage back to a free labour market. All establishments in the new A(E) priority were given emergency priority by local NSS offices in the assignment of workers.

NSS regulations were loosened still further towards the end of 1945. A proposal by Arthur MacNamara in March and April of 1945 to continue NSS employment controls into 1946 was poorly received within government circles[51] and was rejected outright by many business groups across the country.[52] Accordingly, on 21 December 1945, the bulk of the NSS regulations enacted between 1942 and 1945 were rescinded. At the same time a peacetime National Employment Service was established. The system of labour priorities was abandoned in February 1946,[53] with all remaining NSS civilian mobilization regulations annulled by PC 1166 on 31 March 1947.

2 Native Canadian Mobilization

On 3 August 1943, the *Winnipeg Free Press* published an editorial titled "Mobilizing the Red Men" that called for the full military mobilization of Native Canadians. Although the presence of many Native volunteers in the ranks of active duty personnel was acknowledged and lauded, the editorial expressed frustration that the mobilization regulations pertaining to the compulsory conscription of men for Home Defence purposes were not being enforced:

The notion that these aborigines are not subject to the Mobilization Act probably arises from the belief, held by many Indians, that they are still a nation within a nation, an independent people living under treaty with the Pale Faces. There are, of course, a number of Indian treaties. Under them, any Native title or interest in the country was extinguished and the Indians themselves became wards of the state. Some of them have been enfranchised, but in the process they have ceased to be Indians under the law and have forfeited whatever advantage the treaties gave them. There shouldn't be much question as to the enfranchised Indian's liability for military service. As a citizen he must discharge his civic responsibilities. The official view, however, seems to cover those in wardship also and here again there seems to be no just cause for immunity. The Indian ought to be ready to defend the country in which he lives, and considerable numbers of them have volunteered to do so.[1]

But many government officials responsible for the administration of the National Resources Mobilization Act did not share these sentiments. Far from encouraging and promoting the full participation of Indians in the

NRMA system, the basic approach of DNWS and NSS officials towards Natives was one of inconsistency, indifference, and neglect, compounded by prejudice, geography, and profound cultural differences.

The failed attempt to conscript Natives highlights the decentralized nature of the DNWS and NSS military mobilization structure. Divisional Registrars and Mobilization Boards across the country effectively controlled the call-up of Indians with no regard for directives from Ottawa. There was little coordination of policy among mobilization officials and other government departments and agencies such as the Indian Affairs Branch of the Department of Mines and Resources, the Department of National Defence, or the Royal Canadian Mounted Police. Furthermore, DNWS and NSS officials refused to adopt a coherent stance towards the Native community, despite repeated admonitions from the Department of Justice that Indians were to be treated in the same fashion as the rest of the population. The mobilization of Natives presented Ottawa with a unique series of problems in terms of culture and geographic isolation. But Arthur MacNamara simply failed to exercise leadership on this issue and allowed regional NSS officials to deal with Natives as they saw fit. This lax approach saw Natives in some regions pursued vigorously, while the majority of the Indian population was placed beyond the reach of NRMA provisions.

The strident opposition of the Native community to conscription measures only exacerbated the fractured, decentralized, and inconsistent NRMA mobilization structure. No segment of Canadian society was more culturally isolated and marginalized, and decades of mistreatment at the hands of the federal government made Natives unreceptive to compulsory mobilization initiatives.[2] Natives across the country maintained a firm belief that their lack of Canadian citizenship under federal law rendered NRMA provisions inapplicable to them. They looked to a host of historical treaties to buttress their demands for special exemptions from military service. Furthermore, Ottawa had exempted Natives from conscription during World War I because of the ambiguous legal status of Indians. Since this status remained unchanged in the interwar period, Natives opposed any attempt to be mobilized under the NRMA. By the end of the war, only 3,090 Natives had served in the military (including NRMA units) out of a Native Canadian population estimated at 126,000 in 1944.[3] While traditional historical accounts trumpet the enthusiastic support for Indian recruitment from virtually all sectors of the Native community and the Canadian government, they belie a harsh historical reality in the light of the detailed government records that exist pertaining to this issue.[4]

Under Section 3 of the 1940 National War Services regulations, compulsory registration leading potentially to military training and service was mandatory for all British subjects except for a small number of specified groups. Indians were not included among those who were given exemption. Nonetheless, their status under the NRMA remained unclear.[5] In September 1940, Lorne McDonell, the Divisional Registrar in Kingston, sought direction from DNWS officials as to "the liability of an Indian residing on a reserve being compelled to undergo military training."[6] Ottawa replied that the policy concerning Natives would be forthcoming after consultation with the Department of Justice and the Indian Affairs Branch.[7]

The government also heard from various Indian bands protesting any compulsory military service for their members. The most interesting and vitriolic material came from the Lorette Indian Reserve near Quebec City, which thereafter became the centre of Native resistance to mobilization regulations for the duration of the war. On 14 October 1940, Alphonse T. Picard and Maurice Vincent of the Comité de Protection at Lorette informed Ottawa that all Natives were exempt from military service under the Royal Proclamation of 7 October 1763.[8] In response to this claim, the Indian Agent of Lorette was notified forthwith from Ottawa that Indians were subject to military service "in the same manner as all other subjects."[9] The Comité de Protection persisted, but its subsequent protests were given routine bureaucratic replies.

This changed dramatically, however, when the dispute came to centre on a particular individual, Jean-Paul Gros-Louis. Gros-Louis received his military training order on 4 November 1940. That day, his parents protested in a scathing letter to the Department of National Defence. Claiming that their son was already assisting both his family and the country's war effort by working as a labourer at an airfield in Lorette, the parents claimed that there would be no advantage for anyone in compelling him to undergo military training.[10] Picard and Vincent also wrote to Ottawa, arguing again that it was illegal to call up a man who was not a British subject under the 1763 proclamation. Jean-Paul Gros-Louis, they wrote on 12 November, "was free of [the] obligation" of military service.[11] DNWS officials, however, refused to budge and ordered Gros-Louis to report for military training on 10 January 1941.[12] At this stage, a particularly colourful and flamboyant Native protester entered the fray. Jules Sioui, Chief Executive of the Comité de Protection, wrote a belligerent note to the Montreal Divisional Registrar on 30 December 1940, announcing that his compatriot, Gros-Louis, would not submit to the demands of the Registrar. Sioui promised to lead the defence "of my country, my race, my nation, and my people."[13] He remained an irritant to mobilization officials for the duration of the war.

In late 1940 there was also protest in other parts of Canada. In October 1940 W.A. Elliot, Divisional Registrar in Port Arthur, Ontario, asked Ottawa to clarify the status of Indians who were isolated geographically.[14] Resolutions were passed elsewhere in Ontario by tribal councils denouncing compulsory mobilization and demanding that Indian agents "stretch out a long arm and halt all the functions of government."[15] A resolution from the Six Nations band, for example, in Brantford "strongly protested the imposition of thirty days military training upon the single young men of this reservation." Judicial authorities across Canada were eager for DNWS officials to clarify the legal status of Indians under NRMA regulations. On 17 January 1941, five treaty Indians from the Brantford, Ontario, Six Nations Reserve were charged for non-compliance with registration requirements under the NRMA. The cases were postponed pending clarification of the situation by the proper authorities in Ottawa.[16] Earlier in January, a similar situation had arisen in Quebec, and all cases involving the prosecution of Native delinquents were postponed to February 1941.[17]

On 30 January 1941 the government's policy on Native mobilization was explained in DNWS Circular Memorandum No. 141. It was addressed to all Divisional Registrars and Chairs of National War Services Boards responsible for enforcing mobilization regulations. Before drafting the statement, DNWS officials had solicited the legal opinion of the Department of Justice. W. Stuart Edwards, the Deputy Minister of Justice, replied that "Indians, being British subjects, are subject to Section 3 of the National War Regulations, 1940 (Recruits)."[18] This ruling was conveyed in the Circular Memorandum and remained the official position of the government for the duration of the war. Thus, when R.A. Irwin, Divisional Registrar in Toronto, indicated that he was anxious to avoid entering into any controversy with Indians residing on the Brantford Six Nations Reserve, he received an uncompromising reply from a DNWS official who forecast the full cooperation of Indians in the mobilization effort:

I appreciate that you wish to avoid any friction with this group. No one has ever questioned the loyalty of Indians who served bravely in the last war and who are again represented in the fighting overseas. National Registration was a measure enacted by the Government to facilitate the prosecution of our fight for liberty and freedom. In this respect, Indians who have always enjoyed the greatest measure of liberty under Canadian institutions will undoubtedly recognize the importance of giving their whole-hearted support to the measures made necessary by the war.[19]

However, the protests would not go away. In April 1941, Manley J. Edwards, M.P. for Calgary West, wrote to Prime Minister King about a meeting he had had with representatives of the Stoney Indian Reserve.[20] According to Edwards, Indian leaders in the area believed that Treaty Number Seven, signed in September 1877, relegated them to the status of government wards and that as such they were not subject to compulsory military service. Edwards received a curt reply from Ottawa indicating that Circular Memorandum No. 141 containing the Department of Justice ruling had closed the matter.[21] In a document prepared for Cabinet, W. Stuart Edwards reiterated that there was "no provision in these regulations which excepts the Indians from this duty which is imposed on every male British subject ordinarily resident in Canada."[22] At a meeting of the Cabinet War Committee on 20 May, it was decided that no action would be taken to alter the ruling making Indian registration and training mandatory.[23]

Confirmation of government policy followed in response to continued protest from Indian groups. In July 1941, Robert George of Ravenswood, Ontario, claimed that the compulsory call-up of Natives violated the Robinson Treaties of 1850. Indians, he wrote, had "been classed as the lowest of all classes of human beings in this country" as wards of the government, and they should never be forced to submit to compulsory military training.[24] The reply sent to George simply repeated what was in Circular Memorandum. At the same time, the government learned that the leaders of the Shawanaga Reserve in Ontario were insisting that the Supreme Court of Canada rule on the legal position of Natives under the NRMA.[25] This demand, however, was refused by the Department of Justice on the grounds that there was "no reason for adopting the suggestion that a test case be arranged for the purpose of settling some pre-supposed doubt."[26] On 6 August 1941, Circular Memorandum No. 289 communicated this decision to all Chairs of Mobilization Boards and Divisional Registrars. With this, the first stage in the history of Native mobilization in the Second World War came to a close. DNWS officials had made their position clear in Circular Memorandum No. 141. This position had been affirmed by Cabinet in May 1941 and the legal challenge from the Shawanaga Reserve had been dismissed. The government's position was clear, but over the next two years geographic and other complications often took precedence over legal nicety.

One of the most serious problems confronting Divisional Registrars in their attempt to mobilize Natives was geographic isolation. Prior to the summer of 1941, many Registrars had adopted a wait-and-see attitude regarding Indians, and several had indicated that they were not anxious to pursue the issue of Indian military training. The case of Edward Cardinal of Whitecourt, Alberta, illustrates the problems Registrars faced. When a notice ordering Cardinal's medical examination prior to military training was returned by the post office in June 1941,

J.P. McIsaac, the Edmonton Registrar, asked the Whitecourt postmaster why the notice had not been picked up. The postmaster replied that Cardinal frequented an area twelve miles north of Whitecourt around McLeod Lake and that he only stopped by to pick up his mail twice during the year. McIsaac complained to his Ottawa superiors that it was "practically impossible" to locate many Natives, and that their poor medical condition and low level of literacy would make them poor recruits. "The larger majority of these Indians and Halfbreeds," he wrote, were "quite irresponsible," and not worth pursuing.[27]

(McIsaac's opinion about Native health was not unfounded. A large percentage of Native men failed their medical examinations during the war. In June 1942, for example, a mobile medical unit from the Department of National Defence was sent to Moose Lake, Manitoba, to examine forty Native applicants for enlistment. Not one of them passed the medical test.[28])

Problems, geographic isolation in particular, continued through 1941. In November it was acknowledged in Ottawa that the Bella Coola Indians in British Columbia did not have the financial means to travel to medical examination sites at considerable distances from their reserves.[29] Charles Pennock, the Vancouver Divisional Registrar, wrote that the Natives of British Columbia had "a habit of treating our notices and letters with apparent indifference" on the few occasions when they could be tracked down while fishing in the summer or trapping in the fall and winter.[30] The geographic problem was compounded by a poor knowledge of mobilization regulations among the Indians themselves, despite the best efforts of various Indian Agents to make them known.[31]

Registrars' varying responses to these challenges created a patchwork across the country. By February 1942, the Mobilization Board in Edmonton had stopped pursuing Native delinquents, a decision which Ottawa ultimately had no choice but to accept.[32] In British Columbia, Indian agents in remote areas were allowed to act in lieu of the Mobilization Board. With the consent of the Vancouver Registrar, an agent could decide if a Native was fit for active duty and then direct him to submit to a formal medical examination elsewhere. Requests for deferment could likewise be handled by the agent to avoid having to appear before a distant Administrative Board.[33] In Winnipeg, military authorities refused to enrol or enlist most Indians because of language and medical difficulties. On the other hand, they refused to issue the rejection certificates the Indians needed to be hired by local employers.[34] Major E.E. Crandall, District Recruiting Officer in Kenora, Ontario, stated in a letter to recruiting representatives that Natives should be barred from the armed services because experience had shown that Indians could not "stand confinement or training."[35]

These events led to correspondence between representatives of the DNWS and the DND and the first changes of direction in relation to conscription of Natives. The new policy was explained in Circular Memorandum No. 490 of 31 March 1942. Divisional Registrars, acting on the advice of Indian agents, were to ascertain whether a potential Native recruit could speak English or French effectively. Men who spoke neither language would not be called for military training.[36] In June 1942, Indian Affairs Branch officials recommended that a modified policy be adopted in relation to geographically isolated cases.[37] In keeping with this advice, DNWS officials urged Edmonton mobilization officials, among others, to use the "widest measure of discretion" when calling Indians and to report delinquent Indians separately from non-Native delinquents.[38]

Nevertheless, Indian protests continued to be heard across the country. In August 1942, Micmac leaders in Nova Scotia passed a resolution demanding exemption from compulsory military service because of the number of voluntary enlistments in both World Wars, the ambiguous status of Indians as government wards, and the exemption from conscription granted to Natives during World War I.[39] Jules Sioui of the Lorette Reserve continued to harass DNWS and NSS officials. On 28 January 1943, Sioui informed Ottawa that it gave him great satisfaction to counsel Natives to return all military orders unopened. He was proud, he wrote, to defend "the interests, the rights, and the privileges of my nation."[40] The RCMP were immediately called in to begin an investigation of this matter. The result was a report which cast doubt on Sioui's credibility and influence. He was "a known trouble-maker" and had a reputation of being "an undesirable person." He had served three months in jail following conviction of committing indecent acts with young boys and defaming the character of the Indian Agent in Lorette.[41] The NSS response to this report was to instruct the Quebec Registrar to order Sioui to report for registration by 30 April 1943 and to prosecute him immediately if he failed to comply.

Legal endorsement of the government's position on Indian mobilization followed in the summer of 1943. Harris Smallfence of the Caughnawaga Reserve in Quebec had been convicted in late 1942 for failing to appear for a compulsory medical examination. When his case reached the Court of King's Bench on 21 June 1943, Justice Wilfrid Lazure dismissed his appeal. Noting that there were "not two or several kinds of British subjects," Lazure ruled that Indians were covered by all mobilization rules unless specifically exempted from them. This judgment confirmed the stand taken by the Department of Justice in 1941.[42]

For the most part, however, the edifice of government policy towards Native conscription was crumbling. In a February 1943 report which typified the outlook of many military officers, Major Maris Garton, District Recruiting Officer in the Winnipeg Military District, advanced this sweeping and blunt advice:

The attitude of this office has been that while Indians are entitled to offer their services voluntarily for Active Service, extreme care should be exercised as to their acceptance. Experience has shown that very few Indians can stand confinement to camp or barracks for long periods of time and nervous demands incidental to modern warfare. Many Indians who have enlisted have had to ultimately be discharged, very frequently before their training had been completed ... From our experience I would submit that it would not be sound policy to call up treaty Indians for compulsory military training.[43]

Justice J.E. Adamson, Chairman of the Winnipeg Mobilization Board, protested the actions of military officials in Winnipeg to NSS Director Arthur MacNamara. It would not be possible, Adamson wrote, "for this Board or Divisional Registrars to disregard a certain class without changing the regulations."[44] MacNamara replied that while the idea of changing regulations did not appeal to him, he did support the idea that the Winnipeg Board should grant agricultural postponements for Natives.[45] Adamson welcomed this suggestion but recommended that it be taken one step further: "The best practice would be to simply assume that all these men are engaged in agriculture and should stand postponement until we get around to establishing that they are not essential in agriculture."[46] This declaration turned the usual postponement procedure on its head and Adamson admitted that the plan would produce indefinite postponements for Natives in his district. Nonetheless, this was the "practical thing to do."

The same approach was taken in the Port Arthur District. Divisional Registrar E.W. Edwards met with the Port Arthur Mobilization Board on 25 March 1943 and decided that Indians would be "left in their present environment." Edwards continued to support the policy of DND officials such as Major Garton in Winnipeg. In his opinion, Natives were "morose and sulky," and Edwards emphasized that "the number of recruits obtained from the type of Indian in this area is not worth the trouble and expense to us."[47] The decisions taken in Winnipeg and Port Arthur were in direct contravention to the wishes of Department of National Defence officials in Ottawa. Brigadier-General O.M.M. Kay, the Deputy Adjutant-General, informed NSS administrators that excluding Natives from the NRMA recruitment process was a dangerous idea:

There is little which this department can say in regard to the matter in question except that if we are to live up to our approved Army program, it is necessary that we be allotted all physically fit men of military age who are not required as key men in war or essential industry. The difficulty of enforcement in cases such as you refer to is fully appreciated but this Department does not feel that it would be justified in suggesting that there should be any slackening in the efforts to obtain every available man for service in the Armed Forces.[48]

While NSS officials waffled on the issue, Indian groups continued their own campaign against compulsory mobilization. The Walpole Island Indian Reserve near Wallaceburg, Ontario adopted a consistent pattern of resistance. But when A.B. Harris, Divisional Registrar in Toronto, pressed Ottawa as to whether the RCMP should "adopt the same policy of rigid enforcement of the regulations with respect to these people as we do in regard to others," he did not get very far. Thus, instead of ordering the prosecution of Native delinquents at Walpole Island, Harris was asked only that their names be forwarded to NSS officials in Ottawa for further consideration. The problems at Walpole Island, however, did inspire another NSS review of Native mobilization. In connection with this, NSS officials wrote to the Indian Affairs Branch pointing out that many Indians failed to meet Army physical requirements and should somehow be postponed due to their perceived essentiality in agriculture. Senior DMR officials, noting that the question of Indian mobilization had been "a vexing one for a long time," agreed with the NSS assessment and issued a circular memorandum that called on all Indian agents to redouble their efforts to inform Indians of the possibility of applying for postponement through proper channels.[49]

By the summer of 1943, therefore, a patchwork of policies existed. Indians living in remote areas of British Columbia and Alberta were effectively insulated from the reach of compulsory registration, medical examination, and military training provisions. In Winnipeg, Regina, and Port Arthur, a policy of neglect by Mobilization Boards and Divisional Registrars and the refusal of military authorities to enlist Indians had led to the decision to defer drafting Natives in the vague hope that they would be steered to essential industry and agriculture.[50] In Ontario, pleas for some direction from Ottawa had gone unanswered, while in Quebec active prosecution of Native delinquents had been common since the beginning of the war. In the Maritimes, continued Native opposition had not been countered with any effective response by the authorities. In sum, Ottawa's original policy had manifestly failed and the time was ripe for some new initiative.

It came in the form of NSS Circular Memorandum No. 905, distributed to all Chairs of Mobilization Boards and Divisional Registrars on 31 August 1943. The Circular called for a two-pronged approach: vigorous prosecution of Native delinquents, and a renewed effort to inform all Natives of their right to appeal for postponement of military service. Since the courts and the Department of Justice had mandated that Indians had to comply with mobilization regulations, they rendered themselves liable to prosecution and punishment if they failed to respond to the call-up. Postponements could be granted to individual Indians in the same manner as to other individuals. NSS officials were reminded that many Indians would be able to secure agricultural postponements. The circular emphasized that the entire Indian mobilization issue should be approached with "tact, discretion, and patience," and that better results might be obtained by a direct appeal to the "pride, self-respect, and loyalty" of Natives. If reasonable persuasion failed, however, the mobilization regulations should be enforced in both spirit and letter.[51]

The instructions to pursue prosecutions galvanized many Divisional Registrars east of Port Arthur into action, but only for a brief period of time. Acting on the "definite instructions" appearing in Circular Memorandum 905, A.B. Harris immediately issued orders to prosecute delinquency cases on the Walpole Island reserve.[52] From Halifax came reports that various delinquent Natives were being actively pursued.[53] In Quebec, the situation was more aggravated, and DMR officials received many complaints about the increased enforcement of mobilization regulations on the Caughnawaga Reserve.[54] In October 1943 there was a riot on this reserve that "would have made Wild Bill Hickock's trigger finger itch."[55] Eight RCMP officers scuffled with residents and three Indians were shot and wounded. In the aftermath of this disturbance, the Indian Agent in Caughnawaga reported that the reserve was a "haven" for more than 200 draft evaders, but band leaders passed a resolution demanding that the RCMP detachment be removed from the reserve.[56] Some twenty cases were heard in court beginning 12 January 1944; all the Indians subject to prosecution were convicted, fined $25.00 each, and ordered to comply with mobilization procedures.[57]

The stringent polices articulated in Circular Memorandum 905 were soon subverted by NSS officials themselves. The last phase of the war witnessed the dilution of any meaningful mobilization strategy and the abandonment of enforcement measures. The first hint that active prosecution would be halted came in February 1944. Port Arthur Registrar E.W. Edwards complained that his experience showed that expending valuable resources locating and prosecuting Native delinquents was futile.[58] Arthur MacNamara agreed with Edwards' analysis of the situation and suggested that Section 6 of the mobilization regulations, which stated in part that the "Registrar shall *select* the number of men" required to fill manpower quotas, could be used to filter Indian males from the mobilization procedures.[59] Meanwhile, events in Winnipeg continued on their previous course. In February 1944 DND officials in the city complained that a delinquent from the Port Arthur district ordered by Edwards to report in Winnipeg was "a full-blooded Indian and, therefore, cannot be enrolled into the Army under present regulations."[60] Despite stern reminders from DND headquarters that no such formal regulation existed,[61] the Winnipeg military authorities continued to refuse most Indian enlistments for the remainder of the war.[62]

RCMP authorities in the Toronto military district were instructed to drop prosecution of Indian delinquent cases by late 1943, less than three months after Circular Memorandum 905 had been issued. On 18 November 1943, NSS administrators in Toronto, acting on their own authority, informed the commander of the Toronto RCMP Division that the prosecution of Natives would be delayed for several months.[63] Accordingly, all RCMP detachments in the Toronto military district were advised on 22 November 1943 to close all Indian files.[64] Eventually, the issue went all the way to the Commissioner of the RCMP in Ottawa. On 15 February 1944 the Chapleau Indian Agent wrote to the Indian Affairs Branch expressing his bewilderment about the refusal of the RCMP to prosecute delinquents.[65] The Indian Affairs Branch eventually determined that the Toronto police officials were acting on the directions of the Toronto Divisional Registrar, directions that Ottawa had not authorized.[66]

The NSS approach, then, was to ignore gross breaches of the regulations and encourage Registrars to use their own discretion about calling up Indians. In effect, Registrars across the country had complete freedom to interpret NSS policy concerning Natives as they pleased. On 29 February 1944, Circular Memorandum No. 989 asked Registrars to exercise "great care" in selecting Natives from remote or isolated areas without saying exactly where these areas were.[67] The new Toronto Registrar, N.D. Davidson, made it quite clear that he considered that the discretionary powers granted to Mobilization Boards and Registrars rendered the whole issue of active prosecution on Natives irrelevant.[68] By the summer of 1944, Davidson's position was adopted almost everywhere in the country. NSS officials usually insisted that detailed and proper records be kept concerning the most minute facets of mobilization procedure. The disparity among various divisions with respect to Natives, however, forced Ottawa to seek clarification of figures submitted in various weekly and monthly reports. In June 1944, the Regina Divisional Registrar insisted that nothing was to be done regarding Natives and that all Indians would simply be placed in the category "Not Called,"[69] a decision quickly supported by Arthur MacNamara. From Winnipeg, NSS officials continued to inform Ottawa that the Army did not desire Native recruits.[70] In British Columbia, many

medically fit Native men were simply being granted indefinite postponements of military service. In the Kwawkewlth Agency, for example, one
man was overseas, four were on active duty in Canada, two were in
the Army under NRMA provisions, and 106 physically fit men had been
granted deferments.[71]

It seemed that only Jules Sioui could goad NSS officials to support
the strict application of mobilization regulations. Sioui was considered
a clear threat to the established patterns of the administration of Indian
affairs in Canada.[72] Sioui convened a meeting of a few Indian representatives in Ottawa in October 1943 to discuss the problems facing
the Native Canadian community. Although the practical value of this
conference was limited, a larger gathering was scheduled for June 1944,
a meeting that was vigorously opposed by Indian Affairs Branch
officials. Indian agents were advised to remind Natives that they should
fulfill their patriotic duty by supporting the war effort and refraining
from "travelling across the country at the beck and call of any agita-
tor." Despite these exhortations, the June gathering was well attended
and the Minister of Mines and Resources, T.A. Crerar, listened as
delegates from across Canada protested compulsory conscription measures.[73] Sioui's pioneering efforts to establish a national platform for
Indians to voice their concerns[74] received wide media coverage and
generated further Native opposition to NRMA regulations.

In the aftermath of the June 1944 gathering, Sioui was fined $25.00
for contravening mobilization regulation.[75] Undeterred, Sioui appealed
his conviction and subsequently wrote to Indian bands across the
nation urging non-compliance with NRMA regulations, a personal call
that appears to have influenced many Native men.[76] Sioui remained
active in the Lorette Huron community, orchestrating widespread resistance to orders for medical examinations and military training. In
January 1945, Sioui returned eight orders for the medical examination
and one order for military training to the District Officer Commanding
in Quebec City. The RCMP were subsequently ordered to take "immediate and drastic action" by arresting, along with Sioui, the nine other
men who refused to comply.[77] One of the original opponents of
compulsory mobilization on the Lorette Huron reservation was finally
detained; in February 1945, more than four years after he was brought
to the attention of DNWS officials, Jean-Paul Gros-Louis was arrested.
Gros-Louis, along with two of his relatives, posted a $300 bond and
the case was remanded to a later date.[78]

In contrast to their preoccupation with Sioui, NSS officials tolerated
laxity in most regions of the country during the autumn of 1944. At
a general conference of Registrars held in October 1944, Winnipeg
Registrar C.D. McPherson informed Ottawa that, in conjunction with

the Army authorities, the Mobilization Board in his division had simply granted Natives unlimited postponements or else placed them in the "Not Called" category.[79] Port Arthur Registrar E.W. Edwards insisted that active prosecution should not be countenanced in order "to eliminate the tremendous cost and routine in which we rarely gain a single recruit."[80] After Arthur MacNamara toured the West in November 1944, he informed his subordinates that it did not matter to him how the Mobilization Boards dealt with the Indians as long as they found a way to "grant postponement for them all."[81]

The final weeks of 1944 brought new developments arising out of the decision of the King government to send NRMA conscripts overseas. On 22 December 1944, the War Cabinet again considered the issue of Native conscription. Cabinet, ignoring the permissive policies affecting Indians currently in force across the country, emphasized that the Department of Justice ruling of 20 January 1941 mandating the call-up of Natives under the NRMA would remain official government policy. But Indian NRMA recruits could also be exempted from overseas service if DMR officials determined that some Indian claims for exemption from compulsory foreign service were valid.[82] In January 1945, the Indian Affairs Branch distributed a circular letter relieving those Natives covered by Treaties Three, Six, Eight, and Eleven of any requirement for overseas service.[83] On 6 February 1945, by Circular Memorandum No. 1098, NSS officials in Ottawa again attempted to codify mobilization procedures in relation to Natives across the country, but in reality this document simply sanctioned the existing patchwork. Circular Memorandum 1098 directed Registrars not to call Indians who spoke neither English nor French; not to issue orders to any Native living, in the opinion of the Registrar, in remote areas, and to record any Native recruit deemed unacceptable to the Army, regardless of his physical condition, as "Not Acceptable for Medical Reasons."[84] The circle had finally been completed. Almost four years to the day after the Department of Justice had sternly endorsed the necessity and legality of Native mobilization, NSS had rubber-stamped the policies of indifference and apathy that had characterized the actions of many Registrars and Mobilization Boards for most of the period.

The remaining months of the war witnessed the complete halting of any concerted attempt to mobilize the Native population. At the same time Native leaders kept up their resistance campaign. Most dramatically, this took the form of death threats against RCMP constables by the Caughnawaga leaders.[85] On 12 February 1945, the Toronto Registrar was instructed to stay any prosecutions of Indians until further notice. He did so despite another curt reminder from the Justice Department that "the regulations should be enforced in the case of

Indians in the same manner as in the case of other persons liable to military training."[86] Thereafter, Humphrey Mitchell and T.A. Crerar worked out a plan that called for the Indian Agent in each locality to work closely with Natives to persuade them to follow mobilization regulations. But this was a hollow gesture since Mobilization Boards and Army officials were actively refusing to recruit Indians for military service. On 2 May 1945, despite the fact that the regulations remained in force, Arthur MacNamara ordered NSS officials to drop active prosecution of Native delinquents and remove themselves from further involvement with Native Canadians. With the cooperation of the Justice Department, cases that were already in progress were disposed of through the granting of suspended sentences to individuals found guilty by the courts.[87]

Paradoxically, Native Canadian recruitment strategies under the NRMA proved to be an important factor in a more progressive re-orientation of government policy toward Canadian Natives in the postwar era. The presence of Natives within the ranks of NRMA conscripts combined with the distinguished overseas service of Indian volunteers in the armed forces placed the contribution of Indians to Canada's war effort on a par with many other ethnic or racial minority groups. Jules Sioui used the conscription issue to bring widespread public attention to the inferior citizenship status of Natives under the Indian Act, despite the fact that Natives were classed as British subjects during a period of national emergency. Furthermore, Sioui's strident opposition to compulsory mobilization was the primary catalyst in the formation of national Native organizations dedicated to addressing the chronic problems that faced Natives. The Special Parliamentary Committee on Postwar Reconstruction and Re-establishment publicized the social and economic problems facing Canada's Indian population. All of these factors led to the formation of the Special Joint Committee of the Senate and the House of Commons in 1946, and the Committee's investigation into the administration of Indian affairs in Canada resulted in the passage of a new Indian Act in 1951, the first major revision of policies affecting Natives since 1876. While the majority of DNWS and NSS mobilization initiatives had no perceptible impact on the postwar direction of Canadian social and economic policy, the efforts to conscript Native Canadians, though flawed and feeble in most instances, left an important and enduring legacy.

3 Student Deferment

At the June 1944 meeting of the National Conference of Canadian Universities (NCCU), the following motion received unanimous support:

The Conference records its appreciation of the splendid relations which have existed between the universities on the one hand, and the University Advisory Board, the Director of National Selective Service, and the Minister of Labour [on the other hand], and of the fact that the government has always consulted the universities and followed their considered judgment in formulating its regulations respecting the mobilization of students.[1]

The record of cooperation between the government and university officials was indeed exceptional.[2]

The mobilization of Canadian university students differed sharply from the attempts to draft Native Canadians. As the war progressed, an increasingly rudderless, fractured, and permissive mobilization structure placed the overwhelming majority of Indians beyond the reach of NRMA provisions. Conversely, students were subject to increasingly stringent, comprehensive, and standardized mobilization initiatives. Thousands of students in what were deemed to be non-essential subjects had to postpone their studies and enter NRMA units. Students in professional, scientific, and technological disciplines were allowed to complete their studies. NSS officials, however, did not take a leading role in the development of student mobilization strategies. Instead, the NCCU was allowed to essentially regulate its own affairs and determine which and how many students would enter home defence units.[3] The willingness of Arthur MacNamara and leading NSS officials to allow non-governmental agencies to co-opt their role in the formulation and direction of mobilization policy in this area stands out as a key feature of Ottawa's human resource mobilization strategy during the Second World War.

Under the NRMA students, with the exception of some of those studying theology, were eligible for compulsory military service. Training could be postponed pending the completion of their studies. After being granted a deferment, a medically fit student of callable age was required to join his local campus contingent of the Canadian Officers Training Corps (COTC). He had to take 110 hours of military training during term and to attend a two-week military training camp in the summer. The number of students enrolled taking campus military training courses plus the summer military camp increased from 2,138 in 1940 to a maximum of 10,422 in 1941 before declining to 7,440 in the final year of the war.[4]

The military status of students was clarified following the issuance of the 1940 National War Services Regulations. Responding to calls from officials in many administrative divisions, DNWS officials invited all Divisional registrars and Mobilization Board chairmen to attend a meeting with university officials in Ottawa in February 1941.[5] Two key decisions were made at this gathering. First, all medically fit students who turned twenty-one between 1 July 1940 and 30 June 1941 and who had completed 110 hours of training in a campus COTC contingent could attend the two-week military camp in the summer to satisfy the requirement for thirty days of military training. Second, all students who had reached twenty-one prior to 1 July 1940[6] and who had completed 110 hours of COTC training would be considered to have satisfied the thirty-day training requirement. However, students in this category who wanted to attend a two-week summer camp would be allowed to do so. These directives were quickly adopted as the basis of mobilization policy that was first expressed in a DND directive of 5 March 1941[7] and then in PC 1822 of 18 March 1941.[8]

A clear direction had been established, but not all mobilization authorities were satisfied with an outcome that facilitated student deferment. While Divisional registrars were the pointmen for Native Canadian mobilization, Mobilization Board chairmen took centre stage in the debate concerning the call-up of students since they adjudicated the thousands of student requests for postponement of military training from students. The two most vociferous opponents of Ottawa's early policies affecting students were Justice A.M. Manson, chairman of the Vancouver Mobilization Board and, Justice J.F.L. Embury, chairman of the Regina Mobilization Board. Embury repeatedly heaped scorn on the willingness of other Mobilization Boards to defer most theological students. His views were hotly disputed by Major-General Leo R. LaFlèche, the DNWS associate deputy minister and a bureaucrat who was viewed with disdain by many mobilization officials like Embury.[9] While LaFlèche tended to let subordinates handle other mobilization initiatives, he defended the DNWS policy affecting students and criticized Embury for engaging in a "carping which must numb the finer sensibilities." He also offered this vigorous defence of the deferment of theological students:

We are in for a very long and costly war to save our civilization or the right to live as we wish to. If we are fighting for civilization then religious faith is at the top of the list. I shall not be a party to starving the ministry of any denomination. We shall certainly need our churches after this war, when we are in the extremely difficult period of reconstruction which must follow the terrible turmoil the world is in at the present time.[10]

Embury was unimpressed and replied with a scathing denunciation of student deferments in general:

I reiterate the giving of preferential treatment in time of war indiscriminately to students at universities is unfair and wrong. I expect there will be a bit of a row one of these days. If we had less so-called higher education we would have more courage and public spirit. However, my Board can take it. A famous historian once wrote that education is of but little value except to those natures so happily constituted that it is almost superfluous. Let's hope the Russians win the war for us. The way we are going we'd never manage our share for ourselves. Speaking as a resident of my own province, I am ashamed.[11]

Not surprisingly, university administrators hotly disputed this point of view. University of Manitoba President Sidney Smith attempted to counter the critics by documenting the necessity of educating skilled professionals and insisting that any student, regardless of academic discipline, would be expelled from university if he failed to meet stringent academic requirements. The regulations could not be "invoked as a refuge for any young man poor enough in spirit to desire to evade his military obligations"; any student falling short of university requirements would be directed immediately to a DNWS Mobilization Board for prompt action.[12] In the same spirit, University of Toronto President H.J. Cody sought to assure the public that his campus would be "no house of refuge" for delinquent students failing to see the "deadly peril" the war presented to the British Empire.[13] These sentiments were well received in Ottawa, where there was confidence that the right formula had been found vis-à-vis the universities. In January 1942 LaFlèche observed that the mobilization of students had progressed "surprisingly well" and that he was "deeply impressed" with the co-operation received from university officials.[14]

There were, however, some unresolved issues. The most prominent of these concerned compulsory COTC training for medical, engineering, and science students. In October 1941, medical students at McGill University complained to Defence Minister J.L. Ralston that the military training requirements interfered severely with a student's ability to concentrate on a course of study.[15] McGill medical students had made it plain that they would join the armed forces at the conclusion of their schooling and that was all that was required. Their COTC training was cumbersome and "was in no way aiding our nation's war effort." Subsequently, the DND replaced military drill with a course in military medicine for medical students in their clinical years, but public pressure continued to mount to allow medical students to concentrate completely on their studies.[16]

Science and engineering students also expressed considerable opposition to the military training regime, especially the summer camp requirement. Officials of the Wartime Bureau of Technical Personnel asked LaFlèche in December 1941 to waive the two-week summer requirement for science students already enrolled in COTC training during the academic year.[17] They pointed out that war industries were being canvassed to accept any and all technical students for summer employment, and warned LaFlèche of serious financial hardships for science students if they were forced to relinquish employment opportunities to attend military camp. LaFlèche agreed with this assessment that the plight of engineering and science students should receive the "sympathetic consideration" of both DNWS and DND officials.[18] The WBTP next made the case that since science students would not be able to enter employment before the military camps opened in June, they would be deprived of five weeks of employment income.[19] This evidence was compelling and led to action. On 20 January 1942, LaFlèche issued a circular memorandum that allowed the two-week military camp to be waived for science and engineering students provided the District Officer Commanding in a particular area approved of the waiver. This policy was extended to all medical and dental students on 12 February 1942.[20]

Concern about the financial status of students led to further government initiatives. The issue of government assistance to deserving students had already been addressed in an agreement between Ottawa and the provinces. Under the Dominion-Provincial Youth Training Agreement, a payment of $200.00, shared equally between the two levels of government, could be made to a student enrolled in medical or hard science programs. Unfortunately, as late as the start of the 1941–2 academic year, only the four western provinces, Quebec, and Prince Edward Island participated in the scheme; the federal contribution to the scheme was a paltry $21,850.[21] At the urging of DNWS and WBTP officials, a new and more comprehensive agreement was concluded in February 1942. This provided for maximum assistance to an individual student of $300.00. After Ontario failed to agree to sign on to the new student aid plan, Dominion officials concluded separate agreements with the four large Ontario universities to provide scholarships to deserving science and medical students.[22] As a result, the federal contribution in this field doubled to $41,000 before the 1942–3 academic year commenced.[23]

University presidents and deans of engineering and science attended a conference with the NCCU on 11–12 May 1942. The deferment policy for science and technical students was further defined. At a preliminary meeting on 5 May attended by representatives of the DND, the DNWS, the DMS, and NSS, LaFlèche had stated that the existing system lacked consistency and proper coordination and that it was creating an "impossible situation."[24] An alternative scheme would have to be introduced in which NSS civilian officials (at this stage military mobilization was still the responsibility of the DNWS) would have complete authority over the deferment of technical personnel. LaFlèche now also insisted that the time had come to restrict access to courses deemed not to be in the national interest.[25]

On the morning of 12 May, LaFlèche and NSS Director Elliot Little presided over a general session of the conference. In the afternoon, the meeting split up into three groups: university presidents discussed funding for undergraduates and the student mobilization regulations in general; deans of engineering discussed engineering requirements; and deans of science discussed science requirements with WBTP and National Research Council representatives. The result of these deliberations was that nine resolutions emanating from the 5 May preliminary meeting were adopted unanimously. Six of these concerned the transfer of all authority over technical students from the Department of National War Services, which still controlled the call-up regulations under the NRMA, to NSS jurisdiction.[26]

This was a call for sweeping reform. It did not meet with success. A draft Order-in-Council was prepared placing student deferment beyond the reach of the Mobilization Boards. But when LaFlèche ran into concerted opposition from Board chairs such as Manson and Embury, he backed down and in July 1942 he told the WBTP that any proposal to remove students seeking deferment from the direct authority of the Mobilization Boards "would be the beginning of the disintegration of compulsory mobilization in Canada."[27] LaFlèche also came under pressure from political quarters. During the Senate debate on a new vocational training bill in the summer of 1942, Manitoba Senator John Haig claimed that DNWS officials were "exempting the very people who ought to go – the educated people of this country."[28] LaFlèche countered such sentiments with the argument that postponement entitlement was being reduced rather than expanded so as to "impose severe conditions as to scholarity and successful passing of scholastic examinations."[29]

However, two initiatives from the May conference had the effect of moving policy in a more permissive direction. First, WBTP officials were granted the authority to issue permits to all essential technical personnel, permits that would be considered as proof of essentiality in industry by Mobilization Boards. Second, an NSS program of scholarships, including financial aid for first-year students, was introduced. It gave an additional 500 technical students financial assistance. Also, the DND agreed to put on pay and allowance all medical and dental students who were in the final year of their program, physically fit, and willing to enlist upon graduation.[30] The revised regulations for students were embodied in Section 17 of PC 8343 of 16 September 1942. In the view of DNWS officials, the new regulations were "far more severe" than those previously in force and would facilitate "the continuation of the flow of educated men, professional and technical, both for the immediate requirements of the war effort and for the period of reconstruction thereafter."[31]

While this debate concerning technical and professional students was in progress, the issue of deferment for theological students and conscientious objectors was also hotly contested. At the heart of the debate in this period was the question of denominational preference in exemption orders. Under Section 6(d) of the DNWS regulations, Roman Catholic seminarians were classed as clergymen and were, therefore, completely exempt. In March 1941, LaFlèche had refused a request from the Reverend George Dorey of the United Church of Canada Board of Home Missions to exempt United Church theological students who had already completed 110 hours of COTC training from the two-week military camp. Dorey asked for this exemption on the grounds that the camp interfered with summer missionary activity.[32] LaFlèche was unmoved, even though he consistently allowed Catholic seminarians, especially in the province of Quebec, to avoid the mobilization regulations entirely.[33] Dorey shifted the focus of his campaign to the cantankerous Justice Embury in Regina throughout 1942. James McMurtry, a United Church theology student studying at St. Andrew's

College in Saskatoon, had been called for his medical examination and been placed in the lowest possible medical designation. In 1942, however, he was suddenly and arbitrarily upgraded to the medical category of B1 and ordered by Embury to report for alternative service work in Banff.[34] This change, apparently, was made after the Regina Mobilization Board had interrogated McMurtry about his attitude to the war and discovered that he was a conscientious objector. Dorey lodged "an emphatic protest against a military tribunal presuming to pass an opinion" on the beliefs of a United Church theological student.

Daniel Firth, the President of Knox Theological College, University of Toronto, added his voice to the complaints about the alleged special status of Catholic seminarians. He asked LaFlèche to provide a "straightforward answer" – a considerable challenge for the verbose LaFlèche – as to whether bona fide Presbyterian ministerial candidates were eligible for exemption from mobilization. Firth also called for the clarification of the jurisdiction of the Mobilization Boards in relation to theological students.[35] LaFlèche gave his usual blustering reply, denying any discrimination and ignoring his own letters to Catholic officials confirming exemption privileges of Catholic seminarians. Claiming that it was "impossible for me to understand how one can say there is apparent discrimination," LaFlèche attacked Firth for questioning the "unimpeachable character" of Mobilization Board members.[36] In November 1942 the Justice Department ruled that the Mobilization Boards had sole discretion in deciding theological exemptions.[37] Nevertheless, NSS officials continued to mediate the problems that arose after the NSS Mobilization Regulations were issued in December 1942. Moreover, NSS director Arthur MacNamara issued instructions to Mobilization Boards allowing for the exemption of theological students of accredited religious denominations eligible to supply chaplains to the Armed Forces.[38]

No such compromise was reached in relation to Justice Embury's long and unrelenting campaign against conscientious objectors in his district. Embury had such low regard for these men that he once proposed having the press present at hearings dealing with alternative service, but LaFlèche quashed this idea.[39] In December 1941, Embury became embroiled with a group of students at the University of Saskatchewan. Led by Harvey Moats, they claimed that Embury refused to hear their requests for deferment.[40] M.J. Coldwell, the Member of Parliament for Rosetown-Biggar and the Cooperative Commonwealth Federation National President, supported Moats's assertions and reminded Mackenzie King of his statement that conscientious objectors would not be singled out for vindictive treatment.[41] Noting that Moats and his group of students had indicated that they would

take alternative courses in physical fitness and ambulance work instead
of COTC training, Coldwell denounced Embury and the Regina Mobilization Board for showing "an entire disregard of British and democratic
principles."[42]

A bitter debate followed. Board member George Bickerton castigated
Coldwell for his ignorance of the situation in light of the recent
Japanese attack on Pearl Harbor; Coldwell and others "who did not
want to be disturbed in the even tenor of their lives" should step
forward to "defend the principles of democracy and Christianity."
After visiting the United Kingdom and observing the lenient policy
towards conscientious objectors in effect there, Coldwell told Bickerton
that he was determined to see that "no form of incipient Hitlerism
gains ground in this country." Embury claimed that the whole matter
could be resolved if the university dismissed Dr. Carlyle King of the
English department, whom he labelled as a "subversive." When Coldwell
asked for a public presence at Mobilization Board meetings regarding
conscientious objectors, Embury changed his earlier position and
refused on the grounds that the public had "no right to know of them."
He saw no problem, however, in divulging the minutes of the meetings
to Canadian Legion officials anxious to target conscientious objectors
for public example. Eventually, LaFlèche intervened to allow the
Saskatchewan students to complete the academic year free from harass-
ment. In the end, two of the six students pursued by the Regina Board
gave up their fight and joined the Canadian Firefighters Corps in the
United Kingdom. But this did not deflect Embury; in December 1942
he informed NSS officials that 50 per cent of the incoming 1941–42
class of 590 students at the University of Saskatchewan had enrolled
solely to avoid military service.[43]

The first stage of the Canadian government's response to the deferment of university students ended with the NSS takeover of the mobilization machinery in December 1942. Under the supervision of LaFlèche
and DNWS officials, several provisional, halting steps were taken to formulate a policy to protect scientific and technical personnel from induction into the military. The December 1942 NSS mobilization regulations
attempted to address the thorny issue of the exemption of theological
students, although problems continued to be experienced in this area
for the duration of the war. In January 1943 the NCCU expressed support for the "enlightened policy" of the Dominion government in relation to university education and promised its full cooperation in the
national war effort.[44] At the same time, however, NCCU leaders effectively scuttled MacNamara's preliminary proposals to curtail enrolments
in university Arts courses.[45]

In the spring of 1943 the NCCU's promised support was tested by the first nationwide survey of the practices of the thirteen Mobilization Boards in relation to student deferments. The survey was a result of behind-the-scenes pressure from the leader of the Conservative opposition in the House of Commons, R.B. Hanson. Hanson's primary concern was that undergraduates in four-year degree programs were enrolling in professional programs such as law to extend their deferment status. Claiming that such arrangements were "altogether too wide,"[46] Hanson demanded immediate action to avoid the public embarrassment of Labour Minister Humphrey Mitchell in the House of Commons. Hanson expressed particular concern about the situation in Montreal and Toronto, where the Mobilization Boards allegedly used their broad discretionary powers to grant extended postponements.[47]

The survey form distributed by MacNamara to Divisional Registrars across the country asked twenty-two questions.[48] While most Registrars reported similar practices governing postponement of service and treatment of students who failed their academic programs, their answers revealed a patchwork of policies in relation to the duration of deferments. Some Boards only granted postponements for a single term pending clarification of academic progress, while others granted deferments either for the academic year (eight months) or an entire calendar year.[49] Assessments of the overall effectiveness of the student deferment program also varied from place to place. Registrars in London, Montreal, and Saint John reported that the existing system worked adequately. Registrars in Vancouver and Regina expressed dissatisfaction with the status quo. This, however, was hardly surprising given the activities of Justices Manson and Embury, the Mobilization Board Chairs in these cities.

In August 1943 the Board Chairs themselves were sent a questionnaire on student deferment.[50] Three propositions, to be submitted to an upcoming convention of the NCCU, were put to them for comment. These were that: (1) any male student who had less than matriculation standing from high school and who was of the age of eighteen and a half years, or over, would not be permitted to enter a university or complete high school; (2) some limitation should be placed on the numbers of male students entering science courses in universities; and (3) a male student who was aged eighteen and a half or over and who was in Medical Category A should not be allowed to enter or continue any non-science course in a university unless exempted from call-up by the appropriate Mobilization Board.

The answers received from the Board Chairs revealed the wide discrepancies in attitude across the country towards student deferment.

Several respondents in provinces west of Ontario agreed wholeheartedly with all three proposals. Justice J.E. Adamson of Winnipeg insisted that only medical students, engineers, and pure science students should be postponed. While no response was received from the normally bombastic Embury, Justice Manson was heard from in no uncertain terms. Hammering home the point that "Christian civilization" must be defended, he demanded that his Board alone should have the authority to decide on student deferments and that no new rules should interfere with this. In an addendum to his response, Manson showed to full advantage his disdain for existing NSS regulations:

We are deluged with circulars which are a nuisance. We have filed ours away to read after the war. Section 12 [of the NSS regulations dealing with students] should be deleted and an entirely new section drawn. Subsections (1) and (2) might refer to a kindergarten. The university authorities are not in half as good a position to say what courses a student should be allowed to take as are the Mobilization Boards. A course may be available at a university in Canada in the sweet bye and bye and at great expense. The same course may be available in a neighbouring American university now and at a reasonable expense. Subsection (9) should be put in the wastepaper basket. It is more or less innocuous so why keep it?

The two Mobilization Board Chairs in the province of Quebec argued in favour of the status quo. Justice H.A. Fortier of Quebec City and Judge J.C.M. Lajoie of Montreal vehemently opposed any change to the existing regulations. Lajoie insisted that the experience gained in his district in the matter of student deferments should not be wasted by more regulations. In support of this view, Montreal Registrar Raymond Ranger stressed that the need for national unity dictated that no regulation from Ottawa should impinge on Lajoie's autonomy. For his part, Fortier emphasized that Quebec's system of thirty-six classical colleges, which had seven-year programs, could not be compared to the education system to be found in the rest of Canada. The majority of classical college graduates were twenty years old before they even applied to university. Fortier also argued that no distinction should be made between technical or professional students and non-science students.[51]

In the final analysis, MacNamara sided with the advocates of a tough approach after meeting with other mobilization officials in August 1943. In his speech on 30 August 1943 to the opening of the NCCU convention he spoke admiringly of the views of Harold Dodds, the president of Princeton University. Dodds had questioned the value of any student whose "brains were locked up in the ivory tower" and believed that student manpower should be maximized in a period of grave military difficulties.[52] MacNamara agreed and proposed a plan of action, based on the survey of Board Chairs, to the convention. According to this, a male student aged eighteen and a half years or older who had not achieved the standing certified by a provincial department of education for his particular age would not be allowed to enter university. This particular requirement was clearly a sop to the special circumstances of Quebec's classical colleges. Male students in specified university programs such as medicine, science, and dentistry would be deferred as long as their marks were satisfactory. All other male university students in Arts courses would have to make individual applications for deferment. MacNamara admitted that this requirement would prevent non-science students from entering or completing their programs.

The response of the convention to MacNamara's plan was mixed. The NCCU endorsed the first two proposals but balked at the third, which held the promise of freeing the maximum number of students for military service. Instead, the convention adopted a resolution to allow any student who had enrolled for the 1943–44 academic year to complete his year regardless of the course of study. After the completion of the 1943–44 academic year, all students in disciplines deemed non-essential would be re-evaluated and the medically fit among them would not be granted further deferments. The NCCU also recommended that a University Advisory Board (UAB) be established to advise MacNamara on future student policy. While conceding that anyone eighteen and a half years of age or older who was not progressing at the proper pace should not be admitted to university, the NCCU sought to avoid, at least for another year, the flushing out of students in what were considered non-essential university courses.[53]

Remarkably, MacNamara went along with this but he was soon being castigated by other government officials for betraying the interests of Canada's military effort. Even ranking officials in the Department of Labour refused to support his actions. One of these, A.H. Brown, insisted that MacNamara's bargain with the NCCU violated all the principles agreed upon during the pre-conference deliberations with the War Manpower Committee of the Cabinet. According to Brown, the NCCU scheme should have been vetted before the War Manpower Committee before being adopted as official NSS policy. He also maintained that the existing procedure for consulting the NCCU made a University Advisory Board redundant. Major-General H.J. Riley of the NSS Mobilization Division likewise attacked MacNamara for maintaining the privileged status of students in Canada. The beleaguered NSS director also heard from Air Vice-Marshall J.A. Sully, who demanded that no physically-fit student enrolled in a non-science course should be allowed to continue his studies. Exhibiting a will to fight back that he lacked on many other occasions, MacNamara disputed Sully's assertion that the NCCU proposals constituted a licence for students to evade military service. The adoption of the NCCU scheme had "avoided a long drawn-out row which I think the university presidents had anticipated and which, I am sure, the government would not recommend."[54]

University officials, of course, were elated by their victory. Sidney Smith, President of the University of Manitoba, applauded the "wise recommendations" endorsed by MacNamara,[55] while K.P.R. Neville, the Registrar of the University of Western Ontario, maintained that the NCCU resolutions illustrated the "finest kind of co-operative understanding" that two groups working to win the war could have.[56] Mobilization Board Chairs were informed of the new NSS policy concerning student deferments in a circular letter dated 17 September 1943.[57]

Through all of this, the issue of the exemption of Protestant theological students remained prominent. As early as November 1942, D.T. Owens, professor of philosophy at United College in Winnipeg, had complained that the regulatory change allowing exemptions for students in denominations eligible to supply chaplains still granted Mobilization Boards complete discretion with respect to the exemption of Protestant theological students.[58] The next year, Owens returned to the attack, only to have his complaint deflected by MacNamara to other NSS officials.[59] In October 1943, Owens made his case directly to Mackenzie King, railing against the "intolerable inequality" between the draft status of Protestant and Roman Catholic seminarians. Owens demanded that the exemption provisions for theological students be made mandatory for all Mobilization Boards; the current discretionary policy was "unjust, unequal, and inexplicable" and needed to be altered.[60] In his reply on King's behalf, MacNamara insisted that Mobilization Boards were comprised of "responsible citizens with full appreciation of their duties," and as such would continue to have discretion in the matter of exempting theological students. This meant that Boards in Quebec could continue to grant blanket exemption to Catholic seminarians while allowing Boards elsewhere to call or exempt theological students as they saw fit.[61]

In late 1943 the NCCU finally succeeded in constituting the membership of the University Advisory Board. The first meeting of the new group was held on 6 January 1944 to devise a student deferment policy for the 1944–45 academic year. Five of the twelve members of the UAB were university representatives, one came from private business, and four represented NSS. The DMS and the WBTP were represented by one member each.[62] Discussion at the January 1944 meeting centred on the need to defer trained personnel, with the WBTP leading a spirited defence of the deferment of science students. Monsignor Cyrille Gagnon of Laval University, however, called for a more inclusive deferment policy that would cover all courses and allow the university to "train the future leaders of the country." The decision reached at this meeting altered the liberal deferment policies that had been in effect for the first four years of the war. For the first time, students enrolled in non-science courses were to be targeted for call-up if they were medically fit. The existing practice of allowing deferment of all students enrolled in subjects deemed to be in the national interest would continue. Students in eleven specialized programs ranging from medicine to forestry to commerce qualified for special deferment status.[63] But there would now be numerical targets for students enrolled in non-essential disciplines. If medically fit, any male student enrolled in the 1943–44 academic year who did not finish in the upper half of his class would not be allowed to continue his studies. This rule would also apply to students entering university for the first time in 1944–45 and enrolling in subjects considered non-essential. The recommendations of the UAB were duly accepted and Board Chairs were informed of the new policy early in February 1944.[64]

The overwhelming majority of Mobilization Boards and university officials quickly embraced the UAB decision of January 1944 to target specific groups of students for military call-up. University of Saskatchewan officials, for example, reported 121 Arts students in the lower half of their program during the 1943–44 academic year to the Mobilization Board.[65] Mobilization Board Chairs welcomed the precise nature of the regulations calling for the mandatory call-up of medically fit men in the bottom half of their class. Even Justice Manson seemed to welcome the new directives from Ottawa. An interesting case of the application of the new student policy concerned the status of high school students in Victoria who were not achieving a normal rate of progression through the secondary school program. When one such student, Frank Gower, was ordered to report for military training in November 1944, there was a heated exchange of letters between Harold Campbell, Municipal Inspector of Schools in Victoria, and Manson. Campbell implored Manson to allow Gower to complete Grade 12, pointing out that the government now could send NRMA men overseas and that at age nineteen Gower could not be accused of being unduly behind his younger classmates. After Manson declined to reopen the case, T.L. Christie, Secretary of the Board of School Trustees in Victoria, reported the dispute to Ottawa.[66] NSS officials immediately demanded an account of Manson's actions. With obvious delight, Manson countered that he was merely following the instructions issuing from the UAB meeting of January 1944. The provincial education minister had indicated that a student in the twelfth grade should not be older than eighteen years. Since Gower would be twenty in April 1945, he could not be given special consideration. To do so would be to "make fish of one and flesh of another."[67] Faced with this argument, NSS officials withdrew support for Gower's claim for deferment. Before the 1944–45 academic year commenced, 3,600 medically fit students had been reported to Mobilization Boards for assignment under the terms of the January 1944 UAB agreement.[68]

In January 1945 UAB representatives met to consider options with respect to students enrolled in the 1944–5 academic session. Three proposals dealt specifically with the number of students to be deferred. All callable male students who placed in the lower half of their courses would be deemed available for military service. This would effectively eliminate the preferred status of students enrolled in technical and scientific courses. No callable student seeking entrance to a university in the autumn of 1945 would be admitted if his scholastic standing was lower than the average incoming grade of the students accepted in the autumn of 1944. Finally, the number of new students accepted in 1945 would be lower than the number enrolled for the first time in 1943. This sweeping mandate for change was endorsed somewhat reluctantly by Labour Minister Mitchell, who estimated that it would eliminate almost one-third of all students enrolled in Canadian universities and free approximately 4,000 men for military service.[69] Even the UAB recognized that the proposed changes would be controversial.[70]

The progress of the war in Europe during the first months of 1945 allowed the UAB proposals to be placed in abeyance. Then, in May 1945, MacNamara launched a new initiative. Co-operation with university officials, he wrote, had been the key to success and any change in policy with respect to student deferment should be approved and initiated by the UAB. MacNamara's own view was that the requirement for the reporting of the lower 50 per cent of students in non-essential courses could now be abandoned, but that mandatory military training in universities through the COTC should continue.[71] The UAB readily bought the first of these ideas but was lukewarm to the second.[72] This debate was, however, overtaken by the end of the war. At its meeting of 24 August 1945, the UAB called for the repeal of all student mobilization regulations, and this action was taken by the government soon afterwards.[73]

The administration of the deferment of students in post-secondary institutions must be considered as one of the success stories of mobilization in Canada during the Second World War. DNWS officials adopted a flexible and increasingly lenient policy towards science, professional, and technical students in order to guarantee the graduation of skilled personnel for the civilian economy and the armed forces. NSS officials in turn built on this general approach but sought to limit the enrolment of medically fit men in Arts courses in Canadian universities. By 1944 a scientific and measurable standard for student deferments had been established that allowed exemption for students enrolled in select disciplines while permitting strict enforcement of the rules in the case of Arts students who did not meet specific academic goals. These policies, however, were driven by NCCU leaders seeking to prevent the adoption of policies that would strip all medically fit men from Arts courses. Arthur MacNamara worked willingly within a non-governmental framework and cultivated a conciliatory relationship with the NCCU. Student deferment policies adopted between 1940 and 1945 epitomized MacNamara's ideals of compromise and cooperation.

4 War Plant Employees and Other Factory Workers: The Industrial Mobilization Survey Plan

In 1943 NSS introduced the Industrial Mobilization Survey Plan (IMSP), a scheme for identifying surplus workers in war-related industrial establishments who could be released for military service. A year later, NSS supervision of the IMSP was mercilessly satirized in a poem, the "Charge of the Survey Brigade," that was widely circulated among DND officials:

> Surveys to the right of them
> Surveys to the left of them
> Surveys all over them
> Ten thousand papers
>
> Theirs not to reason why
> Theirs not to make reply
> Theirs but to survey or die
> And fill out ten thousand papers
>
> Honour the effort they made
> Honour the time they gave
> Manpower they could not save
> But they filled out ten thousand papers[1]

As the doggerel so aptly suggests, the IMSP was the most ambitious, and the most disastrous, effort by NSS officials to find the right balance between military and industrial needs. It was a concerted and comprehensive attempt to bolster the ranks of home defence forces under the NRMA.

The plan was conceived in the wake of the bitter curtailment debate that dominated the Canadian Cabinet during 1942. The Wartime Prices and Trade Board, with Mackenzie King's blessing, had played a leading role in scuttling Elliot Little's original plan for a draconian nationwide program that would rationalize and restrict non-essential industrial production and free tens of thousands of men for military service and positions in essential industry. After Little resigned, NSS officials indicated that they would prefer to adopt a curtailment plan "affecting only a specific locality or even an individual firm."[2] The IMSP would allow NSS officials to cull non-essential workers from individual companies and to steer them into NRMA units without adopting a national curtailment strategy that would shut down entire industries or plants. In theory, therefore, the IMSP furnished NSS with the means to satisfy both pro- and anti-conscription factions within the Canadian government.

The IMSP was launched immediately after the assumption by NSS of responsibility for military mobilization procedure. On 11 December 1942, Arthur MacNamara asked Department of Munitions and Supply officials to form an interdepartmental committee to establish procedures for surveying all war plants so as to facilitate the orderly withdrawal of all callable men and to prevent the hoarding of manpower. The Manpower Survey Committee included representatives of NSS, the DMS, and the Department of Labour, and met for the first time six days later. At its second meeting, on 21 December 1942, Willard Scott, head of the NSS Survey and Deferment Division, proposed that a trial survey be conducted by DMS and NSS officials in the Toronto area. Scott personally surveyed the John Inglis Company in Toronto and consulted with other companies in the city about the feasibility of the proposed general survey. On 3 February 1943 he submitted a plan for a full-scale survey to the Manpower Survey Committee. It was endorsed by Arthur MacNamara and tested in 110 plants in Toronto, Montreal, and Winnipeg. In July 1943 it was approved by Ottawa for general application across the country.[3]

The IMSP established an Industrial Manpower Survey Committee (IMSC) in twelve of the thirteen NSS Administrative Divisions.[4] Each IMSC had six members, two from NSS and one each from the DND, the DMS, the Divisional Mobilization Board, and the Employment Service. One of the NSS representatives acted as chair. Firms classified by the DMS as being engaged in essential military production were visited by special Employment Service investigators. Each factory was surveyed extensively through a series of plant and worker questionnaires designed to establish the medical category, essentiality, and employment history of each potentially callable male employee. After consultation with a plant manager, the IMSC prepared a comprehensive plan that identified workers who could be called immediately for military service; identified workers who could be given a postponement for a period of one to five months pending the training of replacements; identified workers who could be postponed for a period of six months pending the further survey of the plant, and identified workers who were essential to plant operations. On completion, a survey plan was forwarded for approval to the Mobilization Board in the district where the plant was located.[5]

The IMSP administrative machine was quickly established but a number of issues soon arose to prevent its smooth operation. Serious disputes developed among many IMSC Chairs and Registrars and Mobilization Boards. Second, there was a lack of cooperation by DMS officials in the day-to-day work of the IMSCs. Third, DND officials hampered progress by insisting that they play a greater role in selecting men for military service from firms being surveyed. Fourth, and perhaps most critically, replacements for workers identified as callable for military service proved difficult to find.

In the early months of the IMSP, plans submitted to the district Mobilization Boards were altered in a wholesale fashion. In August 1943, the Toronto Mobilization Board, chaired by Ontario Chief Justice J.G. Gillanders, held back approval of surveys of the Fleet Aircraft and National Acme companies endorsed by Toronto IMSC chair S.R. Frost. In response, NSS officials called on MacNamara to intervene to avoid "looking ridiculous" in the eyes of employers in the other regions that would soon come under survey jurisdiction. NSS requested that Frost be appointed as a full member of the Toronto Mobilization board and that all Board members not sympathetic to the program be excluded from consideration of the surveys. Justice Gillanders assured MacNamara that the issue could be resolved without Frost's help, but mounting pressure from NSS officials in Ottawa and a backlog of fifty completed surveys that needed approval, eventually forced Gillanders to accept both Frost and one other new Mobilization Board member. Gillanders also agreed to streamline approvals by breaking the newly constituted board of nine members into three units, with each unit responsible for approving the surveys assigned to it. For the moment this solved the problem in Toronto,[6] but conflict between mobilization officials and IMSCs would remain alive elsewhere.

DMS officials continued to challenge the IMSP. Since the plants where the surveys were being carried out were war plants under DMS contract, DMS participation at the local level was crucial. In many districts, however, IMSCs had to operate without the help of a DMS representative. Instead, ranking DMS officials in Ottawa chose to lobby NSS officials such as MacNamara and Willard Scott to grant more deferments in individual plants. In October 1943, the DMS reported that it could not supply full-time officers to serve on IMSCs.[7] At the same time, the DMS insisted that its officials have a veto over each plant plan. NSS rejected this claim for "overriding authority" and called on the DMS to participate as a full and equal partner in IMSC decisions at the district level.[8]

Cooperation was not forthcoming, and DMS officials continued to protest the implementation of the IMSP. For example, D.W. Ambridge, director general of the DMS Naval Shipbuilding Branch, charged that the Babcock-Wilcox and Gordie McCulloch plants in Galt had been surveyed unfairly. Willard Scott rejected Ambridge's complaint on the grounds that of the 302 men employed in these plants, only sixteen were to be called immediately. He could not see, Scott wrote, how a "more impartial and scientific approach" could be adopted than that embodied in the survey process.[9] But such assurances did not mollify DMS officials, and in late 1943 they again called upon the Manpower Survey Committee to grant them veto power over all decisions. In rejecting this claim, Brigadier A.E. Nash, the DND deputy adjutant general, again called on DMS representatives to participate fully in all IMSC decisions in order to increase the confidence of Mobilization Boards in approving plans, cut down on the time lag between initiation and implementation of surveys, facilitate the collection of information on plants under contract to DMS, and more effectively distribute available labour between the armed forces and war industry.[10]

In London, Ontario, where the DMS did choose to participate on an active basis, problems cropped up that reinforced its demand for more control. In the first months of 1944, the NSS representative on the London IMSC was completely occupied with his work as the district deferment officer, leaving the DMS representative, Major William Mayall, to assume the responsibility of going before the London Mobilization Board to lobby for individual postponements. Mayall and other DMS officials became exasperated with this arrangement. Willard Scott asked the London IMSC Chairman to name a new NSS representative to the IMSC. Scott also asked DMS officials to stop burdening Mayall with constant requests for individual postponements. This appeal was not heeded, and Mayall continued to appear before the London Mobilization Board demanding large numbers of postponements and the alteration of all survey plans prepared by NSS. Scott complained to MacNamara that the "arbitrary changes" being made by the Mobilization Board under pressure from the DMS were resulting in a serious loss of prestige for the IMSC among local plant owners and superintendents, because they viewed the Mobilization Board, and not the IMSC, as the more important arbiter of the decision regarding which workers were essential in a particular workforce.[11]

DMS concern that too many men were being called up contrasted sharply with complaints from the DND that not enough men were being found for military service. In August 1943, Brigadier Nash of the DND told MacNamara that reports from military officers were highly critical of the way the survey plans were being handled in all three districts in which the IMSP was then in operation.[12] In Toronto, forty-eight plans had been submitted to the Mobilization Board and not a single one had been dealt with (the Toronto Mobilization Board had not yet been reconstituted). In Kingston, there was no representative from the civilian branch of NSS on the IMSC, a circumstance that made it difficult to replace men withdrawn from plants for military service. The Canadian General Electric Company in Kingston had been surveyed three times without a final plan being adopted. Moreover, because of DMS and company lobbying, the third draft plan appeared to be much more lenient than the first one. This debacle had led the Kingston Mobilization Board to invite all employers to participate in its deliberations before giving final approval to any plan, a measure that would have severely limited the number of recruits for military service. Similar bungling occured in Montreal, where the Divisional Registrar had failed to act promptly to fill in the medical information on survey forms and as a result, not a single recruit had been produced from nine surveys.

These problems led Nash and other military officials in Ottawa to call for representatives of the armed forces to conduct the surveys in conjunction with the civilian investigators from the Employment Service. The presence of military personnel in war plants had always been vigorously opposed by many NSS officials, and they foresaw "a nice mess" if the military was given any role in the surveys. From Kingston, IMSC chair W.J. Hyssop reported that military representatives in his district were seeking passes to enter war plants to determine the essentiality of men but were being denied access by DMS officials. On hearing this, MacNamara sternly rebuked Brigadier Nash, reminding him that only IMSCs could screen information submitted to them by the civilian investigators. Military officers were subsequently allowed to visit plants in the Toronto area on condition that their visits did not coincide with those of Employment Service investigators. On 15 October 1943, Major General H.F.G. Letson, the DND Adjutant General, ordered military officials to cease casting public aspersions on the survey process. He also ruled that further military visits to war plants required both the authorization of the plant manager and the approval of district IMSC chair.[13] This simplified matters, but behind the scenes DND officials continued to complain about IMSP procedures for the duration of the war.

A fundamental weakness of the IMSP was the question of how to replace men ticketed for withdrawal from industry. A co-ordinated policy of providing replacements for men deemed callable was never forthcoming, because the survey administration was under the military mobilization rather than the civilian wing of NSS. IMSP officials at the district level insisted that they could not be burdened with the job of finding replacements for the men they chose to identify as suitable for enlistment. As early as July 1943, Toronto IMSC Chair S.R. Frost informed Willard Scott that he wanted the IMSC to assume more of an "executive character" and be free from any duties not directly associated with the identification of callable men.[14] After noting that his IMSC was "not adequately organized" to handle the replacement problem, Frost later called for a "parallel organization" to work with it to coordinate replacements.[15] Ontario NSS officials, however, continued to insist that it was up to individual employers to contact local NSS offices to secure replacements.

Nor could this issue be resolved further up the IMSP hierarchy. Thus, when the Manpower Survey Committee in Ottawa dealt with the matter on 20 October 1943, it was agreed that all survey plans should be adhered to except "where changes in production or other valid reasons warranted variation of the approved plan." Allan Mitchell, Director of the Employment Service, told the MSC that his organization was "not prepared to guarantee replacements."[16] This issue was critical, since a man deemed expendable to his factory under the IMSP could not be issued an order for military training until a replacement had been found for him. Further meetings of the MSC failed to make any headway on the replacement issue, with most members insisting that Willard Scott should continue to report to General Riley of the NSS Mobilization Branch and not to Allan Mitchell of the Employment Service. A proposal to centralize the IMSP process under the direction of either Riley or Mitchell failed to win approval in late 1943. All of these problems eventually forced NSS officials to address a national radio audience on 9 January 1944 to clarify many of the confusing details of the IMSP.[17]

Accordingly, the debate on the replacement issue dragged on into 1944, with DMS officials continuing to line up squarely behind employers engaged in war production who wanted to hold onto their men. In February, Major Mayall informed Ottawa DMS officials that although the IMSP had originally been viewed by employers with a

fair degree of support, "innumerable pleas for relief" were now flooding DMS offices. This was because promised periods of postponement
to train new employees were useless as long as the Employment Service
was unable to supply replacements for men scheduled to be withdrawn.[18] Senior DMS administrators continued to report to Allan
Mitchell that if the survey process was to succeed, it would be necessary for the Employment Service to "fill gaps which might occur."[19]
From London, IMSC Chair J.D. Thomas requested that a district
supervisor be appointed to monitor the whole issue of replacements
for firms under survey. In Thomas's view the existing process was not
"sufficiently co-ordinating men with mechanical abilities to replace
younger personnel." What was needed was a more compact survey
procedure that would allow the Employment Service to monitor men
on deferment and provide replacements.[20] Willard Scott, however,
refused to make this change. Undaunted, Thomas asked him in April
1944 to approve the sending of a nominal roll prepared from each
plant survey to the local NSS office to co-ordinate replacements.[21] Once
again Scott refused, this time with a stinging directive in which he
insisted that it was the sole responsibility of the employer to contact
the Employment Service for replacements. However, he was now willing to admit that the replacements had "never been organized in a
thoroughgoing way" and that the surveys were "squeezing industry
harder" than had been intended.[22]

Inefficient handling of the plan's administration at all branches of the
NSS organization reinforced these negative currents in the operation of
the IMSP at the district level. Problems in Quebec and the Maritimes
typified the organizational paralysis and inefficiency of NSS officials. As
early as July 1943, NSS officials in Montreal reported that it was virtually impossible to secure stenographic help there and that this was leading to delay in the typing of plans to submit to the Mobilization Board
for approval. Jurisdictional problems also arose in Montreal, where the
NSS Regional Superintendent in Quebec supported the claim of the
Regional Placement Officer in the province, H.L. Perry, that control of
the IMSCs in Montreal and Quebec City rested solely with Perry. In the
end, Arthur MacNamara was forced to step in to bring the procedure
in Quebec into line with that in all other districts. In September 1943
General Riley told the Montreal Registrar, Raymond Ranger, that Perry
should be brought into line to avoid the IMSP being viewed as "too
much a child of the Employment Service," a view that could only detract
from the singular goal of releasing men for military service.[23]

The wide array of problems experienced in the implementation of
the IMSP caused some NSS officials to question the merits of the entire
process. In January 1944, G.W. Ritchie, NSS Ontario Regional Director,

told Arthur MacNamara that the IMSP was "far too cumbersome and complicated" and was "almost collapsing from its own weight."[24] According to Ritchie, military officials had been complaining for months that too few men were being obtained from the survey process. Ritchie recommended four changes: the only goal of the surveys should be to identify men callable for military service, and no effort should be made to deal with replacements or to gather information on workers in non-callable age brackets; the number of forms being used should be reduced; the investigators should devote themselves solely to surveys and not be responsible for any other NSS work; and all IMSC members should be controlled directly by MacNamara. Ritchie's proposals for streamlining the process failed to move his Ottawa superiors. However, Willard Scott despatched Alan George, his personal assistant, to travel across the country in the first four months of 1944. His mission was to establish IMSCs in districts where none were currently operating – Halifax, Saint John, Regina, Edmonton, and Vancouver – and to report on the difficulties being experienced elsewhere.

Although George expressed initial optimism about the activities of these newly-formed IMSCs, even they soon ran up against the familiar difficulties. From Saint John, T.C. Crosbie, who was named the local IMSC Chair, complained that the Mobilization Board in his district was not dealing with surveys in an expeditious manner and that the medical examinations of potential recruits from war plants were not being co-ordinated in a proper fashion by the Divisional Registrar, Colonel E.J. Mooney.[25] The Maritime Regional Employment Officer, T.C. McIntyre, expressed similar reservations about the ability of the Halifax Divisional Registrar, Colonel Edgar Mingo, to co-ordinate the medical information required to complete the survey forms for individual workers in his district. MacIntyre complained that twenty-three surveys completed prior to 23 April 1944 had been held up deliberately by Mingo while he called for military service many men who had earlier been scheduled for postponement.[26] In the same vein, George told Scott about the disastrous and inefficient procedures being followed in the Quebec City Administrative Division. Those who had set up the survey system there were completely unqualified and had wilfully adopted wasteful and time-consuming methods that typified "a certain temperament" in the province. George graded the effort as only 25 per cent of what it could and should have been. The Quebec Registrar had not been dutiful in calling men promptly for their medical examinations prior to the commencement of a survey, a circumstance which had produced long delays. The root of the problem in Quebec City lay in the diffusion of industry over a wide area combined with "some politics and the temperament of the people."

The number of personnel in the district, George affirmed, was more than sufficient to manage affairs properly.[27]

Despite these and other serious administrative and jurisdictional difficulties, NSS officials chose, in May 1944, to expand the IMSP process to encompass civilian industries. The idea of surveying civilian plants was broached in October 1943,[28] and increased demands for military personnel in 1944 forced the issue. In addition to securing men for military service, MacNamara sought to end the "considerable hoarding" of labour in civilian industries and to provide for the transfer of skilled workers from less essential to more essential positions.[29] A survey conducted by the Economics and Statistics Branch of the Department of Labour confirmed MacNamara's assessment. Between 1 July 1943 and 1 April 1944 the number of men and women working in war-related work in 600 major firms across the country declined by 40,920 workers, while the civilian-oriented work in these 600 firms showed a net increase of 23,755 men and women. Female war employment in these firms had declined by almost 10,000 persons, while female civilian-oriented employment had increased by a similar number. With MacNamara's blessing, Willard Scott used this data to justify the expansion of the IMSP to all plants, both civilian and military.[30]

A conference held in Ottawa from 31 May to 2 June 1944 gathered all the major players in the survey process to discuss the implementation of the expanded scheme. Although the existing problems in the IMSP structure were again documented and discussed, the proposal to add more work received a surprising endorsement from virtually all those present. On 8 June 1944, Order No. 19, authorized by Humphrey Mitchell, rendered the decisions of the conference effective. This Order stipulated that an IMSC could survey a plant of any size; that every employer was required to abide by the IMSC decisions; that any employer could be directed to appear before an IMSC; and that any male employee between the ages of sixteen and forty-one could be ordered to other employment on the recommendation of an IMSC.[31] Mitchell went on national radio the same day to explain the changes. Claiming that "compulsion of this sort" was only acceptable when "less strenuous measures" had been ineffective, he emphasized that the primary aim of the expanded process was to release some men for military service and to earmark others for compulsory transfer.[32]

It is difficult to gauge the success of the civilian transfer component of the IMSP since no statistics were kept on the number of transfers obtained under its auspices. However, the civilian transfer provisions were deleted from the IMSP within four months. This indicates that the transfer of men from one industry to another did not meet with great success. Close to 18,000 men had been affected by the seven NSS Compulsory Transfer Orders in 1943, and it is doubtful that the new procedure was able to alter the composition of the workforce engaged in non-essential or essential production in any significant fashion.[33] Meanwhile, the military component of the expanded IMSP continued to be plagued by the same problems evident since its earliest days.

In Halifax, problems continued to centre on Colonel Mingo and the organization of NSS in his district. In July 1944, Mingo complained that he could not fill his call-up quota of twelve men per day due to the generous postponements recommended by the IMSC. Mingo noted that large companies seemed to be protecting medically fit men of callable age while smaller companies were being devastated by the IMSP. At the Halifax Shipyards, for example, 235 men had received a postponement of six months and of this number 205 were callable and medically fit.[34] Mingo maintained that the quality of the Employment Service investigators and their reports were "obviously unsatisfactory" and had resulted in the "regrettable ridicule" of all NSS activities.[35] Willard Scott rejected these "childish" accusations by ridiculing Mingo. He surmised that it "would be quite impossible to find common ground" with the Halifax Registrar.[36] Local DND officials also noted that residents of Amherst opposed the "disgraceful" survey of the Canada Car Foundry in which large numbers of non-essential workers had been recommended for postponement by the Halifax IMSC.[37]

In August 1944, Scott despatched Alan George to the Maritimes a second time to solve these growing administrative problems. George subsequently criticized "unqualified" survey officers for hampering the Halifax IMSC. The Halifax Mobilization Board viewed the IMSC postponement recommendations with scepticism, judging that "personal prejudices" influenced the IMSC decisions. This resulted in extensive alterations to the plans submitted to the Board for approval. George concluded that the entire Employment Service structure in the province was inefficient. Furthermore, J.C. Nicholson, the Halifax IMSC Chair, needed to be appointed to the Mobilization Board.[38] MacNamara quickly addressed George's concerns. T.C. McIntyre, the NSS Maritime Regional Employment Officer, was scapegoated for allowing unqualified investigators to survey plants; he was fired along with four of the five Employment Service investigators.[39]

In Ontario, administrative problems also continued to plague the IMSP. London IMSC Chair J.D. Thomas continued to highlight the poor coordination of the surveys. Skilled men who were laid off were not being directed to replace postponed men. He called for the complete overhaul of the replacement system and noted that the number of men being waived from military service on medical grounds was "approaching the extent of a racket."[40] In Toronto, the Mobilization Board and DND officials expressed their disdain for the IMSP. In September 1944, a meeting of the NSS Ontario Regional Advisory Board focussed on the IMSP. A motion to halt all plant surveys unless a Mobilization Board authorized them was tabled. Major R.J. Clapton spoke on behalf of the Toronto Mobilization Board. He claimed that surveys were useless and that the military authorities, in concert with the Registrar and the Board, could handle all postponement matters. H.C. McDermott, the new Toronto IMSC Chair, submitted his report of this meeting to Willard Scott:

I do not recall having listened to any such lofty appraisal of a body of men [the Toronto Mobilization Board] as Major Clapton tried to give them. They are, in his opinion, supermen and require no such assistance as surveys might give them and the Registrar was in full accord with his remarks. The feeling of the Advisory Board is obviously not in favour of the survey. For some reason or other, this attitude seems to be sponsored chiefly by Major Clapton.[41]

Only McDermott and the NSS Ontario regional superintendent supported the IMSP. McDermott believed that Clapton's "continuous hammering" away at the IMSP had turned the ambivalent members of the Advisory Board against the surveys.

In October 1944 Arthur MacNamara finally moved to counter these criticisms of the IMSP after Justice P.M. Anderson, the Regina Mobilization Board Chair, called for the cancellation of the entire program. MacNamara canvassed the twelve Mobilization Board chairs to determine the level of support for the IMSP. He congratulated everyone involved in the administration of the surveys, but announced that although many companies had been surveyed at least twice, the number of men in these plants available for military service was minimal. Layoffs in many war industries had lessened the demand for tight control of the civilian labour force, and the survey results did not "justify the work and effort involved." MacNamara stressed, however, that any curtailment of the IMSP must not be viewed by employers as a sign that the urgent need for military personnel was slackening.[42]

The responses to MacNamara's call for judgment of the IMSP were remarkably diverse. A.S. Cochrane, the Deputy Chair of the Toronto Mobilization Board, agreed with the Deputy Minister's assessment of the IMSP and insisted that any deferment requests should be handled on an individual basis without reference to the survey. Cochrane pointed to the T. Eaton firm in Toronto as an example of the failure of the IMSP. Of the 3,722 callable male Eaton's employees identified on survey forms, only twenty-six had been listed as non-essential, with only six members of this group being over nineteen years of age. Several DMS officials, however, despite their refusal to participate actively in the process, felt that the surveys of civilian plants would prove useful as sources of information related to rehabilitation and post-war employment issues. Mobilization Board chairs in Winnipeg and Edmonton where the IMSP was relatively new remarked that few plants had been surveyed more than once and that the surveys should be continued for at least six months to allow second surveys to be undertaken. Even DND officials commented on the general value of the surveys in the prevention of labour hoarding. They urged MacNamara, however, to streamline the IMSP in view of the fact that many firms had few employees available for military service.[43] After MacNamara considered these responses, the civilian component of the IMSP was abandoned. As well, each IMSC chair now could determine for himself if re-surveys of a specific plant were needed to release available men into the armed forces.[44]

The final alteration to the IMSP occurred with the inauguration of the War Industry Reservists Plan (WIRP). On 2 November 1944, NSS discussed methods for identifying essential skilled men with at least two years' experience as draughtsmen, tool and die makers, tool designers, or wood or metal pattern makers, as well as apprentices. All employees designated as War Industry Reservists working in plants devoted primarily to military production would be granted unlimited postponements. This would allow these essential workers to be exempt from further IMSP surveys. The WIRP was authorized by PC 496 of 25 January 1945. Due to the outcome of the war in Europe, however, the WIRP was terminated less than four months later and only 437 men were classified as War Industry Reservists.[45]

Despite the implementation of the modified IMSP and the WIRP, the survey scheme continued to experience administrative difficulties in the final ten months of the war. NSS still refused to address the replacement issue. In the Maritimes, companies refused to seek replacements for callable men. As a result, the Mobilization Boards in Saint John and Halifax simply extended the postponement period of all employees deemed callable by the IMSC. In December 1944, Willard Scott castigated the NSS Maritime Regional Employment Officer for failing to insist that all employers seek replacements from a local Employment Office.[46] In the same month, the Canadian Legion complained that large numbers of men were on postponement in surveyed plants in the Toronto area. Although Scott agreed with the Legion's complaint, he flatly refused a request from J.C.G. Herwig, the Canadian Legion General Secretary, to allow Legion officials to determine the essentiality of postponed men.[47]

One of the more interesting and acerbic critiques of the IMSP in the closing months of its operation came from Leonard O'Brien, the owner of a lumber firm in Newcastle, New Brunswick and the M.P. for Northumberland. In November 1944, O'Brien had refused to have his firm surveyed. He insisted that the IMSP "was a lot of nonsense" and that the government simply discarded the survey information once it was collected.[48] On 18 January 1945, O'Brien wrote a scathing letter to Arthur MacNamara as an employer and a member of "whatever little is left of a supposedly responsible Canadian parliament."[49] He complained that there was "absolutely no control exercised" over the manpower situation. Several of his essential employees had been called for military service while others had left his employment with impunity. O'Brien claimed that there was a "plethora of strange men running about seeking silly surveys and what not" and that a complete stranger had arrived at his office to examine company records. Since local NSS officials could not identify this individual, O'Brien caustically noted that if "a Jap arrive[d] tomorrow" he would have to "give him haven and be obsequious to him." He dismissed the entire NSS mobilization effort as "a complete debacle" that prevented the efficient mobilization of manpower. While regional NSS officials attempted to settle things with O'Brien in an amicable fashion, his outburst was typical of the dissatisfaction among many manufacturers with the IMSP in particular and NSS operations in general.[50]

The IMSP sputtered to a halt in the closing months of the war. Administrative problems cropped up in virtually every administrative division. Scott expressed particular dissatisfaction with the activities of the two survey committees in Quebec. In February 1945, ninety surveys were delayed in Quebec City after all NSS stenographers had been ordered to take their holidays before the end of the current fiscal year. This decision resulted in the complete shutdown of the Quebec City IMSP.[51] Even at this late date, IMSC officials were being fired in Quebec City for incompetence.[52] Scott condemned the IMSC handling of the War Industry Reservist scheme in both Montreal and Quebec City, terming it "just plain disgraceful."[53] DMS ambivalence about the IMSP remained evident. No DMS representative ever participated in the Quebec City IMSC deliberations. The local DMS official was stationed in Lévis and was not granted travelling expenses to commute the short distance across the St. Lawrence River.[54] Finally, on 30 April 1945, Willard Scott notified all IMSC Chairs that no new surveys were to be started and that any further applications for postponement were to be made directly to the Divisional Registrars. Chairs were asked to complete all surveys in progress up to 30 June 1945. This decision ended more than two years of bureaucratic and procedural wrangling involving the IMSP.

By the time the mobilization survey scheme was terminated, however, a successor scheme, the Industrial Selection and Release Plan (ISRP), was operating. In most respects, the ISRP was the reverse of the IMSP. If the latter plan identified surplus workers available for military service, the ISRP looked to identify key industrial workers in the armed forces for early release. On 24 May 1945, Order-in-Council PC 3683 established the Plan. It was designed as a strategy to circumvent the conventional "first in – first out" armed forces discharge policy that had been formulated in late 1944. Under the ISRP, employers seeking the release of key former employees were given an opportunity to petition government boards to allow for the early discharge of servicemen and servicewomen considered essential for the transition from a wartime to a civilian economy.

PC 3683 established an Industrial Selection and Release Committee (ISRC) in eleven of thirteen military districts across Canada.[55] Each ISRC had six members, with the chairman of the ISRC being a provincial court judge, usually the former IMSC chairman, and the remaining members culled from the former Mobilization Survey Committees. An employer seeking the early discharge of a key employee would apply to the ISRC in his district and the Release Committee would rule on the validity of the application. The ISRC would consider the labour priority of the firm involved in the request, the essentiality of the employee within that firm, and the relation of the key person to the creation of additional employment and increased production. NSS officials tried to improve upon the IMSP by insisting that all applications approved by the local ISRCs be forwarded for final approval by a central Industrial Selection and Release Board (ISRB) in Ottawa. They hoped this centralized structure would control the regional inconsistencies that had plagued NSS operations throughout the war. Composed of nine members, the ISRB was chaired by NSS Associate Director Raymond Ranger (the former Montreal Registrar) and had representation from all three Service branches, as well as the Department of Reconstruction, the DMS, the WPTB, and the Unemployment Insurance Commission. The ISRB would examine applications forwarded from the regional Release Committees and the Department of National Defence would determine the availability of any person recommended by the ISRB. All applications approved would still be subject to the approval of the serviceman requested for release.[56]

On paper the ISRP appeared to be a simple process. Many of the problems that had plagued the wartime IMSP, however, surfaced again in the months following the passage of PC 3683. The regional Industrial Selection and Release Committees tended to stay true to their wartime experience of ignoring specific central directives and set their own policy within the context of intense opposition from many military officials hindered the functioning of the ISRP. The ISRB in Ottawa, however, proved to be the greatest roadblock to the potential success of the ISRP. There was a major recasting of the entire ISRP process within three months of its inception.

Many officials involved with the ISRP criticized the rationale behind the plan shortly after its inception. The provincial court justices chairing each Selection and Release Committee, mindful of their experiences with the IMSP between 1943 and 1945, often proved to be the most vociferous opponents of the plan during the summer of 1945. New Brunswick Chief Justice J.B. Baxter of the Saint John ISRC protested the priority of release outlined by the ISRP.[57] Claiming that it was "practically impossible" to follow the "first in-first out" discharge policy if the industrial ability of a person had any relation to his or her date of release, Baxter insisted that only overseas veterans should be eligible under the discharge provisions of the ISRP. Many ISRC chairmen shared Baxter's views. Administrative difficulties plagued the daily operations of various ISRCs across the country. In London, for example, military representatives on the ISRC complained that they had been "swamped with frivolous applications" that could not be approved.[58] Department of Reconstruction officials also ridiculed the Department of Labour press campaign publicizing the ISRP, claiming that it created the impression that "all an employer had to do was put in an application."[59]

The most significant problem hampering the ISRP before August 1945 was the high rate of rejection experienced by employers seeking release from the military of key former employees. In the first two months of the operation of the ISRP, more than two-thirds of the 14,000 applications for release had been rejected, the majority of them by the ISRB in Ottawa.[60] The refusal of the ISRB to approve positive recommendations of the eleven ISRCs caused a firestorm of criticism to be directed against the entire process and the Department of Labour. In July 1945, Minister of Trade and Commerce James MacKinnon wrote to Humphrey Mitchell complaining bitterly about the ISRP process.[61] In particular, he pointed to the fact that the Ottawa ISRB had rejected 330 of 400 applications for early release of key personnel that had originated with the Edmonton ISRC. Other ISRC officials confirmed MacKinnon's views. T.C. Crosbie, Deputy Chairman of the Saint John

ISRC, wrote to Raymond Ranger on 13 July 1945 castigating Ranger for the actions of the ISRB.[62] Crosbie complained bitterly that the Maritimes had been "left out of the national picture" despite the fact that all decisions taken in Saint John had been in compliance with the provisions of PC 3683. Crosbie denounced the ISRB for rejecting applications even before the DND had ruled on the availability of a key worker, and he insisted that no group of officials in a "mid-Dominion location" could reasonably sit in judgment of Maritime industrial needs "unless gifted with clairvoyance." Crosbie joined MacKinnon in calling for the abolishment of the ISRB and the direct referral of all ISRC cases to the DND.

Business leaders also contributed to the avalanche of criticism being directed against the ISRP scheme. For example, Fred Halls, president of Fine Papers Ltd in Toronto, complained that one of his key former employees had been rejected for release, despite the fact that the government had been spending thousands of dollars publicizing their "wonderful plans" for full employment.[63] Hall sarcastically volunteered his services to help the government reach the full employment objective if only the ISRC would release the men he asked for. Howard Ellis, personnel manager of the Massey-Harris Company, complained to the Toronto ISRC that government advertising campaigns promoting the ISRP had created the impression that all an employer had to do was fill out an application and a key man would be released.[64] Ellis stated that while none of his applications had been for non-essential personnel, not a single former employee had been authorized for early release from the armed forces, mainly because of the rejection of applications by the Ottawa ISRB.

In late July and early August 1945, key government officials became increasingly aware of the widespread dissatisfaction with the ISRP. Justice A.S. Cochrane of the Toronto ISRC proclaimed his distaste for the entire procedure to Arthur MacNamara after being the target of repeated attacks from employers who had had applications for employee release turned down. Cochrane noted that his Committee was being subjected to "very severe criticism" since it could not adequately explain why the Ottawa ISRB rejected so many applications for early release.[65] The Toronto ISRC went one step further by passing a motion on 18 July stating that no appeal of an Ottawa ISRB decision would be dealt with until a formal policy statement was issued by Ottawa explaining the high rate of rejection. Public distrust of the ISRP reached the Prime Minister's Office, with Mackenzie King's private secretary J.W. Pickersgill noting the "mounting tide of criticism" of the early discharge scheme.[66] Defence Minister General A.G.L. McNaughton confirmed Pickersgill's appraisal of the situation and offered the most authoritative condemnation of the Ottawa SRB. McNaughton felt that the procedure could be simplified by eliminating the authority of the Ottawa ISRB entirely and allowing each regional ISRC to forward requests for release to the District Officers Commanding or General Officers Commanding across Canada.[67] Although the heaviest criticism was laid at the door of NSS officials, DND officials were not blameless in the problem of early release. In Vancouver, the ISRC chairman noted that only three of the 1,000 personnal authorized for release in his district by 2 August had actually been discharged.[68]

NSS officials bowed to pressure for the reformation of the ISRP process in mid-August 1945, allowing the second phase of the ISRP to commence. Administrative Bulletin No. 22 of 14 August 1945 followed General McNaughton's suggestion by removing the central ISRB in Ottawa from any decision-making capacity, although Raymond Ranger and the ISRB continued to act as a monitoring agency for the nationwide Selection and Release process.[69] Each of the eleven ISRCs would forward its decisions to DND officials in the corresponding military district. To appease employers who were upset about original ISRB decisions, all negative decisions of the ISRB were referred back to the ISRCs for re-evaluation. A crucial second discharge method was added to the revised ISRP procedure. An individual member of the armed forces could now apply directly to his or her commanding officer for release to his former employment if he or she was entitled to re-instatement under the 1942 Re-instatement in Civil Employment Act, which allowed a veteran to return to the job he or she had held immediately prior to enlisting. Arthur MacNamara emphasized that the spirit of the original PC 3683 should be followed under the revised procedure, and special consideration given to men destined for essential industries such as coal mining and logging.[70]

The removal of the ISRB from the Selection and Release Plan machinery and the increasing willingness of DND officials to expedite the discharge of personnel, particularly from Home Defence units, allowed the ISRP to clear a large backlog in the three months following the re-organization of the ISRP. From the second week of August to the end of October 1945, more than 22,000 members of the armed forces were released, compared to only 4,900 in the first ten weeks of the operation of the ISRP.[71] The option of individual applications from service personnel was the most dramatic factor in the sharp rise in discharges under the ISRP. Despite the acceleration of discharges, however, the ISRP continued to be plagued with administrative difficulties and DND officials continued to question the continuation of the early release program. In the light of accelerated discharge rates for service personnel in general, Colin Gibson, Minister of National

Defence for Air, complained that the ISRP posed a "grave threat to overseas morale and the equitable administration of the repatriation policy" of the RCAF.[72]

DND opposition to the ISRP combined with the large numbers of men and women released from military service caused NSS officials to question the usefulness of continuing the Selection and Release program. At a meeting of the Ottawa ISRB on 13 September 1945, military officials argued that the scheme should be abandoned.[73] Even ISRP administrator Raymond Ranger recommended that the program be terminated in the light of the fact that employers had had four months to apply for the release of key employees and the 65,000 general discharges from the armed services in September alone made the prospect of employment shortages unlikely. Ranger's call for the cancellation of the ISRP fell on deaf ears. In a posture that characterized NSS supervision of human resource mobilization in Canada, Arthur MacNamara deflected the calls for a prompt disposition of the ISRP. Instead, he launched an extensive consultation process in October and November 1945, which sought the views of the constituencies with an interest in the industrial discharge process.

The responses tended to favour the cancellation or the scaling down of the ISRP. WPTB officials argued that the public in general, and employers in particular, remained in the dark about its purposes and procedures.[74] The WPTB had surveyed primary textile employers about their experience with the ISRP and found that early release had been requested for only 127 of 600 essential men. Primary textile producers pointed to the high rate of rejection in the early months of the ISRP and the fact that most producers had no understanding of the mid-August policy reformation. While the complete shutdown of the ISRP would only validate public opinion of the process, the WPTB did support a dramatic scaling down of the ISRP and the substitution of a "simple procedure" in its place.

Officials from the Departments of Reconstruction and Munitions and Supply were less conciliatory and insisted that the ISRP could be dispensed with altogether. All applications for early release could be handled by their respective departments.[75] DND officials also favoured the discontinuance of the plan. Deputy Air Minister H.F. Gordon admitted that the ISRP had "fulfilled an important purpose." The volume of discharges, however, made any preference for key industrial workers irrelevant.[76] Support for the continuation of the ISRP came only from a handful of ISRC chairmen across the country.[77] However, when Humphrey Mitchell drafted an Order-in-Council on 23 October 1945 calling for the revocation of PC 3683, MacNamara and his officials prevailed upon Cabinet to defer any decision into 1946.[78]

Despite the fact that applications under the ISRP slowed to a trickle in late 1945, the third and final stage of the Industrial Selection and Release program continued to be beset by departmental divisions and conflicts. Early in December 1945, Montreal ISRC Deputy Chairman H.E. MacDonald complained bitterly that military authorities continued to hamper the development of cooperative links between the Department of Labour and the Department of National Defence.[79] MacDonald's chief concern was that DND intransigence left NSS officials isolated in terms of public opinion, since the ISRP was a responsibility of the Labour Department. Public perception of the Selection and Release Plan had not been helped by a most negative article on the topic in the 24 November issue of the *Globe & Mail*. Ralph Allen wrote a scathing piece on the attitude of men stationed overseas towards the early discharge, based on industrial occupation, of their compatriots. Up to the middle of November 1945, 2,210 overseas personnel had been returned to Canada and discharged under the ISRP, but Allen noted that a hairdresser and an ice-cream maker had been repatriated in this group. DND officials used the *Globe* article to highlight the purportedly inferior applications being accepted by Release Committees across Canada.[80]

The ISRP limped into the first months of 1946 beset by criticism from all sides. The WPTB pulled all representatives from any ISRP administrative bodies in January 1946; the DND followed suit in February 1946. Regional ISRCs tried to function, but found it difficult without DND support. The deputy chairman of the ISRC in Winnipeg noted the military's intransigence. The RCAF, for example, rejected thirty-five of forty-two applications his ISRC recommended in January 1946.[81] A meeting of the ISRB on 23 January 1945 recommended the discontinuance of the ISRP for the third time,[82] only to have Arthur MacNamara intervene again and insist that the program continue. The ISRC structure was changed slightly in February 1946 to streamline each committee,[83] but applications continued to drop precipitously. For the week of 11 April 1946, only sixty-one applications nationwide were received by Selection and Release Committees, down from 373 applications for the week of 3 January 1946.[84] The ISRP was rendered even less relevant when the Canadian Army abandoned its point system for discharge on 15 April 1946, and prepared to discharge all non-essential personnel upon request. Finally, Arthur MacNamara bowed to the inevitable and informed Humphrey Mitchell on 23 April 1946 that the ISRP should be terminated. PC 2093 of 28 May 1946 rescinded the provisions of PC 3683; two days later, the ISRP ceased operations.[85]

A statistical review of the IMSP and the ISRP reveals the scope of each plan. Tables 2 through 5 illustrate the regional variations in IMSP survey figures for firms that had been surveyed once, twice, three times and four times. Nationally, 4,331 individual firms had been surveyed at least once under the mandate of the IMSP; these firms had a total male employment of more than 825,000. Including re-surveys, 8,123 surveys were completed with the large majority of men surveyed residing in Ontario and Quebec. Due to the severe problems that plagued the IMSP, the number of men stripped from industry is difficult to gauge. If all men who were to be called immediately or who were called after a postponement of one to five months are considered to have actually been taken into the military, the IMSP channelled 76,493 men out of industrial employment into NRMA units. Administrators of the IMSP readily acknowledged that most men given short postponements pending the training of replacements were never called for military service. Thus a large proportion of the number of men identified as being replaceable over a one-to five-month period, a total of 28,917 men, were undisturbed in their employment. Those men classified as being available for immediate call were not necessarily called by Registrars and those who were called could be rejected by the Army for medical or other reasons. In Manitoba, for example, 1,452 men were ordered to report for military training between 1 October 1943 and 31 March 1944 after they passed the preliminary medical examination. Remarkably, 854 of these men were denied enrolment in the armed forces for a variety of reasons, including psychiatric problems and illiteracy.[86] Furthermore, in the final eight months of the war in Europe, some men who were scheduled to be inducted into NRMA units as a result of the IMSP simply volunteered for duty in the Navy; these men were subsequently allowed to remain in civilian employment until positions opened for them in that service branch.[87] It is doubtful, therefore, if more than 10,000 men were inducted for NRMA duty under IMSP provisions. One final observation concerning the IMSP should be emphasized. Many workplaces were disrupted through the withdrawal of male employees, but no regulations existed to force a single man recruited under the IMSP to enlist for overseas duty.

Although the number of men released from industrial employment is difficult to assess, an examination of the data in Tables 2 through 5 reveals interesting patterns. The percentage of callable men in the workforce remained surprisingly constant. The percentage of employees in callable age classifications ranged between 26 per cent and 28 per cent for companies undergoing a first, second, third, or fourth survey despite the fact that those companies surveyed a fourth time were canvassed in the final months of the war. The number of men in callable age groups classified as medically unfit for military service, however, skyrocketed during the course of the war. Only 47 per cent of the men in plants surveyed a first time were classified as medically unfit, while

Table 2
IMSP Statistical Summary for All Plants Surveyed Once, 1943–45

Category	Ontario	Quebec	Maritimes	Prairies	BC	National
Surveys	928	1,052	676	1,057	618	4,331
Men Employed	292,964	291,708	65,083	80,035	96,543	826,333
Subject to Call	72,835	95,812	19,250	19,167	22,213	229,277
Low Medical						
or Discharge	41,063	43,218	12,082	11,947	12,438	120,748
(% of S to C)	(57.1%)	(45.1%)	(62.8%)	(62.3%)	(60.0%)	(52.7%)
Balance	31,772	52,594	7,168	7,220	9,775	108,799
N: Available						
for call	9,071	12,871	2,366	2,380	2,785	29,473
(% of Balance)	(28.6%)	(24.5%)	(33.0%)	(33.0%)	(28.5%)	(27.1%)
1–5 month						
postponement	6,705	8,459	1,027	975	2,481	19,647
(% of Balance)	(21.1%)	(16.1%)	(14.3%)	(13.5%)	(25.4%)	(18.1%)
6 month						
postponement	13,636	29,714	3,042	1,615	3,096	51,103
(% of Balance)	(42.9%)	(56.5%)	(42.4%)	(22.4%)	(31.7%)	(47.0%)
Essential or Other	2,360	1,550	733	2,250	1,413	8,576
(% of Balance)	(7.4%)	(2.9%)	(10.3%)	(31.1%)	(14.4%)	(7.8%)

Source: NA, RG 27, Volume 986, File 4, NSS History of IMS Plans

Table 3
IMSP Statistical Summary for All Plants Surveyed Twice

Category	Ontario	Quebec	Maritimes	Prairies	BC	National
Surveys	648	718	236	528	330	2,460
Men Employed	217,509	233,147	36,199	54,970	68,414	610,239
Subject to Call	54,576	78,154	10,307	11,916	15,442	170,395
Low Medical						
or Discharge	37,929	56,622	7,096	8,509	10,768	120,924
(% of S to C)	(69.5%)	(72.4%)	(68.8%)	(71.4%)	(69.7%)	(71.0%)
Balance	16,647	21,532	3,211	3,407	4,674	49,471
N: Available						
for call	3,899	5,748	1,067	692	1,299	12,705
(% of Balance)	(23.4%)	(26.7%)	(33.2%)	(20.3%)	(27.8%)	(25.7%)
1–5 month						
postponement	3,095	1,909	361	370	1,098	6,833
(% of Balance)	(18.6%)	(8.9%)	(11.2%)	(10.9%)	(23.5%)	(13.8%)
6 month						
postponement	8,568	13,223	1,534	1,004	1,704	26,033
(% of Balance)	(51.4%)	(61.4%)	(47.8%)	(29.5%)	(36.4%)	(52.6%)
Essential or Other	1,085	652	249	981	573	3,900
(% of Balance)	(6.6%)	(3.0%)	(7.8%)	(39.3%)	(12.3%)	(7.9%)

Source: NA, RG 27, Volume 986, File 4, NSS History of IMS Plans

Table 4
IMSP Statistical Summary for All Plants Surveyed Three Times

Category	Ontario	Quebec	Maritimes	Prairies	BC	National
Surveys	450	359	21	147	156	1,133
Men Employed	169,667	119,187	5,036	25,564	44,230	363,684
Subject to Call	39,715	40,255	1,729	3,999	9,431	95,129
Low Medical						
or Discharge	29,895	33,007	1,321	2,527	7,070	73,820
(% of S to C)	(75.3%)	(82.0%)	(76.4%)	(63.2%)	(75.0%)	(77.6%)
Balance	9,830	7,248	408	1,472	2,361	21,319
N: Available						
for call	2,694	897	97	270	810	4,768
(% of Balance)	(27.4%)	(12.4%)	(23.8%)	(18.3%)	(34.3%)	(22.4%)
1–5 month						
postponement	1,040	397	19	170	525	2,151
(% of Balance)	(10.6%)	(5.5%)	(4.7%)	(11.5%)	(22.2%)	(10.1%)
6 month						
postponement	4,996	5,544	228	375	900	12,043
(% of Balance)	(50.8%)	(76.5%)	(55.9%)	(25.5%)	(38.1%)	(56.5%)
Essential or Other	1,100	410	64	657	126	2,357
(% of Balance)	(11.2%)	(5.6%)	(15.6%)	(44.7%)	(5.4%)	(11.0%)

Source: NA, RG 27, Volume 986, File 4, NSS History of IMS Plans

Table 5
IMSP Statistical Summary for All Plants Surveyed Four Times

Category	Ontario	Quebec	Maritimes	Prairies	BC	National
Surveys	154	29			16	199
Men Employed	51,805	4,103			5,664	61,572
Subject to Call	13,978	1,443			1,294	16,715
Low Medical						
or Discharge	11,256	1,169			1,028	13,453
(% of S to C)	(80.5%)	(81.0%)			(79.4%)	(80.5%)
Balance	2,722	274			266	3,262
N: Available						
for call	521	17			92	630
(% of Balance)	(19.1%)	(6.2%)			(34.6%)	(19.3%)
1–5 month						
postponement	259	12			15	286
(% of Balance)	(9.5%)	(4.4%)			(5.6%)	(8.8%)
6 month						
postponement	1,718	232			149	2,099
(% of Balance)	(63.1%)	(84.7%)			(56.0%)	(64.3%)
Essential or Other	224	13			10	247
(% of Balance)	(8.3%)	(4.7%)			(3.8%)	(7.6%)

Source: NA, RG 27, Volume 986, File 4, NSS History of IMS Plans

Table 6
ISRP Statistical Summary–24 May 1945 to 31 May 1946

ISRC Location	Applications Received	Applications Rejected	% Applications Rejected
London	3,701	1,128	30.5
Toronto	11,365	2,178	19.2
Kingston	1,982	288	14.5
Montreal	5,809	530	9.1
Quebec	1,160	66	5.7
Halifax	1,626	356	21.9
Saint John	1,442	124	8.6
Winnipeg	2,904	502	17.3
Vancouver	5,818	835	14.4
Regina	1,731	240	13.9
Edmonton	2,047	312	15.2
Miscellaneous	2,507	64	2.6
Nationwide	42,092	6,623	15.7

Source: NA, RG 27, Volume 3018, File Report on the Operations of the ISRP, "Report of the ISRP, 24 May 1945 to 31 May 1946"

more than 80 per cent of men in callable age categories were deemed medically unsuitable for military service or had been discharged in plants surveyed a fourth time. The survey patterns in Quebec stand out from other regions. The percentage of men granted six-month postponements in Quebec exceeded the ratio in the rest of the country, increasing from 56 per cent for first surveys to close to 85 per cent for firms surveyed four times. The national average was 47 per cent for firms surveyed a first time and 64 per cent for plants surveyed four times. In Montreal, not a single postponement of one or two months pending replacement was asked for between 1943 and 1945. Significant proportions of callable men in the Prairie Region were labelled as essential because men on agricultural postponements were working on a seasonal or temporary basis in industrial employment.

Table 6 provides a statistical summary of the ISRP.[88] More than 35,000 men and women secured an early release under the ISRP, a figure representing almost 8 per cent of all persons discharged from the armed forces between 30 May 1945 and 30 May 1946, with the majority of these releases coming from NRMA units or active duty forces stationed in Canada. Many ISRCs deviated substantially from the national rejection average of 15.7 per cent of all applicants. The high rejection rate of applicants for industrial release in London illustrates the problems Ottawa NSS officials experienced with ISRC officials in that city. Conversely, Quebec City and Montreal rejected few applications for early release, following the lenient deferment policies that had been established during the war in the province of Quebec. More than 69 per cent of all early releases came from the Army. Close to 11 per cent and 20 per cent of ISRP releases came from the Royal Canadian Navy and the Royal Canadian Air Force, respectively. Almost 64 per cent of all released service personnel were skilled or semi-skilled workers. The top eight individual occupational categories in terms of releases were: 1)professional and managerial workers: 5,204; 2)clerical workers: 3,747; 3)construction workers: 3,611; 4)metal workers: 2,677; 5)mining workers: 1,938; 6)food workers: 1,593; 7)sales workers: 1,461; 8)textile workers: 1,173.

A statistical review of the IMSP confirms the somewhat inconsistent nature of the NSS mobilization effort. The IMSP was the primary NSS initiative designed to supplement NRMA regulations. Unfortunately, its chronic mismanagement superseded the remarkable logistical accomplishment of surveying thousands of firms and hundreds of thousands of workers. The IMSP was the most comprehensive of the measures adopted to mobilize Canadian human resources, but examining its implementation reveals fundamental weaknesses inherent in both the NSS regulatory structure and the Canadian administrative state during the war.

5 Coal Labour in Nova Scotia

Coal was critical to the Canadian war economy. Wartime consumption of all types of coal increased from 29.4 million short tons in 1939 to a peak of 43.8 million short tons in 1944. Domestic production of coal, however, declined from a wartime high of 18.2 million short tons in 1941 to 16.5 million short tons in 1945.[1] Bituminous coal output in Nova Scotia declined by almost 30 per cent from a wartime high of 7.38 million short tons in 1941 to only 5.1 million short tons in 1945. Declining coal production in the Maritimes forced Ontario and Quebec to become almost wholly dependent upon American coal imports. Between 1939 and 1942, American coal imports skyrocketed from less than 14 million tons to more than 25 million tons, a level that stayed fairly constant for the remainder of the war. Nova Scotia's Dominion Coal Company (DCC) accounted for close to 60 per cent of all bituminous coal mined in the province in 1941, with 4.35 million short tons produced in the company's Sydney mines. The company's production fell to less than three million short tons by 1945. Productivity likewise declined in the Nova Scotia mines. In 1941 the average coal output per man day was 2.049 short tons; by 1945 this figure declined to 1.579 short tons per man day.

A severe shortage of skilled labour lay at the root of the precipitous decline in bituminous coal output in Nova Scotia during the war. The inability of National Selective Service to stabilize and augment the provincial coal labour force so as to prevent production shortfalls represents a striking failure.[2] No industry across the nation was subject to more regulatory control than the bituminous coal operations in

Nova Scotia. The government particularly focussed on the massive production facilities of the DCC. However, the regulatory effort foundered, and for a number of reasons.

Bitter inter-departmental divisions between the Department of Labour and the Department of Munitions and Supply prevented the formation of a coherent and progressive policy affecting coal production. Wage control and labour relations strategies adopted by the Mackenzie King government were not adequate to improve the economic conditions of coal workers in Nova Scotia, and examination of the figures shows that they in fact had a regressive effect. By the time NSS was formed in 1942, thousands of physically fit and skilled coal miners had voluntarily entered the armed forces; it proved difficult to extricate these men from the military once production declines became critical. Restrictive legislation affecting mobilization of coal miners was passed by parliament, but NSS officials refused to use the resulting broad powers to their maximum advantage.

Perhaps the most crucial determinant in the failure of NSS policy to increase bituminous coal production in Nova Scotia was the active and determined opposition of provincial rank and file coal miners in District 26 of the United Mineworkers of America (UMWA) to government control of their working environment.[3] No sector of the Canadian labour force matches the turbulent and troubled history experienced by Nova Scotia's coal miners, particularly during the inter-war period. Decades of intense and bitter confrontation between District 26 miners and the coal companies and, in most cases, the companies' government lackeys carried over into the war years. NSS proved completely unable or unwilling to either compel coal workers to enter essential producing positions or to coax bituminous coal miners to accept government control of their working environment through significant wage concessions and a restructuring of the longstanding adversarial pattern of labour relations in the industry. The war provided Ottawa with a unique opportunity to cure the historical malaise plaguing the bituminous coal industry in Nova Scotia. Ottawa, however, bungled the opportunity. An ineffective and often misguided federal response to the coal production crisis only exacerbated and strengthened an established pattern of union militancy that prevailed in the province.

While civilian labour force controls were not established until 1942, the centralized regulation of production of essential industrial commodities such as coal was contemplated as early as the first weeks of September 1939.[4] On 18 October 1939, James McGregor Stewart was appointed as Coal Administrator within the Wartime Prices and Trade Board. Stewart supervised the administration of the Domestic Fuel Act, which allowed for a bounty to be paid on domestic coal for use in the iron and steel industry, and executed all government Orders-in-Council relating to the movement and distribution of both domestic and imported coal. All undertakings for the mining of coal were declared essential services in June 1941. The next initiative was the establishment of the Emergency Coal Production Board (ECPB) in November 1942 under Stewart's control. In an effort to revive the flagging coal industry, the ECPB established a subsidy system that covered the operating losses of the coal companies together with the amount of their standard profits or 15 cents per net ton of coal produced, whichever figure was lower. This system was changed in 1944 to a flat subsidy system based on the productivity and financial position of provincial coal companies. In March 1943, the ECPB gained added power with the transfer of all coal functions from the WPTB to the Department of Munitions and Supply. The Coal Administrator now became the DMS Coal Controller, with Ernest J. Brunning replacing Stewart as Controller in July 1943. Thereafter, the Controller supervised an increasingly complex and thorough series of regulations governing most aspects of coal supply and distribution in Canada. The Controller did not, however, have any direct statutory control over labour supply. Nevertheless, the ubiqui-tous C.D. Howe and such equally zealous DMS subordinates as Brunning proved able to wield a great measure of influence over NSS labour policies in the Cape Breton coal fields.

If DMS officials proved to be a persistent irritant to their Department of Labour counterparts, NSS officials were also hobbled by two of the prime wartime domestic policy initiatives of the King government–wage control and other labour relations strategies.[5] In December 1940, Order-in-Council PC 7440 dictated that the prevailing wage rates between 1926 and 1929, or higher levels established during the 1930s–a time period which saw successive rollbacks in the wages of coal miners–would be considered "generally fair and reasonable" limits for wages during the war. Workers could be protected from inflationary pres-sures through the payment of a cost-of-living bonus. In October 1941, the government promulgated PC 8253, which replaced PC 7440, and broadened the reach of the policy initiatives to virtually the entire workforce. Through this Order, the National War Labour Board (NWLB) was established in Ottawa to be chaired by the Dominion Minister of Labour and to consist of an equal number of business and labour representatives. The NWLB adjudicated wage disputes of a national character in a wide range of industries including coal mining, while nine regional boards handled disputes of a purely provincial nature. Employers were forbidden from raising wages without the consent of the NWLB or a regional board, and the cost of living bonus could be denied to a sector of workers if their wages were considered to be too high. This bureaucratic, politically influenced, and unwieldy process, which essentially froze wages for the duration of the war, was stridently opposed by organized labour.

Organized labour was similarly displeased with the development of wartime labour relations policies. The cornerstone of Mackenzie King's labour policy was the submission of all labour disputes to compulsory conciliation. The 1907 Industrial Disputes Investigation Act (IDIA) prohibited strikes and lockouts in specific industries pending investigation by a conciliation board. Although declared unconstitutional in 1925 for infringing on provincial jurisdictions, the IDIA remained in effect for provinces which passed enabling legislation declaring the IDIA to apply in a given province. In 1939, using the sweeping powers of the War Measures Act, Mackenzie King moved quickly to apply the IDIA to 85 per cent of Canadian workers. Order-in-Council PC 2685, enacted in June 1940, encouraged employers to negotiate in good faith with unions, but continued to mandate the submission of industrial disputes to conciliation boards while refusing to enshrine the principle of unfettered collective bargaining in Canadian law. In 1941, the formation of the Industrial Disputes Inquiry Commission added another layer of conciliation and investigation to the cumbersome IDIA process. Furthermore, in September 1941, the government mandated that all legal strike action in any war industry required a second strike vote in addition to the vote that had sent the dispute to the Industrial Disputes Investigation Commission in the first place. Until the passage of Order-in-Council PC 1003 in February 1944 and the recognition of collective bargaining rights in Canada, therefore, Canadian workers and their unions were forced to deal with an exceptionally bureaucratic conciliation apparatus designed to stave off strike action. Additionally, wage levels were largely pre-determined by administrative fiat by the equally cumbersome NWLB and regional war labour boards. In response to these restraints, the Canadian economy witnessed a sharp spike in industrial unrest, culminating in an unprecedented wave of strikes in 1943.

Coal miners in Nova Scotia had emerged from World War I in a moderately strong position and secured wage increases in 1919 and 1920. The British Empire Steel Corporation (BESCO) and its successor, the Dominion Steel and Coal Company (DOSCO), enjoying a virtual monopoly on the production of coal and steel in the province, sought to drastically pare these wages throughout the 1920s and 1930s. BESCO unilaterally reduced wages by more than one-third in January 1922. The subsequent appointment of two conciliation boards could not stop festering wage grievances between miners and operators, and a major coal strike in 1922, a sympathy strike with Sydney steelworkers in 1923, and a two-month strike in 1924 crippled coal production in Nova Scotia. All these events led to the massive five-month strike of 1925 that was characterized by widespread violence and property damage but which ended with a pay cut for the miners. A further wage cut of more than 12 per cent in 1932 led to further agitation for improved pay scales throughout the 1930s, but District 26 miners ended the Great Depression in a worse economic position than they had held in 1920.[6] Wage grievances were further exacerbated by the appalling working and living conditions endured by the miners.[7] The parsimony of the coal companies guaranteed that any industry initiative to improve productivity would meet with resistance.[8]

Nor could miners turn to government for a sympathetic hearing of their problems. In every strike in the inter war period, the provincial and federal governments intervened on the side of the coal operators. Government conciliation efforts were hopelessly inadequate in addressing the concerns of miners, and to suppress coal disturbances the full might of the state was used through militia and police units. The standard government response to industrial unrest in the coal mines was to appoint a royal commission. Sir Andrew Rae Duncan presided over two commissions in 1925 and 1932 that failed to result in any improvements in the lot of coal miners. Indeed, the findings of the more significant 1925 Duncan Commission set the stage for a 10 per cent wage cut from the standard 1924 rates that remained in effect until the end of 1928. Similarly, the 1932 Duncan Commission sided with the coal industry and recommended sweeping wage reductions and mine closures.

When war broke out in 1939, the Dominion government looked to longstanding opponents of miners within industry and government circles to act as advisors in the determination of policy affecting the coal industry. A prominent recruit was Michael Dwyer, a former Minister of Mines and Labour in the provincial Liberal government of Angus MacDonald and the president of the Nova Scotia Steel and Coal Company. Dwyer was a consistent opponent of rank and file militancy within the coal mining community. Dwyer was the NSS Maritime Regional Superintendent between 1942 and 1945 and he believed that harsh and arbitrary action against UMWA militancy was necessary to boost coal production. When the Dominion government appointed yet another Royal Commission in 1944 to study the coal industry in Nova Scotia, it turned to Justice W.F. Carroll to act as chairman. Carroll was well known to District 26 miners, having waged an unusually bitter and vitriolic election campaign in Cape Breton against UMWA militant J.B. McLachlan during the 1921 Dominion elections.[9]

The struggles of UMWA miners against business and government officials were matched by bitter internecine conflict within the UMWA itself. In March 1919, the UMWA succeeded the Provincial Workmen's Association and the Amalgamated Mine Workers of Nova Scotia as the legitimate bargaining representative of the miners. Under its international president, John L. Lewis, the UMWA was a conservative business union that demanded strict adherence to negotiated contracts.[10] When rank and file militancy swept the provincial coal industry during the early 1920s under the leadership of J.B. McLachlan, Lewis revoked the charter for District 26. After the 1923 sympathy strike he appointed a provisional district executive that governed the district until the autumn of 1924. Continued splits among the District 26 miners and their conservative and timid UMWA leaders led to the 1932 formation of the breakaway Amalgamated Mine Workers of Nova Scotia, which provided an effective challenge to the UMWA until the dissident organization was itself re-integrated into the UMWA in 1936.[11] The actions of the militant wing of the UMWA workforce in District 26 dominated the union response to government initiatives designed to spur coal production during World War II. When Dominion government officials looked to the ranks of the UMWA to join mobilization boards, it invariably chose men heatedly opposed to militant union activism. The most important conscript in this regard was John W. McLeod, who acted as the special NSS consultant on coal mining in the Maritimes from 1943 to 1945. McLeod had been the president of District 26 between 1924 and 1927, a period which included the failed 1925 strike and the subsequent rollback in wages. McLeod worked as a Dominion Coal Company official after leaving the District 26 executive. He proved to be a bitter opponent of miner radicalism and during his tenure with NSS he advocated compelling coal miners to go back to work. He also promoted the levying of harsh penalties against District 26 militants.

The outbreak of war in 1939 quickly exacerbated tensions between rank-and-file District 26 workers and their conservative union bosses and company officials. Coal miners in Nova Scotia were working under the provisions of an unsatisfactory contract that had expired in February 1939. They voted down a proposed deal in August 1939. The District 26 executive and the Dominion Coal Company had established a dispute-settlement mechanism in 1938 that called for all grievances to be submitted to an arbitrator whose decision was binding. John McLeod occupied this position. His decisions and the entire grievance mechanism were opposed by most UMWA members. Dissatisfaction with the contract and the grievance structure spurred a wave of illegal strikes in the coal industry, with thirty-nine and fifty-five strikes occurring in the provincial coal industry in 1939 and 1940, respectively.[12] After a provincial inquiry condemned UMWA militancy in November 1939, a major conference brought together UMWA, DCC, and provincial and federal government officials in Glace Bay in January 1940. Against the wishes of many militant miners, the District 26 leadership and the Dominion Coal Company subsequently applied for a federal conciliation tribunal to report on the situation. Chaired by Ontario Supreme Court Justice C.P. McTague, the tribunal report appeared in March 1940 and recommended paltry wage increases for the datal workers (an employee class encompassing all underground workers not working directly at the coal face) and, with few exceptions, nothing for the skilled contract miners working directly at the coal face. The McTague report also condemned the time-honoured practice of submitting wage agreements to the UMWA membership for ratification. A second conciliation panel, under the chairmanship of Justice W.H. Harrison, refused to endorse wage parity with DCC employees for workers in two DOSCO subsidiaries, the Old Sydney Collieries and the Acadia Coal Company.[13]

A majority of the miners rejected both sets of proposals at the District 26 convention held in August 1940, despite pleas from federal and provincial officials and the UMWA executive. The convention also refused to support the submission of the conciliation terms to a referendum of coal workers. The District executive was instructed to enter negotiations to exact wage concessions from the coal companies, with a strike ballot to be taken if an improved agreement could not be reached by 30 October 1940. After the conservative District 26 executive was returned to office, by a narrow margin, in the district elections in October, they submitted the McTague and Harrison recommendations to a referendum–contrary to the wishes of the August convention. The vote witnessed the acceptance of the terms of the conciliation reports, although the militant Glace Bay locals rejected them, and the locals working in the Old Sydney and Acadia Coal mines refused to cast ballots. Worker unrest grew throughout District 26, so another conference of all interested parties was held in Halifax in December. UMWA representatives agreed that a conciliation tribunal to be chaired by McTague would arbitrate the details of a new contract if company and union leaders could not agree to a new contract by 15 January 1941. Four days after the Halifax meeting, however, Order-in-Council PC 7440 was issued, and the failure to obtain an agreement before the deadline guaranteed that the dispute would be settled by McTague, who was now responsible for ensuring that any wage agreement complied with the "fair and reasonable" standard based on wages between 1926 and 1929 stipulated by PC 7440. In March 1941, McTague rejected the UMWA demands and sided with the company's view that it could not afford to pay wage increases. Some specialized workers of the Old Sydney and Acadia Coal companies were awarded small wage increases, but the full cost-of-living bonus called for by PC 7440 was denied to District 26 workers due to the supposed poor financial condition of the industry. If the union accepted the conditions of the proposed contract within thirty days, McTague called for the wage increases and a portion of the bonus to be retroactive to 1 February 1941.

Rank-and-file members of District 26 were outraged by this decision, but the District executive refused to submit the McTague decision to a referendum, voting instead by a margin of five to three to accept the contract. Immediately, miners in the Glace Bay, New Waterford, and Sydney Mines sub-districts walked off the job for four days. The miners in these areas formed the basis for an increasingly militant protest against the actions of the district executive. After a petition was received calling for the removal of the District 26 officers, John L. Lewis appointed two men to travel to Nova Scotia to investigate the situation. He simultaneously condemned the work slowdowns and stoppages that were limiting production in the province. In July, Lewis charged District 26 International Board Member Silby Barrett with the responsibility to end the slowdowns. Barrett had a chequered reputation among the members, having run the union's affairs in District 26 after Lewis had revoked the charter for the district in 1923. Barrett's suspension of thirteen prominent slowdown leaders only aggravated the situation, but a tough stance from the coal companies that saw the dismissal of 400 men in Cape Breton who refused to renounce curtailment plans eventually forced the District 26 miners to consider ending the slowdowns. After the government and the coal companies offered some face-saving concessions, including the reinstatement of dismissed miners and the payment of a portion of the cost-of-living bonus to DCC miners, the slowdown campaign ended in September 1941.

The slowdown strikes cast a long shadow over NSS efforts to increase coal production in Nova Scotia between 1942 and 1945. Many of the most radical UMWA men were elected to office in District 26 in the 1942 elections, including Freeman Jenkins as President and Tom Ling as Vice-President, and these men were strongly opposed to NSS regulatory control.[14] One of the key issues in the slowdown strikes remained unresolved into 1942: the three largest operators–the DCC, the Old Sydney Collieries, and the Acadia Coal Company–all had different basic wage rates. A report issued by the National War Labour Board in March 1942 called for continued "supplementary negotiations" between the companies and District 26 officials to "level up" the wage rates in these three firms. The report also recommended that the

Dominion government be responsible for paying increased wages if the companies were unable to do so,[15] a recommendation that enabled UMWA officials in District 26 to lobby company and government officials for increased wages for the duration of the war.

Almost 2,000 skilled and physically fit Maritime coal miners left the danger, financial uncertainty, and drudgery of their mining occupations behind them during this period and volunteered for active duty in the armed forces.[16] NSS officials was unable to find a way to get these vital men to return the mines and could never provide an adequate supply of qualified replacements.

From the time of its launch in March 1942, NSS possessed little control over the civilian labour force. Until the passage of Order-in-Council PC 7595 in August 1942, it could do little to address complaints of drastic labour shortfalls in coal mines across Canada that were voiced during the summer of 1942. One possibility that was contemplated early on by NSS was a more lenient postponement policy for essential coal employees who were called up. This was resisted by DNWS officials, who remained in charge of military mobilization procedures until September 1942.[17]

Meanwhile, WPTB officials were warning of an impending national crisis in the coal mines. The most urgent problem was "the provision of an adequate and contented staff of mine labour."[18] The WPTB insisted that this problem could not be addressed by simply transferring unskilled or inexperienced men to the mines; that strategy would result in no increase in coal output. This observation was undoubtedly correct, but it would be largely ignored by NSS officials for the duration of the war. The datal workforce in the Nova Scotia coal fields continued to expand during the war while the more highly skilled production workers declined in numbers. Between 1940 and 1944, coal face workers declined by almost 29 per cent, while the number of datal underground workers increased by more than 8 per cent.[19] The hard reality was that while many datal workers possessed the skills and qualifications to work at the coal face, NSS did not have the authority to compel them to do so.

While the calls of the WPTB for immediate action could be deflected by NSS officials, UMWA demands could not be ignored. In the spring of 1942, festering labour resentments led the DCC to place full-page advertisements in the *Sydney Post-Record* urging coal workers not to support their union. District 26 officials countered by attempting to establish production committees to register grievances with company officials. District 26 President Freeman Jenkins blamed the "bungling and indifference" of DCC executives for the decline in coal production.[20] Charles

Millard, Canadian Director of the Steel Workers Organizing Committee, maintained that the Dominion government's "vicious labour policy" of wage control was directly responsible for the decline in coal production. This trend, union leaders argued, could only be reversed if labour was made an equal partner in coal production. Some NSS officials in Ottawa viewed the proposed establishment of labour-management production committees as the "germ of something which may prove to be of the utmost benefit,"[21] but others interpreted the UMWA proposal as nothing more than a publicity gimmick designed to counter the DCC advertisements and to regain a measure of public sympathy after the 1941 slowdown strikes. J.W. McLeod claimed that management had every right to be wary of entering into negotiations for the establishment of production committees. The UMWA men now calling for production committees had been the leaders of the "infamous and shameful" slowdown strike that had strangled production in 1941 and caused many miners to enlist in the armed forces to escape District 26 radicalism.[22]

If the idea of production committees was a non-starter, the NWLB call for a levelling-up of wages was irresistible. After company and District 26 representatives failed to agree on how this would be done, NWLB officials recommended that a conference be held in Ottawa with Department of Labour, company, and union officials.[23] At this gathering, which took place on 7 and 8 October 1942, preliminary agreement was reached on a union claim for more than $793,000 in wage stabilization. Since the Old Sydney Collieries company was able to pay its share of the levelling-up funds, a balance of approximately $550,000 would have to be paid by the government to many employees of the DCC and the Acadia Coal Company. Silby Barrett, the ranking UMWA official present at the Ottawa meeting, returned to Nova Scotia insisting that these wage disbursements had been promised on an annual basis and that no strings had been attached concerning production figures. Detailed negotiations between the UMWA and the companies followed, but when these proved difficult, Barrett threatened further job action.[24]

This development led Humphrey Mitchell to inform the union leaders in December 1942 that the government's arrangements with the companies over wage subsidies would be designed to bring long-term stability to the entire coal industry. The intention of the government, he wrote, was that the disbursements would be within the range authorized at the October meeting in Ottawa; that the agreement would "result in a materially improved rate" of coal production; and that wages negotiated with the companies would be fixed for the duration of the war subject to cost-of-living increases granted by the NWLB.[25] Noting that the NWLB had already granted close to $2,000,000 in cost-of-living increases to DCC employees since the start of the war, Mitchell insisted that future production levels must be commensurate with the goodwill the government had shown. In sum, wage increases and labour stability were firmly linked.

Silby Barrett and Freeman Jenkins, however, denied that they had promised to forego further wage increases for the duration of the war and insisted that the wage increase to be granted in the levelling-up scheme must be retroactive to 1 October 1942.[26] While Mitchell agreed that the issue of retroactivity could be discussed, he insisted that Barrett had already agreed to a wage freeze for the duration of the war once the levelling up was completed. In these circumstances the further negotiations among union and DCC and ACC officials that commenced on 4 January proceeded with great difficulty. Barrett claimed that he had been "fooled completely" by Mitchell while in Ottawa, and DCC officials were incensed that the levelling-up negotiations were viewed by the union as the starting point for massive wage increases.[27] At the end of the day, however, the union and the companies made an agreement whereby $560,000 of Dominion government money would be distributed to selected employees of the DCC and the ACC.[28]

Ottawa also sought to address the crisis in the coal industry by modifying its military recruitment policies. In October 1942, a directive provided that, on request, any employee in the iron, steel, and coal mining industries could postpone his military training to 15 February 1943.[29] Plans were also developed in late 1942 to release military personnel with coal mining experience back to the mines. This scheme initially applied to Western provinces only, but was eventually extended to encompass the Maritimes as well.[30] Since the tangible results of the release of large numbers of men from the armed forces would not be apparent until the second half of 1943, complaints from WPTB officials continued to pour into NSS offices in the final months of 1942. The Canadian National Railways began to dip into reserve coal stocks in October 1942.[31] In that same month, James McGregor Stewart noted that increasing dependence on American coal was placing Canada in a highly vulnerable position in view of the massive wave of labour unrest sweeping American coal fields. Stewart insisted that "severe curtailment" of all types of consumption in Canada coal usage would be necessary if the requisite numbers of men were not found and placed in coal employment.[32] WPTB officials felt that NSS should be more diligent in directing skilled men to coal employment. NSS Director Elliot Little, however, insisted that a piecemeal approach directed at individual workers would be "only a drop in the ocean" and would have "no perceptible effect" on the coal labour situation.[33]

Despite overwhelming evidence to the contrary, Arthur MacNamara, after relieving Little of his duties as NSS director, continued to proclaim publicly throughout December 1942 that National Selective Service had "practically cured" the labour and production problems in coal mines across the country.[34] MacNamara admitted that Little had envisioned sweeping measures designed to coerce men to report for essential employment, but he made known that no such action would be taken in the immediate future. Newspapers across the country, however, refused to support MacNamara's rosy assessment of the coal situation. The *Montreal Standard* called on the public to be ready to deal with an acute manpower shortage in coal employment and to "really shiver" in the coming winter months.[35] Noting that 4,000 coal employees nationwide had joined the armed forces, the *Standard* noted that "no existing legislation" could "replace them or compel them to return." Only Little's plan for the massive consolidation of the civilian labour force could solve the problem.

Continued WPTB demands for action on the coal labour issue finally spurred serious debate within NSS in January 1943.[36] The immediate background to this was a survey, urged by MacGregor Stewart and agreed to by Defence Minister Ralston, of all Army men stationed in Canada to determine the availability of experienced coal miners.[37] Around the same time, a WPTB survey showed that 1,700 men, including 938 certified miners, were urgently needed in Nova Scotia.[38] In these circumstances, Arthur MacNamara succumbed to Stewart's demands for concerted action and agreed, on 14 January 1943, to appoint a special committee to deal with the coal labour situation. In doing so, however, the Deputy Minister made the remarkable assertion that the massive labour shortfalls in the coal industry could be overcome "without a great deal of difficulty."[39] Chaired by C.F. Needham, the Coal Labour Survey Committee (CLSC)[40] met for the first time on 19 January. It remained the primary NSS advisory panel on coal labour problems for the first six months of 1943. In February 1943, the CLSC was empowered to investigate all matters relating to the production of coal. A variety of measures were discussed, though not immediately adopted. Chief among these was a proposal for stepping up the release of miners from military service and for a nationwide publicity and morale-building campaign on behalf of the industry.

On 5 March 1943, the responsibility for managing the production of coal was transferred from the WPTB to the DMS. The formidable C.D. Howe quickly made his presence felt within Department of Labour circles. Howe attacked the CLSC for not providing concrete solutions to the coal labour crisis and warned that the "alarming" possibility of massive production declines must be met with vigorous action.[41] He also attacked the optimistic assessment of the labour situation that had been provided to him, a document in which Humphrey Mitchell had claimed that more than 3,300 men had been placed in coal employment across the nation.[42] Howe noted that this figure did not take account of separations from coal employment and that the majority of the coal placements had been farmers in the Western provinces who would be leaving coal employment to return to their farms on 1 May 1943.[43] Noting that 2,748 coal miners–1,700 of them in Nova Scotia–had enlisted between 1 April 1942 and 31 March 1943,[44] Howe asserted that the employment outlook in the industry was actually worse in the spring of 1943 than it had been at any time during the war.

Despite Howe's condemnation of the NSS record in relation to coal labour, no comprehensive measures were planned by NSS administrators in March and April of 1943 and business continued as usual. Working with the National Film Board, the CLSC continued to develop plans for the inauguration of the proposed publicity campaign. In the same spirit, the special provisions concerning the postponement of military training for coal miners were extended to the autumn of 1943. But these were limited measures, as were proposals to undertake a survey on absenteeism, to revive the production committee idea, to reduce the income tax rate for coal miners, and to issue to the public "a full and frank statement" of the difficulties facing the government in this "most difficult of all labour supply problems."[45] The policy of returning military personnel to the coal mines was not very successful. Although 500 Army men had volunteered to return to coal employment in Nova Scotia, only fifty-nine were actually released.[46] The RCAF refused to countenance the temporary release of any personnel not destined for essential agricultural employment. In the week ending 27 March 1943, only ninety-nine placements had been made in Nova Scotia coal mines, although there was a net labour demand for an additional 1,471 workers.[47] Moreover, problems continued to be evident in the workplace. Absenteeism remained an issue, and datal men with mining certificates were refusing to move to producer positions at the coal face; they could earn the same wages in lower-risk jobs because of the increase in wages paid to all coal employees since the start of the war.

In effect, the first phase of the NSS response to the crisis in the coal industry in Nova Scotia came to an end in April 1943. UMWA wage demands had been addressed, at least temporarily, through the levelling-up scheme agreed to in January 1943. Some preliminary attempts to address labour shortages had been made through the automatic granting of postponement to coal miners and through the release of limited numbers of Army personnel. The Coal Labour Survey Committee had been formed to gather information and to report on all aspects of the labour crisis. Preliminary plans had been made to launch a national advertising campaign to boost morale and to highlight the necessity of men volunteering for coal employment, although no campaign had been formally approved or funded. Also, NSS officials were put on notice that more serious measures might be needed to address the situation in Nova Scotia. At a meeting of the CLSC in April 1943, committee members agreed that to secure the required numbers of workers might require some form of compulsion. From now until the end of the war, in response to the employment problems of the coal industry, NSS launched the greatest single effort by the government of Canada in World War II to control a segment of the labour force.

Not surprisingly, C.D. Howe provided the spark. Howe went directly to Cabinet in May 1943 with a scalding denunciation of NSS and a demand that the labour situation in the coal mines be rectified. Claiming that it was "unthinkable" for the War Committee of the Cabinet not to take "drastic action to forestall so great a calamity," Howe insisted that coal production problems could be "wholly attributed" to the failure of NSS to provide an adequate labour force in the mines.[48] The War Committee rejected some of Howe's demands, but his basic argument was accepted. At the 4 May meeting of the Cabinet, it was agreed that authorization was needed to prevent miners from leaving coal employment and to compel all men with coal-mining experience who were working in other industries to return to the pits. There were brief consultations with company and union officials, and then Order-in-Council PC 4092 was issued on 17 May 1943, adding Section 210A to PC 246, the NSS Civilian Regulations which had been issued in January 1943. Now anyone with coal-mining experience but who was working in another industry had to register at a local NSS office reporting his coal experience. Also, all employers with knowledge of former coal miners in their employ had to submit that information to NSS officials. No man with coal-mining experience was allowed to remain in other employment beyond 1 June 1943 without the approval of an NSS officer. All men rejected by the armed forces on medical grounds or because of conscientious objection could be directed to coal employment under Section 202 of PC 246. No coal miner would be accepted by the armed forces for enlistment until 1 February 1944, and all miners seeking postponement from military service were not to be issued orders for medical examination or military training.

A nationwide publicity campaign accompanied the promulgation of PC 4092. Department of Labour press releases insisted that only a domestic solution would satisfy Canada's hunger for coal, and that the "extraordinary measures" of PC 4092 would solve coal production problems.[49] Full-page advertisements describing the desperate situation in the coal fields and the government's remedial measures appeared in major newspapers in all coal producing provinces during June 1943. The CLSC planned and coordinated a series of National Film Board productions about the coal industry.[50] Humphrey Mitchell capped the advertising offensive with a national radio address on 14 July. Claiming that he had no intention of "unduly disturbing the public mind," Mitchell exhorted men engaged in coal mining to fulfil their "patriotic duty" and avoid any dispute that would disrupt production. He emphasized that the income taxes levied by the Dominion government did not, as UMWA leaders asserted, discriminate against coal mine workers.[51] In an apparently inept example of scheduling, Mitchell's broadcast was immediately preceded by a CBC "Production Front" broadcast that originated from the coal mines of New Waterford and Sydney. Reporter Allan May noted that the "chief cause" of resentment among the members of District 26 was the federal income tax. After interviewing several miners, May concluded that the miners were justified in their grievances. To say the least, his assertion was an inauspicious prelude to Mitchell's plea for labour peace and increased production.[52]

Not surprisingly, the Dominion government's efforts to resolve the coal production crisis provoked vigorous public debate. The *Glace Bay Gazette* condemned compulsory regulation, claiming that "more discontent" and "more aggravation" would result from the "ostrich policy" that the government was following.[53] Only improved working conditions, salaries, and income tax concessions, the *Gazette* asserted, would improve production, and any forced repatriation of former coal miners would only add a disgruntled class of employees to an already volatile labour mix. In August 1943, the *Globe and Mail* joined the attack. According to *Globe* editorialists, the decision of the DMS to ration coal for home heating showed "the failure of NSS to function even in extreme urgencies."[54] Production statistics provided by Humphrey Mitchell in the House of Commons countered positive NSS reports on the coal labour situation; the government's action "to restore coal production [had] been done too late, although the government was warned time without number over the past eighteen months by its own officials that just such a situation lay ahead."

In a bid to address one of the UMWA's primary grievances, NSS officials formulated plans during the summer of 1943 to introduce a modified system of income tax deductions for coal miners. In August 1943,

District 26 officials protested to Humphrey Mitchell that increased rates of taxation on overtime work held back production, promoted absenteeism and dissatisfaction, and even denied UMWA men the chance to provide the "necessities of life."[55] In fact, discussions had already commenced among officials of the Departments of National Revenue, Finance, and Labour on the possibility of introducing a flat annual taxation rate for coal miners. Under existing tax rules, the wages a worker made in an individual pay period were assumed to be indicative of the wages earned over the course of a whole year. A miner working significant amounts of overtime, therefore, jumped temporarily to a higher tax bracket and a greater proportion of his wage was deducted from his cheque. To remedy this, government officials proposed that coal employees pay a constant flat-rate tax based on projected annual earnings. After consultation with UMWA representatives, a modified income tax deduction for coal miners came into effect on 31 August 1943. All coal firms employing more than twenty-five employees were required to fill out forms indicating the expected annual earnings of each worker. The yearly pay was then correlated with existing tax tables and a constant tax rate was applied to the pay packet of each worker regardless of the number of hours worked or wages earned during the course of a two-week or monthly pay period.[56]

The National Film Board publicity reels produced and released in the final six months of 1943 encountered a major stumbling block in the form of coal-mining labour history. The NFB, like NSS and Department of Labour officials, could never point to a time of harmonious relations between employers and employees, nor could they trumpet the economic prosperity or well-being of miners, because these workers had occupied the lowest rungs of the socioeconomic ladder for many decades. Only an appeal to patriotism and the solidarity of the working-class community could be offered to convince men to return to the coal companies. The prime NFB publicity reel was titled "Coal Face Canada" and featured Bruce Adams as the local boy who returned from the Army to work in the very mines where his father had been killed six months earlier. After chronicling Adams' misgivings about returning to an environment he despised, the film documents his remarkable change of attitude as he explored the town and reacquainted himself with the people. As the film's narration explained:

Bruce went on through the town, [and] he realised for the first time what we've done for ourselves. He saw our libraries, financed by the miners, for studying labour problems and learning the how and why of things. He began to look more closely at the signs on the store fronts along Main Street, and what he saw there showed him a new kind of life. He was learning that there's almost no limit to what you can do when you work together. He was getting his bearings, finding democracy right on his doorstep ... The next day Bruce Adams reported for duty with the night shift. He's still with us. He knows how we live and work and how we feel about the future. He's learned that, in our own way, we're fighters too. And he's working with all the men of Coaltown to build the world we want.[57]

Despite the government's income-tax concessions and the big publicity campaign, the desired results of PC 4092 were not realized. Between 1 June and 31 August, 1,105 ex-coal miners in the Maritimes registered under the provisions of PC 4092. Of these, 351 were referred to coal employment, 444 were allowed, for medical or other reasons, to remain in their existing jobs, and, as of 1 September, 310 awaited disposition.[58] According to Michael Dwyer, the NSS Maritime Regional Superintendent, the entire registration process had "completely bogged down," with men simply producing medical examination certificates claiming an inability to perform coal work that were "not worth the paper they are printed on."[59] Men deemed fit for coal employment were appealing their medical examinations to NSS appeal boards. In the Minto area, sixteen of nineteen appeals were granted by NSS officials. In the New Glasgow area, Divisional Registrar Colonel Edgar Mingo set up an Army Medical Board with only one doctor instead of the normal two. Out of forty ex-coal miners examined, thirty-seven were judged to be medically fit to return to coal employment, but all thirty-seven men appealed the decisions on the grounds that two doctors were not present. Mingo sent two new doctors to examine the men, and this new Medical Board judged thirty of the thirty-seven appellants to be medically unfit for coal employment.[60]

In July 1943 Arthur MacNamara issued a directive that gave coal mining priority over all other industries in the use of available unskilled labour. Mine operators, however, pointed out that they were swamped with unskilled help and that only an increase in the number of men qualified to work at the coal face would increase the output in the coal mines of Nova Scotia. To enlarge already bloated staffs would be to no avail.[61]

The effort to release coal miners from the Army that was introduced in late 1942, continued to yield frustrating results. Of the 2,200 miners who had been authorized for release by September 1943, 700 had either withdrawn their applications to return to the pits or been sent overseas, 100 had left and then returned to the Army, and only 970 had gone to mines across the country. The remainder awaited allocation.[62] There were several attempts to smooth the process of release, but many DND officials resisted any suggestion that military personnel should be compelled to return to coal employment.[63] At the same time, UMWA demands continued. Residual issues arising out of the levelling-up of wages at the DCC, ACC, and OSC were settled during the summer of 1943, but District 26 officials lobbied hard to level up wages at three other companies in Nova Scotia.[64] In the autumn of 1943, exasperated Department of Labour officials authorized all District 26 claims for levelling-up of wages in the Nova Scotia coal industry in the vain hope that this further concession to union demands would result in a corresponding increase in coal production.

Frustrated officials began to lobby Arthur MacNamara for more draconian measures to remedy the coal labour situation. Allan Mitchell, the Director of the Unemployment Insurance Commission and rarely an advocate of compulsion, noted that PC 2254 of 21 March 1942, the Order-in-Council establishing National Selective Service, empow-ered the NSS director to coordinate the mobilization activities of all government departments in order to further the war effort "in all its phases." He believed that this permitted new and sterner measures to secure the release of skilled miners from the armed forces:

I do not believe that the coordination of manpower policy which is defined in the above wording has been put into effect. If this were so, we would not be carrying out the present cumbersome system of trying to secure soldier miners from the armed forces, but would merely through the centralized control exercised at Ottawa over manpower issues issue an Order that all soldier miners were to report at given military depots for transfer back to the mines.[65]

MacNamara's response highlighted his aversion to full-scale compul-sion of workers. Noting that only Russia, Germany, and Japan would countenance such measures, MacNamara asserted that the existing NSS efforts in the coal mines of Canada were "pretty drastic" and that Mitchell's plan was neither "feasible nor practical."[66]

The last major NSS initiative launched in the second half of 1943 centred on the extension of training classes to facilitate the transfer of datal men to the coal face. Coal mining methods had changed radically since provincial mining laws had first been enacted. The old "room and pillar" method allowed two men to work together in one room, with these men responsible for all facets of the face operation including boring holes, blasting, cutting the coal, loading the coal, laying track, looking after ventilation, and putting up safety timbers. Because of the large area required for this method, it was difficult for foremen to pro-vide close supervision, and producers had to be extremely skilled in all phases of coal work. The "longwall" mining method in place in most Nova Scotia mines during the war, however, allowed many men to work together at the coal face under the supervision of a single foreman with no auxiliary duties such as laying track.[67] NSS officials were well aware that this mining method allowed for the use of non-certified miners along side skilled miners with first-class mining certificates.

To encourage datal men in this direction, NSS representatives attempted to inaugurate a series of training classes in the larger coal mines in Nova Scotia. But while the companies indicated a willingness to participate in the training scheme, UMWA officials refused to endorse it. Preliminary discussions between the companies and District 26 leaders in September 1943 resulted in the establishment of a small training class in Caledonia at the expense of the DCC.[68] In the final months of 1943, however, any hope of continued UMWA cooperation evaporated in the face of the union's continuing demands for wage increases. The District 26 contract with the coal companies had expired on 1 February 1943, and a UMWA brief submitted to the NWLB had not been addressed. At the District 26 convention in October 1943, UMWA officials resolved not to support any training schemes. Wage increases of $15-17 million annually, the union claimed, would settle all production shortfalls in the province.[69] In the same month as the convention, UMWA officials advised MacNamara that all "fly-by-night" NSS training schemes should be abandoned in favour of immediate wage increases. The training option was abandoned until the spring of 1944.[70]

In the first five months of 1944 NSS did not attempt any new initiatives to increase the production of coal in Nova Scotia. District 26 miners had been granted a $1 per day increase in wages through an NWLB decision issued in December 1943,[71] and additional income tax concessions were granted to all coal miners in July 1944.[72] The provisions of PC 4092 barring the enlistment of coal miners were extended to 1 August 1944. In June 1944, a second attempt was made to start training classes at the DCC in cooperation with the union. Two classes were eventually begun with a limited number of participants in the No. 1-B and No. 24 mines.[73] Although company officials continued to support the training option, the DCC noted that the dollar-per-day pay increase had only resulted in higher rates of absenteeism and had further decreased the incentive for datal workers to move to producing positions at the coalface.[74] The government of Nova Scotia attempted a remedy with an Order-in-Council issued in March 1944 that allowed males as young as seventeen to work at the face if they were supervised by an experienced miner. More than 800 ex-coal miners were eventually returned to the Maritime coal fields under the registration provisions of PC 4092[75] and more than 2,000 soldier miners were working in coal mines across Canada by June 1944.[76] None of these measures, however, resulted in an increase in the production of bituminous coal in Nova Scotia.

Coal company officials launched a concerted campaign in June 1944 to impress their labour problems upon DMS officials in Ottawa. DCC General Manager T.L. McCall detailed the severe problem of absenteeism resulting from the increased wages being paid to District 26 employees.[77] McCall claimed that "the pick of our producers physically and as to loyalty" had enlisted in disgust after the slowdown strikes of 1941, and that their replacements, secured through NSS, had been of poor quality. The absentee rate in DCC mines had increased from a daily average of 18.2 per cent in May 1942 to 29.7 per cent in May 1943. In the week in May 1944 that the DCC had paid the retroactive one dollar-per-day wage increase, the absentee rate coal-face producers had reached a staggering 41.2 per cent. In McCall's view, price controls gave well-paid producers an incentive to stop working once they reached an acceptable level of earnings. Datal workers also remained a problem; 625 of them in the employ of the DCC either possessed first- or second-class mining certificates or possessed skills that would qualify them to gain the necessary certificate to work in producing positions at the coal face, but they were not being transferred to where they were needed.

E.J. Brunning, the new DMS Coal Controller, quickly brought this particular account of the failure of NSS efforts to the attention of Arthur MacNamara and other ranking officials in the Department of Labour. In view of production shortfalls in the United States and the possibility of increased demands on American coal after the Normandy invasion, the "serious deterioration" in the Maritime coal fields necessitated immediate action.[78] In 1939, Brunning noted, producers had composed 36.4 per cent (2,274 workers) of a total workforce of 7,209. By April 1944, however, only 24.7 per cent (1,554 workers) of the workforce was directly engaged in production. Comparing the first five months of 1939 with the first five months of 1944, production had declined by 16 per cent and the number of producers by 31 per cent. As a result of various NSS initiatives, the mines were "flooded with non-producers"; the high rates paid to datal workers provided no incentive for them switch to production positions. Brunning called for an immediate NSS investigation into the production crisis; it was essential to induce datal men to move to the coal face and to change wage rates so as to achieve this.

In July 1944, more than two years after the idea of production committees had been rejected by NSS leaders as a publicity ploy of the UMWA, a desperate Arthur MacNamara endorsed the union's proposal.[79] The first steps to get the committees going were taken at a meeting of Department of Labour officials, coal company executives, and UMWA leaders at the Isle Royale Hotel in Sydney on 12–13 July.[80] A wide variety of grievances were aired at this gathering. Company officials complained that absenteeism and deliberate union slowdowns were hampering production despite the large wage concessions that had been made to District 26 members. Union representatives countered by noting the squalor of the coal environment, the lack of pension and recreational opportunities for miners, and the closing of liquor stores in coal areas on Saturdays, a decision made by the Nova Scotia government on the recommendation of Humphrey Mitchell. After two days of rancorous debate, four understandings were reached: Joint Production Committees would be established and would meet twice per month; pressure would be exerted on the Nova Scotia government to open liquor stores on Saturdays; companies would improve recreational and community facilities in company towns, and the formation of a coal commission would be sought to oversee the implementation of improvements in the industry.

Although NSS officials viewed the establishment of Joint Production Committees as an alternative to more coercive measures, pressure continued to build in July and August of 1944 for more decisive action. Beginning on 30 July, workers at the Acadia Coal Company in Stellarton walked off the job for five days, an event that led ACC officials to document forty cases of illegal work stoppages between August 1943 and August 1944. According to the company, in February 1944 fourteen miners employed at the ACC No. 7 mine had returned to the surface early despite being warned that they would be paid only for the hours they had actually worked. When the men received their pay packets two weeks later and discovered that their pay had indeed been docked, they and fifteen other men had refused to work. Three entire shifts had subsequently failed to report for work over the next two working days and 325 tons of output had been lost.[81] Production at the ACC mines had declined by more than 10,000 tons in the first six months of 1944 compared with the same period in 1943, and absenteeism had only increased in response to the income tax concessions made in July 1944.[82]

The flood of criticism directed towards the government's handling of the coal labour force, the continued union problems, and the declining coal production figures, led some NSS officials to openly challenge their director Arthur MacNamara to authorize coercion. In August 1944, for example, C.F. Needham called for "drastic disciplinary action" to be taken against miners and suggested, for the first time, that Compulsory Transfer Orders be used within mines to force datal men to work at the face.[83] Needham noted that the Dominion Coal Company producing class of 1,900 workers was 900 short of the required number while there was a surplus of datal men working in the DCC mines that included more than 600 certified miners. DCC officials likewise lobbied MacNamara through the DMS Coal Controller for tough action. The Company's position was that all previous NSS initiatives, including the wage increases and income tax rebates, had only exacerbated the problem.[84] Several of MacNamara's key advisors, however, lobbied against calls for coercion of the coal workforce. M.M. Maclean, the Director of Industrial Relations, asserted that Needham was "not intimately informed" of the issues involved in the coal situation. Needham was simply parroting J.W. McLeod's viewpoint, a perspective that was "entirely out of touch" with both union and company sentiment. This ignored volumes of correspondence from company representatives endorsing Needham's views. According to Maclean, the Joint Production Committees would solve the problem.[85] MacNamara agreed, and, while admitting to Needham that he was "stymied" on the whole issue, he would go no further than to suggest that the NWLB investigate the possibility of a further increase in the wage differential between datal and production workers.[86]

Senior NSS officials in the Maritimes, however, supported the views of Needham and McLeod. On 24 August, NSS Regional Superintendent Michael Dwyer told MacNamara that the records of the previous forty years showed that every wage increase had been followed by an increase in absenteeism and a decrease in production. In Dwyer's view the time had come for the establishment of a permanent labour board with "final and supreme authority" over the coal industry.[87] The development of a new labour policy "with some teeth in it" would initially be resisted, but the majority of the workers would agree to the new rules and not allow the "radicals to win if a strong hand [was] brought to bear in the first place." Dwyer undoubtedly made a strong case, but once again M.M. Maclean dissuaded MacNamara from acting on it. Dwyer, Maclean argued, had a "very biased" viewpoint and had swallowed the company line. The Joint Production Committees would solve the problem of absenteeism.[88]

This second phase of the NSS response to the coal labour crisis can be considered to have ended in August 1944. The most compulsory labour mobilization measures of the war had been instituted through PC 4092 of May 1943, but coal production continued to decline steadily in the sixteen months thereafter. Massive publicity efforts did not begin to solve the shortage of skilled miners. The release of coal miners from the armed forces was numerically the most significant source of men to augment producer staffs, but proceeded with difficulty and could not fill the void created by the initial loss of these men to the armed forces. Training classes were only marginally successful and were not supported by UMWA officials. Wage and income tax concessions designed to alleviate tensions among District 26 members led to greater levels of absenteeism rather than production gains. In desperation, the Department of Labour turned to Joint Production Committees as a way out but in practice these also failed to solve the problem. The result was that, having rejected various calls for tough and concerted action, Arthur MacNamara and other NSS officials were reduced in the last year of the war to operating a tepid campaign of consultation and conciliation.

By contrast, DMS officials continued to attempt to spur the government to take a more interventionist approach. In September 1944, Coal Controller E.J. Brunning lobbied C.D. Howe to wield his influence because massive government subsidies to the coal industry were not resulting in production increases. The "chief reason" for the financial losses and production shortfalls coal companies in Nova Scotia were experiencing was the poor balance of producers within the coal labour force.[89] Brunning called for an Industrial Mobilization Survey to be carried out in all coal mines to indentify medically fit datal men qualified to work at the face; they would be forced to do so or else face compulsory military service. NSS immediately rejected this proposal. M.M. Maclean condemned it as a "great mistake,"[90] while H.C. Goldenberg, Chairman of the Manpower Survey Committee in Ottawa, noted that any survey designed to comb men out of coal employment would "create nothing but confusion and misunderstanding" since many men had been directed to the mines and frozen in that employment.[91] For Maclean and Goldenberg the Joint Production Committees remained the only viable solution to the production problem. Brunning, however, refused to back down and insisted that a "correct proportion" of datal men to production workers be established. Dismissing the Joint Production Committees as irrelevant, he insisted that only the threat of conscription could force datal men to work at the coal face.[92]

After C.D. Howe pressured Humphrey Mitchell to adopt Brunning's plan, a meeting of senior DMS and Department of Labour officials was convened in Ottawa on 25 September 1944. At this meeting, Arthur MacNamara admitted that compelling qualified datal workers to work at the coal face was an attractive option, but working against it was the possibility of widespread discontent among UMWA members. M.M. Maclean now finally admitted that the Joint Production Committees "would be too slow in adjusting the production problem," and that the training schemes established in March 1944 would not solve it either.[93] On their side, the DMS representatives present proposed that a survey of datal men in Nova Scotia coal mines be carried out to gain an accurate and comprehensive picture of the composition and qualification of the datal workforce. Agreement was reached on this, and a Coal Labour Survey form, modelled on the Industrial Mobilization Survey Plan forms, was drafted within a week. Each datal worker was required to report his qualifications for a production position and his reasons for remaining in datal employment. Employers were required to fill out a second form assessing the essentiality of each datal worker. Letters announcing the survey were sent to all company and union officials on 2 October 1944. The first survey was undertaken at the DCC and eventually eleven Nova Scotia coal companies and 8,677 workers were canvassed.

In the face of increased official scrutiny of coal mining operations and the datal workforce, UMWA officials suddenly sought government support for a new conciliatory labour strategy. The Royal Commission on Coal, chaired by Justice W.F. Carroll, had been formed in October 1944 to investigate the problems plaguing the coal industry across Canada.[94] District 26 President Freeman Jenkins informed E.J. Brunning on 5 October 1944 that the UMWA had adopted a Summary of Proposals calling for: (1) the union promotion of improvements in social conditions, housing, and recreation; (2) the creation of central production committees; (3) the union encouragement of "energetic" education programs; (4) the development of company initiatives to improve management techniques; (5) the development of special machinery for union-management cooperation; (6) the formulation, with government assistance, of mechanization plans; (7) the support of government labour experts in union education plans; and (8) the granting of the union shop. Jenkins asked that the Summary of Proposals be accepted by DMS and the Department of Labour and that they in turn exert pressure on the coal companies to make it a joint labour-management brief to the Royal Commission.[95] Not surprisingly, some NSS officials jumped at the chance to facilitate union-company cooperation. M.M. Maclean told MacNamara that the UMWA document contained a "sound diagnosis" of the problems of the coal mining industry.[96] In late October, Maclean advised that a special conference of all interested parties should be convened to explore ways to adopt the UMWA plan.

MacNamara, however, rejected Maclean's calls for cooperation with UMWA officials. In a rare display of emotion, MacNamara informed his subordinate that he was disgusted with UMWA actions during the war and that the results of the Coal Labour Survey should be tabulated before any further action was contemplated.[97] In an even rarer move, MacNamara expressed his feelings about the union to UMWA officials themselves on 5 November 1944. Reiterating his belief that UMWA men were responsible for production declines, MacNamara rejected the union proposals and insisted that the Coal Labour Survey would form the basis of a solution to the industry's problems.[98] The UMWA replied quickly; the union proposals, they insisted, should be considered an "integral part" of a larger process–including the survey–designed to increase production and stabilize the coal labour force.[99] The Coal Labour Survey would not solve anything since the questions it contained were "mostly superfluous" and were viewed by the miners as being related to military service (a claim confirmed by several senior NSS officials).[100]

Some NSS officials sought to place the blame on other departments. Chief among them was L.E. Westman, the NSS Associate Director–War Industries, a position created in the summer of 1944. In two detailed memoranda, one to E.J. Brunning (October 1944) and the other to Arthur MacNamara (November 1944),[101] Westman admitted that virtually every NSS initiative had been a failure. The return of soldier miners to datal work rather than to production positions had been of limited value. Pay increases had bloated datal staffs, while the training schools had not been a factor of "any great consequence." Only three training classes were currently in operation at the Dominion Coal Company with a combined enrolment of fewer than fifty men. Westman blamed the Department of Munitions and Supply for the production declines. The real problem in Nova Scotia was not wages and labour supply, but working conditions. Until these were addressed the "chronic problems" of the industry could not be solved.

As might be expected, the DMS rejected Westman's analysis. Although DMS officials admitted that the number of Army men working in the Nova Scotia mines was limited, they emphasized that those released from the military were the "steadiest workers in the pits."[102] Again, while it was true that the number of men taking training classes had been "very low," there was a "greater interest" than ever in this option. As for conditions underground, the mines were in "the best of physical condition," and DCC officials were doing a "wonderful job of maintaining the facilities." The DMS view was that only the use of mechanical loaders in the larger mines could solve the labour problem, but these machines could only be introduced after a period of "long and careful experiment." A "mental condition" existed among Cape Breton miners that affected their outlook, and only the "utmost cooperation" between labour and management could overcome this.

NSS and DMS officials converged in hoping that the Coal Labour Survey would be the preliminary step to an eventual shift of datal men to production positions, but in practice the survey suffered from many of the same problems that plagued the Industrial Mobilization Survey. Its success of the depended on two key considerations, a good response rate from the UMWA datal men and the subsequent interviewing of all men deemed qualified to work at the face. It was hoped that the majority of surveys would be returned by mail during October 1944, but the response rate during that month was "far from satisfactory."[103] By 7 November only 35 per cent of the surveys had been completed; this forced NSS officials to issue 3,000 follow-up letters to miners urging them to fill out the forms.[104] By 7 December, 75 percent of the surveys had been completed, but, with the final report scheduled for delivery on 15 December, the NSS representative supervising the survey asked that the plan to interview datal men be abandoned.[105] DMS officials immediately opposed this request; the entire rationale behind the survey was to use the biographical information on the forms to identify and interview the most promising datal workers. The DMS agreed with UMWA officials that the form contained many questions which were "not germane to the main point" of the survey.[106] In the middle of January 1945, the decision was made to interview approximately 550 Dominion Coal Company employees.

Remarkably, the interviews never occurred. In a February 1945 weekly report to MacNamara, Willard Scott, NSS Associate Director–Industrial Mobilization Survey, insisted that personal interviews were unnecessary because survey tabulations made it "sufficiently clear" why datal men were not going to the face.[107] More than 3,400 datal men possessed first- or second-class mining certificates, but close to 65 per cent of the individuals in this group were over forty years of age. Moreover, 63 per cent of the 6,373 men who had completed the forms were either physically unfit for face work or had been declared essential by their employers. Although close to 800 of the men eligible for transfer had indicated that they would refuse, for a variety of reasons, to work in production positions, Scott maintained that a tighter control of the datal workforce would iron out many of the existing problems.[108] Specifically, he called for the adoption of five measures: the institution of a five-day week; the close monitoring of extra shifts for datal workers to cut down on absenteeism and over-time; the alteration of PC 4092 to allow NSS officials to compel men to positions within coal mines; the return to the armed forces of soldier miners who refused to work at the face; and the implementation of provincial measures to reduce the time needed to obtain a first class mining certificate. In a more subtle manner, Scott was advocating C.F. Needham's August 1944 suggestion that NSS control be extended to the supervision of individual workers in coal employment, with qualified workers being forced to move to the face.

Scott's views had considerable support among NSS officials, but Arthur MacNamara's actions ensured that nothing concrete would result from the Coal Labour Survey. NSS Eastern Coal Consultant J.W. McLeod agreed with Scott that NSS should have power to compel certain men to work at the face, but he also maintained that the 799 soldier miners working in Nova Scotia, 392 of whom were performing datal work, should be left alone.[109] Both company and NSS representatives supported the proposals for a five-day work week and a clampdown on overtime shifts. MacNamara, however, failed to act and sent the completed survey tabulations to the Royal Commission on Coal for information purposes only.[110] The coal companies were not even given the opportunity to move men who had indicated on the survey forms a willingness to switch to production jobs. This was because individual responses to the survey could not be released to management without the permission of the UMWA.[111] As a result, many experienced men remained in datal posts in companies where no shortage of producers existed. In the mines of the Cumberland Railway & Coal Company, for example, 145 qualified datal men were willing to work at the coal face, but no production vacancies were available in that company's operations.[112] At the same time, other companies in need of production workers did not have access to the information needed to identify them.

In truth, MacNamara had the support of many senior NSS officials in his *de facto* abandonment of regulatory control of the coal labour force. On 14 March 1945, L.E. Westman told the Deputy Minister that "various expedients" might be tried to reduce the demand for 1,100 producers in the coal mines across Canada, but that it was "questionable whether the net result would justify the means."[113] At the same time labour relations in the Nova Scotia coalfields continued to deteriorate. On 20 February 1945, after the NWLB rejected a union proposal for increased wages, a strike vote was called by District 26 President Freeman Jenkins.[114] Despite Humphrey Mitchell's public warning that the vote would not further the miners' cause and that a strike was forbidden under the provisions of the Wartime Wages Control Order, the vote carried and a series of tie-ups and work stoppages ensued. The most notable stoppage in production occurred in June, when UMWA miners in Glace Bay went on strike in support of a group of waitresses at the Glory Café who had been fired and were being denied their pay until they returned their uniforms. Local unions determined that café owner Yee Yen was "in league with other café owners in a move to smash the waitresses' union"; this made full UMWA support of the waitresses mandatory.[115] Two days were lost in the mines as a result of the job action.

NSS basically adopted a hands-off approach to the problems of the industry for the remainder of the war. Absenteeism continued to increase, while production continued to go down. By June 1945, absenteeism had reached a daily average of 30 per cent in the Nova Scotia coal industry, a rate characterized by NSS officials as a "deliberate and calculated" attempt to produce more overtime work.[116] Production declined by six per cent per month from January to June 1945, a situation made worse for the country by a simultaneous import cut of 10 per cent in American coal.[117] In June, Humphrey Mitchell offered an increase of 25 cents per ton to the existing subsidy for coal, with the sum realized thereby to be divided among union members if the UMWA would agree to a contract for twelve months.[118] Key NSS officials, however, cautioned that decreasing production rates would be a "foregone conclusion" if datal wage rates were increased as a result of Mitchell's offer.[119] NSS representatives welcomed the end of the war in the Pacific as an opportunity to extricate the Dominion government from the morass of the previous three years. With the return of thousands of men to Cape Breton and the nationwide early release of more than 600 coal miners from the armed forces under the Industrial Selection and Release Plan,[120] freezing regulations and compulsory direction of ex-coal miners were dropped in September 1945. In November, despite although the industry was still in a "precarious condition," PC 4092 and the emergency regulations governing the coal labour force were repealed.[121]

6 Halifax Longshoremen

Business in the Port of Halifax quickly boomed after the outbreak of war in 1939 and the city assumed a prominent position as one of the essential wartime ports involved in the critical and costly convoy operations in the North Atlantic theatre that kept Britain alive in the early years of the war and supplied the enormous needs of Allied forces in Europe throughout the conflict. The number of deep-sea or ocean-going vessels arriving in or departing from Halifax increased from 3,116 in 1939 to 7,067 in 1943. Inward cargo tonnage handled in Halifax increased from 1.27 million tons in 1939 to a peak of 2.66 million tons in 1943, while outward cargo tonnage processed in Halifax increased from less than one million tons in 1939 to a wartime peak of 3.67 million tons in 1944. The war transformed Halifax from a relatively minor Canadian port to the most important shipping centre in the country. In 1939, Halifax handled less than eight per cent of the cargo tonnage in all Canadian ports. By 1943, however, Halifax was responsible for processing almost 27 per cent of the nation's shipping cargo.

An adequate and stable supply of longshoremen in Halifax allowed the port to process this increase in cargo tonnage. In an overheated national, regional, and municipal civilian economy experiencing severe shortages of labour, National Selective Service officials were able to double the number of longshoremen working on the Halifax docks during the war. With the consent of Halifax dock workers, control of labour in the port was centralized in the hands of a single powerful individual by the end of 1942. The inefficient traditional system of constituting irregular gangs of workers on the docks was completely abandoned in favour of permanent gangs of longshoremen despatched from a central hiring hall. When labour shortages continued to hamper loading operations, the federal Cabinet passed two orders-in-council on 25 June 1943. The first required all ex-longshoremen to register with NSS and await possible direction to the Halifax docks. The second created a reserve pool of labour and guaranteed a generous weekly minimum wage. Combined with other measures such as the provision of bunkhouses and canteen facilities for dock workers, these government initiatives promoted the expeditious and efficient handling of cargo in Halifax during the critical years of the war. Utilizing the sweeping powers granted to them to co-ordinate the civilian labour force, NSS officials were able to fundamentally transform patterns of longshore work that had prevailed in Halifax for decades. Moreover, this transformation endured into the postwar period. The story of the Halifax docks in World War II constitutes an important chapter in the neglected history of longshoremen in Canada.[1] It exemplifies the positive side of government intervention in the labour market in wartime Canada.

Like the coal miners, Halifax longshoremen were the target of compulsory registration provisions and the beneficiaries of wage concessions that, in theory, were designed to increase labour supply and boost productivity. But the wage concessions to coal miners were reactive and not accompanied by restructuring of the poisonous working environment in the coal fields. Wage policies affecting longshoremen were proactive in their intent and scope and they were closely linked with improvements in the working environment of the Halifax docks. While skilled coal miners required more training than longshoremen, the tepid attempts to institute training classes in Nova Scotia coal mines could not match the NSS efforts to establish surplus civilian labour pools and Army labour units as key components of a dock labour strategy.

Halifax dockworkers were unionized under the Halifax Longshoremen's Association (HLA), a branch of the International Longshoremen's Association (ILA), and the HLA kept a tight rein on membership. Any government attempt to alter historical patterns of longshore employment could be expected to be opposed by Halifax dockworkers. The issue of casual labour lay at the heart of HLA opposition.[2] Prior to 1930 two main groups were working on the Halifax docks. The first was comprised of permanent members of the HLA, primarily Irish Catholics benefiting from various circles of patronage and nepotism. Many of the permanent HLA members worked in shipping company gangs that had first crack at any work available on the docks. The second group, the majority, consisted of a floating pool of casual labour who were summoned to work whenever additional dock labour was needed. Men were selected for temporary employment through the "shape-up," also known as the "have a look" hiring method. Job seekers would generally arrive at a dock at three specific times for the shape-up, usually at 7:00 a.m., 1:00 p.m., and 6:00 p.m. A walking boss, an experienced stevedore who supervised the loading at a ship, would select the men needed to fill out permanent HLA gangs or form additional gangs. A dehumanizing and corrupt practice, the shape-up was nevertheless tolerated by both the union and the shipping companies.

During the 1930s, however, an important change occurred. Shipping companies granted the HLA control of the hiring process. In an effort to decasualize the longshore labour market, the HLA used a hiring hall to coordinate the employment of longshoremen, a practice that already had been adopted in other Atlantic ports such as Saint John. Longshoremen were formed into groups on a theoretically equal basis, providing that any man applying for work was a permanent HLA member or a temporary member, known as a cardman. The hiring hall employed an alphabetical rotation system to despatch men to job sites. A man seeking work on a particular day would place a pin beside his name on a board at the hiring hall containing the names of all longshoremen eligible for employment. The HLA despatching officer, using the job board as a guide, sent men to the various piers on a rotating basis. This method allowed a restricted number of longshoremen to work a maximum number of days during the year. The shape-up remained in place as a necessary method of securing workers in times of peak labour demand, particularly once the war began in 1939 and port traffic in Halifax increased. To ensure the smooth handling of wartime cargo Department of Labour and NSS officials were intervening in a complex labour environment. While wartime administrators sought to saturate the Halifax docks with a guaranteed supply of labour regardless of union affiliation, HLA members sought to retain control of the hiring process to guarantee steady employment to permanent longshoremen. These conflicting positions were not satisfactorily addressed in a comprehensive fashion until late 1943.

The first meeting between Department of Labour officials and the parties concerned with longshore operations in Halifax occurred in February 1941. At this gathering, Minister of Labour Norman McLarty heard a variety of complaints from the shipping companies about the intransigence of some HLA workers and the failings of the "have a look" system of hiring. As a result of this discussion, the HLA agreed to admit more temporary members into the union for the duration of war, to increase the number of day gangs, and to begin a limited number of night shifts. As well, the HLA and the employers agreed to the appointment of an arbitrator to settle future differences between them.[3] By PC 1706 of 10 March 1941, Vincent MacDonald, Dean of the Law Faculty at Dalhousie University, was named to this position. Despite these changes and HLA promises to increase union membership on a voluntary basis, poor turnout was causing a decline in the volume of tonnage handled. In August, McLarty met with employer representatives about the continuing failure of the HLA to supply enough workers. Only 208 cardmen had been added to union ranks, and the employer representatives maintained that only 800 of the 1,300 registered longshoremen showed up regularly for dock work. While MacDonald's appointment as arbitrator was applauded by the spokesmen for the shipping companies, they also noted that he did not have the statutory authority to needed change.[4]

In December 1941, the HLA and the employers reached on their own a Working Agreement designed to alleviate the problems which had arisen.[5] This agreement guaranteed a day wage rate of 77 cents per hour and a night wage rate of 88 cents per hour (exclusive of war bonuses) but left the HLA responsible for finding sufficient numbers of workers to ensure the prompt unloading and despatch of ships. The HLA committed itself to use "all its powers to prevent irregularity of attendance." This was promising; but employers soon reported that haphazard hiring schemes and irregularity of attendance rendered the Working Agreement invalid, despite the election of a more co-operative HLA President, Peter Garnier. George Huband of the British Ministry of War Transport informed C.D. Howe in January 1942 that words could not express the "extreme seriousness" of the Halifax situation.[6] Howe suggested that the labour shortage in Halifax would be solved by sending more reliable dockworkers from Montreal to the troubled Atlantic port. Despite the addition of 350 cardmen to the HLA, the longshoremen in Halifax still could not handle the increasing traffic.

The Department of Labour appointed MacDonald to study the situation and submit a plan for a complete reorganization of work in the port. MacDonald subsequently met with the Shipping Committee of the Halifax Board of Trade, the HLA, and a variety of other Port officials.[7] He submitted his comprehensive report on 12 February 1942. MacDonald concluded that the "haphazard hiring system" of rounding up individual men at dock gates when ships arrived and firing them the moment work ended was outdated. All traces of the "have a look" system would have to be replaced with a system that permitted the hiring of gangs of skilled workers. MacDonald laid much of the blame for the port's problems at the feet of HLA members. Some unionized workers, for example, opted to work on the more remunerative evening and night shifts, leaving the more critical day shift starved for labour.

Union longshoremen also tended to sign up to handle specific types of cargo, leaving less attractive work for casual labourers. Altogether, MacDonald made fourteen recommendations and he advised that the changes required should be made through Order-in-Council rather than through negotiation between the employers and the union. The HLA should be required to admit enough cardmen to its permanent membership to bring this group to a strength of 1,200. It should also be required to grant an additional 800 temporary cards to bring its overall strength to 2,000. A controller should be appointed to wield supreme authority in all port matters, and a Central Despatching Agency formed to deal with absenteeism and to organize properly constituted work gangs.

As a result of MacDonald's report, PC 1758 was issued on 9 March 1942. It called on the Minister of Labour to prepare a "wartime plan for the re-organization of ship loading and unloading operations in the Port of Halifax." Under this plan, a Controller of Loading Operations would be empowered to co-ordinate all dock activities; the "have a look" hiring scheme would be abolished and longshoremen would be called at regular times; all cardmen would be admitted to the HLA with full privileges and additional temporary cardmen would be recruited to bring the longshore labour pool to 1,700 men, and the daily hiring of individual workers at the job site would be abolished and all longshoremen hired in fixed, permanent gangs through a Central Despatching Agency. Men who refused to work without a valid excuse would lose their dock permits.

After newly-appointed Minister of Labour Humphrey Mitchell travelled to Halifax for discussions with the HLA, part of Ottawa's plan was put into effect by PC 3511 of 30 April 1942. Under this Order, the Controller was given authority over all Port matters with the exception of wage rates. The "have a look" system was abolished and all existing and future cardmen were given "complete equality with permanent members" of the HLA with respect to hiring and working privileges. A Central Despatching Agency (CDA) was established and gangs were required to work at night when so directed. For the position of Controller the government recruited Vincent MacDonald; John J. Green of the Eastern Canada Stevedoring Company of Montreal was named Port Loading Superintendent, and Charles Train was brought from the Vancouver dockyards to organize the central despatching system.[8]

MacDonald wasted no time getting to work. He immediately demanded that the despatching of longshore workers be taken completely away from the offices of the Unemployment Insurance Commission (UIC) and that he be given a "free hand" in organizing the CDA.[9] Although the offices of the UIC were not formally incorporated into the NSS structure until September 1942, plans were already afoot to use them as employment offices under NSS regulations. Arthur MacNamara's view was that the CDA should be incorporated as a UIC office to assist in record keeping;[10] some UIC officers in the Maritimes, however, supported MacDonald's call for autonomy. MacDonald opposed UIC involvement in the CDA in part because stevedores were not covered under the Unemployment Insurance Act. But he was also anxious to have the same degree of control over the CDA as he had over all other port functions.[11] Ultimately, despite MacNamara's continued resistance, MacDonald got his way and the CDA functioned as an autonomous unit for the duration of the war.

MacDonald also had trouble early on with the HLA, which attempted to block the appointment of John Green as Port Loading Superintendent. On 2 May, HLA President Peter Garnier informed Humphrey Mitchell that the HLA would not accept the appointment of Green to any post in the Halifax system.[12] At a meeting of the HLA on 17 June the terms of PC 3511 were rejected specifically because Mitchell had refused the union's demand that Green be replaced.[13] MacDonald thought that it would be prudent to "remove this unnecessary spot of friction,"[14] but MacNamara and Mitchell refused to give way. Pressed for a justification of his rejection of Green, Garnier told Mitchell in July that the HLA had been promised that the Controller, the Port Loading Superintendent, and the Chief Despatcher would not be connected in any way either with the union or the employers.[15] Green's association with the Eastern Canada Stevedoring Company in Montreal violated this guarantee. His American citizenship was another liability as there were many qualified Canadian candidates for the job. Eventually, Mitchell had to back down; in July it was announced that Green would be replaced as Port Loading Superintendent by Captain W.F. Spring of Vancouver.[16] One of the primary reasons for choosing Spring lay in the fact that Vancouver had been operating under a central hiring hall for some time.

Throughout the autumn of 1942, HLA officials continued to resist the radical revision of existing longshore hiring methods. MacDonald's work was made more difficult, moreover, when he decided to leave the office of Controller at the end of 1942 to become Assistant Deputy Minister of Labour. In anticipation of this change, E.L. Cousins, Wartime Administrator of Canadian Atlantic Ports within the Department of Munitions and Supply,[17] was asked to assume the position, but he declined.[18] On 26 November 1942, by PC 10323, Captain R.G. Perchard, Deputy Harbour Master of the Port of Montreal, was named to the job. MacDonald, however, remained the leading figure in pushing forward the reorganization plan.

In December 1942, the HLA voted to accept the new hiring system for a three-month trial period, but the union refused to admit 1,500 temporary cardmen.[19] Under pressure from the ILA leader in New York, who had been visited by Vincent MacDonald,[20] Peter Garnier endorsed the three-month trial period to avoid an open split with the HLA's parent union. To facilitate matters, Department of Labour officials next agreed to a HLA request that three of its members be named to the new despatching agency.[21] Humphrey Mitchell applauded this development as a "welcome change" in the HLA position,[22] while MacDonald was willing to go along with it in order to avoid a repetition of the "passive non-cooperation which [had] previously delayed the scheme for months." Even the *Halifax Star*, a consistent opponent of HLA resistance to plans to re-organize the Halifax docks, editorialized that the HLA decision to accept the hiring hall on a trial basis would "undoubtedly help greatly to facilitate the speedy handing of vital ship cargoes at this port."[23] But rank-and-file opposition to the plan mounted in the first months of 1943. On 8 February HLA members voted to reject the entire longshore reorganization scheme, but further pressure from the government and the ILA forced them to approve MacDonald's plan.[24] PC 24/1280 of 17 February 1943 allowed the Department of Labour to appoint the staff, including HLA members, of the CDA effective March 1.[25] It was on this date that the three-month trial period began.

The regulations MacDonald devised for the CDA had thirty-two sections and involved sweeping change.[26] They confirmed the primacy of the Controller and the use of the CDA at 59 Hollis Street as the sole clearinghouse for longshoremen. Each longshoreman had to register with the Chief Despatcher and be cleared to work through the issuance of an identification card by the Controller. Regularly constituted work gangs were under the control of gang foremen, who would receive instructions from the CDA to order the members of their units to report directly to job sites. Companies seeking men for day, evening, or night work had to submit orders at a specified time before the men were required. Men absent from a gang with a good excuse were to be replaced by men from a Surplus Board under the direct control of the CDA. The Controller determined the number of gangs needed to operate port traffic and could constitute extra gangs from the Surplus Board. In contrast to previous practice, gangs could be shifted from ship to ship once work on a particular vessel had been completed. Longshoremen could not pick their own assignments and had to accept any positions offered to them. Representatives of both the employers and the HLA had access to the Chief Despatcher to ensure that the regulations were being carried out. Despatching hours for men on the Surplus Board were 8 to 9 a.m. for the day shift, 1 to 2 p.m. for the evening shift, and 7 to 7:30 p.m. for the night shift. Payment of workers on the Surplus Board commenced at the moment of despatch, and each man was allotted thirty minutes to arrive at the job site.

Despite the comprehensive nature of this scheme, the CDA failed to meet the demand for longshoremen because of the acute manpower shortage both in the city and the Maritimes generally. It was only a matter of days before E.L. Cousins informed C.D. Howe that critical labour shortages were plaguing the efficient operation of the CDA.[27] Previous studies had shown that 807 permanent HLA members had been augmented by 794 cardmen, but only 1,350 men had registered with the new Hollis Street hiring hall and, on average, only 1,200 were working each day. On 13 March a shortage of 442 men was recorded. A conference with Halifax officials, Cousins reported, had resulted in ten CNR boarding cars being obtained to house workers being brought to Halifax to work on the docks. This had helped matters, but 2,500 men were needed to handle all cargo demands. Subsequently, Cousins became the driving force behind the construction, over the objections of area residents,[28] of a bunkhouse complex to house 750 men needed to augment the HLA workforce. This complex was located on MacLean Street, and the men living there had their way paid to Halifax by NSS. By the beginning of May 1943, 2,043 men were officially registered at the CDA, but daily turnout continued to be problematical. On 15 May, Colonel A.N. Jones, Chairman of the Halifax Steamship Committee, informed Humphrey Mitchell that the longshore labour situation was "the worst we have experienced here for all times." Jones reported that there had been a shortage of 477 longshoremen the previous day and that by 7 p.m. sixteen ships had been idle. This was a situation that demanded "prompt action" to avoid the impeding of the war effort. A day later G.P. McLaren of the British Ministry of War Transport complained that thirty-two vessels were waiting to be loaded. Unless NSS officials provided 1,000 men and started night work, War Transport officials "would be backed up into an impossible situation" and would have to use American ports.[29]

All of this prompted Vincent MacDonald to countenance a more direct and compulsory program of action. This eventually included the introduction of mandatory night shifts, the freezing of longshoremen in their employment, the compulsory transfer of labour to dock work, the establishment of a minimum wage, and the formation of a reserve labour battalion to keep men on the job and provide a ready surplus of workers when traffic in Halifax reached peak levels. On 17 May MacDonald met with representatives of the employers. Afterwards, he rated the operations of the hiring hall as being "reasonably satisfactory," but criticized the "constant uncontrollable drift" of longshoremen to other industries. The next day he met with MacNamara and other key NSS officials to consider what further steps could be taken to ameliorate the situation in Halifax. As a result of this consultation, NSS offices throughout the Maritimes were instructed to give longshore labour demands the highest priority and advertising blitzes were authorized to publicize the need for experienced dock workers. MacDonald himself was entrusted to devise plans for the guaranteed wage and the reserve labour battalion. He was likewise assigned the tasks of speeding up work on the bunkhouses and informing the HLA that the hiring hall scheme would continue once the trial period expired on 31 May 1943. In the meantime, statistical evidence continued to flood into NSS headquarters about the extent of the problem in the Nova Scotia capital. From 1 May to 23 May 1943, loading operations were short an average of 325 men per day, only 10 per cent of gangs worked in the evening, and no work was done at night. Twelve ships were diverted to American ports during the month of May, and British Ministry of War Transport officials urged that a meeting of all interested parties be held to devise some new way to address the labour crisis.[30]

On 31 May MacDonald wrote to MacNamara about the continued opposition of the HLA to the hiring hall procedure.[31] This, together with the continuing shortage of labour and the diversion of ships to American ports, indicated the "immediate necessity of further government action." In MacDonald's view, what was now required was a labour reserve to augment the established longshore workforce. Many HLA members opposed the CDA despite the "indispensable service" offered by its three union despatchers. MacDonald noted that HLA hostility centred on the "radical change" in the methods of hiring men, a change that was characterized as "unnecessary regimentation," but he judged that HLA resentment could be overcome by vigorous government intervention to silence the "vocal minority of irreconcilables" who opposed the hiring hall scheme. On 26 May 1943, in fact, the HLA had voted by 126 to 74 to discontinue support for the hiring hall scheme even though 2,043 stevedores were registered at the Hollis Street office. According to MacDonald, 300 additional men were needed for day work and 500 for night work to end the delays in Halifax.

Acting on this analysis, and facing continued HLA resistance to the hiring hall,[32] MacDonald next drafted two Orders-in-Council which were eventually issued on 25 June as PC 5160 and PC 5161. PC 5160 required any ex-longshoreman who had been employed on the docks for an aggregate period of twelve months since 31 December 1938 and who was in an age bracket eligible for military service to separate from his existing employment and accept a longshore position in Halifax or another eastern port designated by NSS. The Order also forbade an employer from taking an ex-longshoreman into his employ. Conversely, it froze all active longshoremen in their existing jobs. Ex-longshoremen had until 21 July 1943 to comply with the terms of the order.

PC 5161, known as the Stabilization of Longshore Labour (Halifax) Order, set forth four other measures to "secure or maintain longshore labour at its proper level." First, a group of workers would be identified to form a Reserve Pool. These workers would be housed in the bunkhouse complex under construction and would be available for work on the docks as needed. Second, a guaranteed wage of $45.12 per week, based on a forty-eight hour working week, would be provided to all longshoremen. Third, deficiency pay to top up weekly wages would be awarded to all longshoremen available for work either in the Reserve Pool or the CDA. Finally, the Controller was authorized, once the number of longshoremen reached the required level, to establish a rotation schedule to ensure that night work was carried out. Originally, the arrangements for the Reserve Pool were to take effect on 1 August 1943, but delays in the construction of the bunkhouses pushed this date back to 7 September 1943. To facilitate night shifts, the construction of a restaurant for dockworkers was now also authorized. The sum of $21,500 was set aside for this, and the catering firm of Crawley & McCracken was contracted to provide meal service for both the restaurant and bunkhouse.[33]

Once the labour stabilization plan was in place, MacDonald acted to ensure that the British Ministry of War Transport would guarantee a flow of traffic that justified the expense involved in setting up the Reserve Pool and guaranteeing a minimum wage. Early in August 1943, he told Captain Eric Aikman of the Ministry that all efforts would be wasted if an "appropriate volume of tonnage" was not forthcoming.[34] Aikman, however, insisted that MacDonald would have to "produce the goods" before War Transport authorities could route more traffic to Halifax.[35] He pointed out that in July, seventeen ships unaffected by repairs had loaded 76,879 tons of cargo in 165 ship days. These figures averaged out to 4,522 tons and 9.7 days per ship, a very poor record indeed. Whereas cargo should be loaded at an average rate of 1,000 tons per ship per day, a rate of only 466 tons per ship per day had been achieved in Halifax. This translated into eighty-eight ship days lost. The "cold, conservative facts" of the case, Aikman insisted, dictated that Halifax could not be allocated additional tonnage until the port's longshoremen proved themselves ready for the challenge.

Other complaints were also heard about the terms of PC 5161. National Harbours Board officials informed MacNamara that since entrance to the Reserve Pool was not limited to ex-longshoremen, many other classes of workers could be expected to join the Pool because of the guaranteed wage.[36] NSS would have to be vigilant in this regard. The Shipping Federation of Canada likewise worried about the long-term effect of what was being done.[37] In the Federation's view, a minimum wage of more than $45.00 per week was outrageous considering the fact that many of the men in the Reserve Pool would not be skilled or experienced stevedores; these workers should be kept at $30.00 per week maximum. Concern was also expressed about Section 13 of PC 5161, which stipulated that the government could recover some expenses of the stabilization plan by levying assessments against employers. According to the Shipping Federation of Canada, this should not be done without prior consultation with the affected companies.

Despite the inauguration of the Reserve Pool in early September, slack shipping schedules hindered the effective implementation of the stabilization plan. During September, the number of gangs not working on any given day ranged from a low of seven to a high of forty-nine, with the average being twenty-one.[38] Given these numbers, E.L. Cousins continued to criticize NSS efforts in Halifax, claiming that the "matter of labour supply had improved but little."[39] Cousins condemned the British Ministry of War Transport for expecting that men should be "available at all times irrespective of the irregularity of vessel movement." Cousins also noted the intransigence and apparent indifference of many HLA members to the orders of the Controller.[40] When the Controller had ordered the HLA to admit 150 extra cardmen to union ranks, HLA officials stated that they would "give the matter consideration" but nothing had been done. As usual, Cousins lashed out at union opposition and countenanced a more direct course of action that would see the Despatcher be the sole dispenser of union cards; HLA opposition to government regulation should no longer be tolerated and tepid policies accommodating HLA concerns should be modified.

Yet another continuing problem, despite construction of the bunkhouse complex, was the housing situation facing would-be workers.[41] In July, MacDonald had asked DMS officials if some prefabricated houses built by Wartime Housing Limited in Halifax could be allocated to longshoremen returning to the city under PC 5160. These were needed because the bunkhouses were not suitable for married men with children. This request was refused on the grounds that few men would be recruited under PC 5160. In truth, many letters from longshoremen requesting housing in Halifax were finding their way into MacDonald's hands. Isaac Sullivan, for example, wrote that he was willing to comply with PC 5160 and return to Halifax, but only if accommodation could be found for himself, his wife, and his five children. Cyril Rent, who had come to Halifax from Cape Breton, complained that he had been forced to sell all his farm livestock, acquired over a lifetime, because his wife had not been able to take care of them in his absence. In compensation, he demanded that he be given a house in Halifax so that his wife and five children could live with him. In response to this and other such requests, MacDonald continued to plead with DMS officials to release housing for longshoremen, but he was consistently rebuffed.[42]

Nonetheless, by November 1943 the total registered strength of the dock labour force had been brought up to 2,343 men – 750 regular HLA men, 530 duration cardmen, 766 temporary cardmen, and 297 Reserve Pool men. This was double the number available three years earlier.[43] Much had been accomplished, but much remained to be done. There were still pockets of HLA resistance to the Despatching Regulations and the hiring hall, and the total number of registered longshoremen did not approximate the actual number of men working on a regular basis. The Reserve Pool, moreover, would never live up to its promise; only 200 ex-longshoremen had been secured under PC 5160 for the Halifax docks. Most significantly, the entire NSS operation of the longshore labour system continued to be attacked in the remaining months of the war by a variety of port officials, most notably by E.L. Cousins.

In his capacity as Wartime Administrator of Canadian Atlantic Ports, Cousins had a keen interest in the operation of American ports. In particular, he sought to inform himself about the Army labour battalions being used in the United States to solve longshore difficulties. In May 1943, the US Coast Guard informed Cousins that skilled Army port battalions were stationed in many Atlantic ports and that the specially trained men in these units received regular Army pay.[44] While asserting that the military personnel were not used to replace civilian stevedores, Coast Guard officials admitted that the "line of demarcation" between the two groups was not clear. Cousins had next asked John Green, the man the HLA had rejected as Port Loading Superintendent, to scout the American ports and the Army battalions on his behalf. In May Green reported that the use of trained, disciplined military workers seemed to galvanize civilian longshoremen to perform better, out of a fear that all loading operations might be consigned to the Army men.[45] In July 1943, the Department of Labour had agreed to allow a 600-man Army Port Company (APC) to begin training so as to be ready in the event of labour strife on the Halifax waterfront. Thereafter, DMS and DND officials exerted increasing pressure on NSS to deploy the APC in Halifax. Arthur MacNamara, however, was firmly of the view that only an illegal work stoppage would justify this deployment.[46]

In January 1944, knowing the disdain that C.D. Howe felt for many aspects of NSS operations, Cousins sought to enlist his help in wresting control of all loading operations from the Department of Labour. In a memo to his Minister, Cousins elaborated on four key points.[47] First, he insisted that the APC be deployed immediately; 300 Army men should be allowed to compete directly with regular stevedores to settle the debate over the efficiency of military workers. Second, Cousins ridiculed the members of the HLA as being hopelessly inefficient and wholly dominated by the union leaders. It was common practice, for example, for a gang arriving at work short of men to refuse to do anything until it was brought to full strength by the Despatching Hall. Third, Cousins claimed that despite all the efforts of NSS to secure enough men, only 1,400 men were regularly on duty. In the circumstances, the high cost of the minimum wage and the Reserve Pool was absurd; the NSS stabilization operation should be curtailed and the guaranteed weekly wage reduced to $25. Finally, Cousins called for a sweeping reorganization of the administration of the port, with the centralization of all functions in the hands of the individual most eminently qualified to carry them out. This, of course, was himself. Cousins closed with his usual denunciation of the HLA and NSS and promised that the "general inefficiency" of Port operations and the "general defiance" of union men would be eliminated under his skilled leadership.

NSS officials, however, were not about to see their authority usurped in this fashion. Claiming that inefficiency was "a relative term," MacDonald told Humphrey Mitchell that the longshore stabilization scheme was beginning to yield dividends and that the use of Army personnel would "inject into Halifax an element of potential friction" that might produce a retaliatory slowdown by all civilian longshoremen. While admitting that the guaranteed wage was too high, MacDonald rejected Cousins' demand for more centralized control; the broad power already vested in the Controller was all that was required. MacNamara added his consistently cautious and considered view to labour matters by claiming that Cousins' recommendations should be "examined very carefully," although he conceded the latter's point about the level of the minimum wage. Armed with these opinions, Mitchell told Howe that military personnel could not be used without the approval of the HLA. He also challenged the claim that military labour would be more efficient than civilian labour. Except "under the stress of battle engagement or preparation for same," this was unlikely to be the case.

Although he had no jurisdiction in the matter, Howe countered that it was "inconceivable" why trained Army personnel were being denied the opportunity to work in Halifax. Claiming that the record of the Port of Halifax was the "worst on the Atlantic Coast," he insisted that only properly trained men could solve the problem. Howe challenged Mitchell to put the APC in direct competition with the HLA to determine which group was more productive. The Reserve Pool constituted a "first class scandal"; a "poor class" of men showed no desire to work while taking advantage of the minimum wage. Military labour should be brought in at once because it could "not be any worse than stevedoring labour generally working under present Halifax conditions." M.M. Maclean, Director of Industrial Relations in the Department of Labour, counterattacked by accusing Howe of having a "narrow viewpoint" and favouring a policy in relation to the APC that was both dangerous and unrealistic:

This is the usual sort of wishful thinking we find prevalent among many employer executives. In this Halifax situation what we [would] get is a riot. The difficulties we have been encountering can be accounted for almost wholly by the policy of the shipowners down through the years. On Mr. Howe's statement that the men in the labour pool are of a poor class and have no desire to work, there is apparently no evidence to support him. If there is discovered to be any abuse of the guaranteed wage policy, it can be effectively dealt with by appropriate safeguarding regulations.[48]

After Cabinet requested more information on the matter, MacDonald wrote a thorough report in February 1944. He highlighted the shortcomings of the Reserve Pool and the HLA's agreement to allow Army men to be employed in Halifax and outlying ports, but only when union men could not be found.[49] This agreement put the potentially explosive issue of Army labour to rest. In March 1944, over 300 Army men moved into the Maclean Street bunkhouse complex. Their presence augmented the Reserve Pool, which remained below 300 men for the duration of the war.[50] Despite continuing criticism from Cousins, NSS officials had overcome the most serious wartime challenge to the success of their longshore stabilization plan.

One final administrative shuffle in Halifax occurred in March 1944, when Port Loading Superintendent Captain R.F. Spring replaced Perchard as Controller. As the war progressed, Halifax longshoremen seemed to treat Controllers with an increasing level of respect. MacDonald was resented; Perchard was grudgingly accepted, and Spring was welcomed. Spring's popularity among HLA officials grew in June 1944 as a result of yet another dispute with the employers. The Halifax Steamship Committee had wanted walking bosses, who were HLA members, included in the deficiency pay and guaranteed wage arrangements, but MacDonald had insisted that walking bosses be employed directly by the companies. The Steamship Committee now complained bitterly to Arthur MacNamara about the increase in the number of walking bosses ordered by the Controller.[51] MacNamara refused to interfere, while MacDonald was furious that Steamship Committee officials had gone over his head to the Deputy Minister of Labour. MacDonald told the Steamship Committee that the shipping companies had requested full control of the walking bosses in September 1942, and that the increase in the ranks of the Bosses had occurred only because their previous numbers had been "notoriously low."[52] He also pointed out that the shipping companies were the recipients of large sums of government money and had to play by the rules. In sum, Spring's decisions were final.

The remainder of the war saw few changes in the Port of Halifax. Operations were now going well, though there were small irritations. Crawley & McCracken, for example, were disappointed with the bunkhouse scheme. They had entered into the catering agreement on the assumption that 750 men – 500 longshoremen and 250 freight handlers – would be housed in the bunkhouses. In fact, the total had rarely exceeded 400, and a decline set in once the APC arrived.[53] When complaints continued to be voiced about the minimum weekly wage, pay was reduced to $30.40 per week. This was done through PC 3370 of 8 May 1944 and the change took effect on 17 June. Although generally satisfied with the operation of the CDA, the HLA continued to push for minor concessions, such as the elimination of night work. Spring, however, refused the HLA demands. At a meeting with Ministry of War Transport officials in January 1945, the performance of Halifax longshoremen was "not unduly criticized" by British officials.[54] As one NSS official now reported, the overall labour situation on the Halifax docks was "comfortable" despite a lack of improvement in the housing situation in the city.[55] During May and June 1945, after the end of the war in Europe, an increasing number of gangs became idle and many temporary HLA members returned to seasonal occupations. By 10 July 1945, the number of working gangs was reduced by ten.[56]

During that same month, the first discussions took place concerning the dismantling of the wartime regulations. Spring insisted that the existing despatching system could "be maintained with advantage"; to return to the "have a look" hiring system would be disastrous.[57] The shift to peacetime operations should "take place gradually and in an orderly fashion"; the Reserve Pool should be phased out and negotiations should be started with the HLA to release numbers of duration and temporary cardmen. At a series of meetings in August, both the HLA and the employers advocated the continuation of the CDA and the position of Controller. This was done through PC 5980 of 11 September 1945, which revoked PC 5161 effective 3 November 1945. The wartime system was thus brought to a "clean cut finish."[58] Thereafter, MacNamara had little to do but monitor the last vestiges of the NSS presence on the

Halifax docks. With the abandonment of the Reserve Pool, the disposition of the bunkhouses became an issue. PC 6493 of 12 October 1945
allowed the Minister of Labour to continue to operate this facility, but
by 31 May 1946 only twelve longshoremen were still living in the
MacLean Street complex, as well as approximately 200 Army personnel
and various other workers.[59] The decision was made to close the bunkhouses effective 31 August 1946.[60]

In May 1946, Spring reported to MacNamara that he was pleased
that all disputes involving longshore labour had been settled "more or
less amicably," and that the HLA, after being given control of the hiring
hall in the autumn of 1945, had conducted its business in an "orderly
manner." At MacNamara's request, Spring next asked the HLA and
the employers for their candid opinions concerning the extension of
the Controllership. Responses showed the high esteem in which Spring
was held by all concerned. The HLA spokesmen described Spring as a
"distinct asset" to the Port and a "very capable man" who should be
kept in his job. The Halifax Steamship Committee told Spring himself
that he enjoyed the unanimous support of all Committee members.
In late 1946 and early 1947, mainly to rising salaries and the costs
of running the Despatching Agency, which totalled approximately
$57,000 per year, some thought was given to divorcing the Department
of Labour from the operation of the Halifax docks. This, however,
was not done and the "worthwhile arrangement" that had been made
during the war was allowed to continue. Finally, in 1950, the union
was given complete control of its own affairs except for "periodic
inspections" by Department of Labour officials. At the same time,
responsibility for administering longshore affairs in Halifax was
handed over to the Employment Service of Canada.[61]

In review, it is clear that the most critical government measures taken
to stabilize the longshore labour force between 1940 and 1945 were
the establishment of the Reserve Pool and the introduction of a guaranteed minimum weekly wage for all longshoremen. Table 7 shows the
cost of the guaranteed wage system and the relationship between public
and private contributions to the total wage bill. Altogether, the Department of Labour spent almost $1.275 million between September 1943
and August 1945 in wage supplements for longshoremen. This sum
represented more than thirteen percent of all stevedoring wages paid
while the Reserve Pool was in operation. In addition, the government
paid the salaries of various port officials, and met the costs of the pier
restaurant, the bunkhouses, and the Central Despatching Agency.
Although the government share of the Reserve Pool wages would
logically be high, the guaranteed wage system also forced Dominion

Table 7
Government Payment of Wages under PC 5161, 1943–45

Date	Total Earning & Deficiency Pay ($)	Total Reserve Pool Pay ($)	Total Despatch Hall Pay ($)	% NSS/ Total Pay	% NSS/ Total RP Pay	% NSS/ Total DH Pay
Sep-Dec '43 avg	474,651.07	69,896.75	404,754.32	18.7	56.4	12.2
Jan-Mar '44 avg	404,292.73	59,971.83	344,320.90	9.1	35.1	4.6
Apr '44	381,765.05	25,396.77	356,368.28	7.9	31.7	6.2
May '44	439,717.04	29,176.97	410,540.07	4.4	17.7	3.5
Jun '44	440,652.76	34,151.64	406,501.12	45.2	51.1	44.7
Jul '44	338,583.62	16,191.50	322,392.12	15.3	22.9	14.9
Aug '44	259,779.33	13,749.21	246,300.12	33.9	52.5	32.9
Sep '44	434,836.45	23,875.70	410,960.75	12.3	34.2	11.1
Oct '44	289,169.53	23,796.04	265,373.49	24.8	35.4	23.8
Nov '44	296,180.89	28,066.86	268,114.03	28.9	43.2	27.4
Dec '44	453,040.77	48,225.02	404,815.75	9.4	17.6	8.5
Jan '45	448,030.47	56,218.80	391,811.67	1.4	6.2	0.7
Feb '45	472,525.82	47,049.47	425,476.35	1.3	9.7	0.3
Mar '45	592,170.23	53,251.88	538,918.35	2.4	16.8	1.0
Apr '45	416,862.26	28,551.40	388,310.86	3.8	13.6	3.1
May '45	311,926.80	14,262.19	297,664.61	9.3	16.0	9.0
Jun '45	373,900.25	14,747.15	359,153.10	8.7	39.1	7.4
Jul '45	295,840.88	12,308.07	283,532.81	5.2	39.5	3.7
Aug '45	292,608.89	15,288.20	277,320.69	16.4	42.1	15.0
TOTALS	9,649,073.51	943,539.36	8,705.534.15	13.2	36.0	10.8

Source: NA, RG 27, Volume 665, File 6–5–6–3–6, Monthly Reports

officials to spend close to $1 million during the war to stabilize the wages of the regular longshoremen registered at the hiring hall. This was almost three times the amount spent on the workers in the Reserve Pool. The sudden increase in government costs in the summer of 1944 is attributable to the fact that large numbers of ships loaded in preparation for the Normandy landings never returned to Halifax in the months following the invasion.[62] The maximum number of men enrolled in the Reserve Pool was 272 in January 1945; the minimum number was 104 in May 1945. Efforts to increase the number of men registered at the CDA were clearly successful. The maximum number of men registered was 2,343 (November 1943); the minimum number recorded (when wartime traffic was ebbing) was 1,646 (August 1945).

The wartime history of the Halifax docks is an example of successful centralized control by NSS and the Department of Labour to manage a difficult situation. By using its powers systematically and adroitly the government was able to maintain essential levels of employment, albeit at considerable cost to the public purse. In this case, moreover, wartime regulation facilitated postwar labour peace. The wartime reorganization of longshore hiring methods in Halifax and the centralized direction of dock employment there was such a resounding success that all the interests involved agreed voluntarily to continue government regulation into the postwar period. Nothing like this happened in the coal, textile, and meatpacking industries, all of which saw serious postwar labour disruptions within two years of the end of the war. Not until 1949 did serious labour strife return to the Halifax docks, and the wave of unrest that materialized in 1949 sprang from causes unrelated to wartime government control of the dock labour force. Although Ottawa waited almost four years after the commencement of the war in 1939 to adopt a labour stabilization plan for the Halifax docks, the results it obtained when it finally did act represent the pinnacle of NSS achievement in managing the wartime labour force.

7 Meatpacking Labour

Canadian slaughterhouses and abattoirs processed an unprecedented supply of meat products during World War II. The number of hogs slaughtered in Canada increased from 3.6 million in 1939 to more than 8.7 million in 1944, while cattle slaughters increased from fewer than 900,000 in 1939 to almost 1.9 million by 1945. The total dressed weight of meat in the four major livestock categories of cattle, calves, hogs, and sheep increased from approximately 1.1 billion pounds in 1939 to almost 2.3 billion pounds in 1944. The United Kingdom consumed most of this. Exports of bacon, pork, and ham, for example, increased from 1.86 million carat weight in 1939 to more than 7 million carat weight in 1944; in the same period beef exports to Great Britain skyrocketed from less than 9,000 carat weight to more than 980,000 carat weight. By the end of 1944, two-thirds of all pork and bacon products consumed in the United Kingdom came from Canada.[1]

An ambitious plan to supply vast quantities of meat to the United Kingdom was formulated with no thought to providing slaughterhouses with an adequate labour force. Canadian Department of Agriculture officials encouraged farmers to rapidly expand their livestock herds, but failed to work in tandem with their National Selective Service counterparts to plan for the labour supply. There were labour shortfalls and an astonishing rate of labour turnover in meatpacking plants; an extraordinarily tight and constantly shifting labour market prevailed across the country.

The attempt to increase the number of workers in the meatpacking industry reveals several important features of NSS control of the civilian mobilization process. NSS policy was susceptible to external pressure.

This case also highlights the acute problem of labour turnover during the war, despite the September 1943 imposition of a supposed labour freeze for essential male workers. In the packing industry as in most labour sectors, separations from employment were a consistent feature of the wartime labour force, and the labour priority rating system – the administrative anchor of NSS mobilization policy – was largely ineffective.

Problems with the labour supply in meatpacking plants first manifested themselves in 1943. The situation was heightened by the seasonal nature of employment in the industry.[2] The rush on packing plant operations began in the autumn of each year. For cattle and sheep, the busiest four-month period occurred from September to December. In this period, for example, close to 58 per cent of all sheep slaughters in 1943 occurred. For hogs, the pressure on abattoirs commenced in the last weeks of the calendar year, with the first four months of the following year being the busiest. From January to April 1944, for example, 41 per cent of all annual hog slaughters occurred; this ratio increased to almost 44 per cent in the first four months of 1945. Meatpacking, moreover, had few positive attractions for potential workers. Poor working conditions and low wages deterred many men from pursuing packing employment voluntarily. Slaughterhouse and packing employment stood twenty-seventh on the scale of remuneration in 1943 but slipped to twenty-ninth in 1944. Over the same two years wage rates declined from 71 to 68 cents per hour.[3] The combination of low wages, unattractive working conditions, and seasonal fluctuations in demand meant that the industry was poorly placed in the wartime competition for workers.

NSS first become aware of labour shortages in the packing industry in the spring and summer of 1943. In May and June, Winnipeg packing plants had difficulty securing the deferment from conscription for skilled employees, despite the fact that the number of postponements sought in relation to the total packing workforce in the city was low.[4] NSS officials initially resisted calls for increased protection for the packing labour force. In June, Deputy Minister of Agriculture G.S.H. Barton told Arthur MacNamara that more than 1,000 men out of a national packing labour force of slightly more than 13,000 had left their jobs. The majority of those who had quit were farmers who worked in abattoirs and slaughterhouses during the winter months. While NSS had funnelled a significant number of unskilled men and women to packing employment, skilled labour was "impossible to find." As a result of the shortage of experienced workers, hogs were now being shipped from Alberta to Winnipeg.[5] With many male employees moving to more lucrative employment, the time had come, Barton insisted, to order all skilled packinghouse workers to stay in their jobs.

Despite confirmation from his own officials that the industry was now short some 1,589 male and female workers,[6] MacNamara resisted this advice. While admitting that wages and working conditions were not attractive in the industry, he maintained that tough regulations would only result in greater resentment than already existed among workers and therefore do more harm than good.[7] For the moment, NSS relied on Industrial Mobilization Surveys and the postponement of skilled packing workers from the call-up to satisfy the employment needs of the industry. This strategy encountered stiff resistance from the companies. In August, for example, J.S. McLean, the president of Canada Packers in Toronto, reported that he was "extremely nervous" and "genuinely alarmed" by the Department of Agriculture livestock delivery forecasts. These indicated a volume of work that had never been known in the history of the company.[8] Following joint submissions from the Wartime Prices and Trade Board and the Department of Agriculture, and meetings between Barton and MacNamara, NSS took further action. This came on 19 August in the form of a recommendation from the Inter-Departmental Labour Priorities Committee that thirty-six meatpacking plants across Canada be granted an A priority rating, to be reviewed by 1 December, for men and women.[9]

From the perspective of the meatpacking companies, however, this was not enough. In September, Joseph Harris, the plant manager for Canada Packers at St. Boniface, Manitoba, told J.S. McLean that something more would have to be done quickly to "avoid the worst mess the industry" had ever known. Claiming that a "national tragedy" loomed, Harris forecast that NSS officials would do nothing until stockyards across the country were cluttered with livestock that could not be slaughtered.[10] MacNamara's routine response to such criticism was that "every industry [had] the same idea" – the guarantee of a stable labour force and no such guarantee could be given. Moreover, the packing companies were notoriously slow in giving local NSS offices advance notice of livestock shipments that would necessitate the hiring of more workers.[11] Nevertheless, MacNamara agreed to two changes to help the industry. First, by PC 6625 of 1 September, employees in all establishments with an A or B labour priority rating were restricted from leaving their jobs.[12] Second, on 23 September 1943, instructions were issued that employees in seven critical industries, including meatpacking, were to be given "special consideration" when postponement requests came before Mobilization Boards. Noting that 21 per cent of the men who normally worked in meatpacking were now in the armed forces, MacNamara told his officials that packing staffs needed to be significantly increased to handle increased livestock flows.[13]

These were promising measures, but tensions continued between packing plant officials and local NSS offices. From Regina, S.L. Hinchliffe, the manager of the city's NSS office, on the day the new instructions were issued to Mobilization Boards, wrote that the Burns plant had laid off three men and that he could no longer accommodate requests for dozens of men on twelve hours notice.[14] Company officials immediately countered that each of the three men in question had either left voluntarily or been fired for negligence. Hinchliffe's report was designed only to "cover up the shortcomings of Selective Service" and his "baseless statements" posed a grave danger to efficient packing operations.[15] In the same spirit, S.E. Todd, the managing director of the Industrial and Development Council of Canadian Meat Packers (IDCCMP), also disputed an NSS report from the Maritimes that the Swift's plant in Moncton employed forty-five travelling salesmen. According to Todd, Swift's employed only seventeen salesmen. Todd was also quick to point out that the industry had adopted many labour saving methods ordered by the WPTB. Cellophane wrapping had been discontinued on seven of ten base products; the number of salesmen had been reduced by 35 per cent; the number of rope strands on hide bales had been reduced from three to two; the number of products packaged in tin had been reduced from forty-two to seventeen; and the number of products sold in less than carcass quantities had been reduced, thereby cutting back on the labour needed for processing, handling, shipping, and ordering.[16]

Todd was also active in investigating the possibility of using Army labour to help the packing industry. In October, the IDCCMP drew up a preliminary list of eighty-eight Ontario men with experience who were in the armed forces. After consultation with military officials, packing representatives learned that only four men on the list would be available for release. Armed with this survey result, Todd lobbied for the placing of meatpacking on the same priority as coal mining in terms of securing the release of skilled employees.[17] NSS officials agreed to consider this request, and the IDCCMP subsequently submitted a forty-two page list of former packing employees dating back to 1939.[18] National Defence officials, however, refused to consider the wholesale release of packing workers, though small numbers of skilled butchers were released in December 1943.

NSS officials questioned whether the packing industry really needed all the workers it constantly sought.[19] In March 1944, MacNamara diplomatically asked G.S.H. Barton to provide a more exact accounting of future livestock movements in order that NSS "might feel justified" in devoting so much attention to the needs of meatpackers.[20] In New Brunswick, NSS officials continued to question the employment practices in the Swift's plant in Moncton, especially the refusal of plant managers to hire men over forty-five and their decision to limit daily operating hours. Swift's managers vehemently rejected this criticism. According to

J.A. Ford, the manager of the Moncton plant, men were leaving packing employment all the time with the full consent of local NSS officers. The optimistic employment forecasts of Moncton NSS officials were misleading because Swift's had been forced to accept many women and young men who were "entirely unsuited" for packing work.[21]

The first stage of the NSS response to the crisis in meatpacking employment ended in March 1944. The recruitment of 2,851 agricultural workers to work in packing houses and various regulatory initiatives meant that the agency was able to meet the need presented by the increase in livestock shipments in late 1943 and early 1944. The nationwide freezing of employees in essential firms reduced the rates of separation from packing employment. Moreover, to March 1944, more than 1,000 key men in the packing industry were granted deferment of military service.[22] Finally, increased labour priority ratings allowed unskilled labour to be channelled into packing employment. Comparing the first eight weeks of 1944 with the first eight weeks of 1943, cattle and calf slaughters increased by 36 per cent, hog slaughters by 77 per cent, and sheep and lamb slaughters by 34 per cent.[23] NSS officials were confident that the crisis in the industry had passed. Accordingly, at an ILPC meeting in late January 1944, the labour priority rating for meatpacking workers was reduced from A to B.[24]

This decision proved shortsighted, however, for in the spring of 1944 packing plants faced a new round of labour shortages. The main reason for this was the return of agricultural workers and farmers to their normal occupations. Under NSS regulations, all agricultural men working temporarily in other employment had to return to farms before 1 April 1944. During the first week of March, Department of Agriculture and IDCCMP representatives succeeded in having the issue of meatpacking labour placed on the agenda of a meeting of the NSS Administration Board scheduled for 14 March. Remarkably, it was decided at this meeting that agreements with the provinces concerning the disposition of farm labour could not be violated. The problems of the packing industry would have to be solved by other means. Two possibilities were to import workers from Newfoundland and to continue of the policy of postponing the military call-up of key meatpacking workers. Administration Board members took the position that the root cause of the trouble in the meatpacking business was not a faulty regulatory framework but poor wages and working conditions.[25] Nonetheless, the priority ratings for packing workers were raised to A at the ILPC meeting of 16 March 1944.[26] NSS officials also extended the postponement of essential packing employees.[27]

This was considered a tepid response, and it evoked a concerted industry attack. On 29 March Todd complained to Barton that a "rapidly deteriorating" employment situation left managers with a "very pessimistic" opinion of the government's ability to handle the situation which had arisen with increased livestock shipments.[28] The Swift's plant in Edmonton, for example, was scheduled to lose 50 per cent of its workforce through the departure of agriculturalists. Claiming that he had avoided making "alarmist representations" in the past, Todd now asserted that labour shortages would be "crippling." In forwarding Todd's analysis to Arthur MacNamara, Barton noted that plants had been able to process livestock runs during March by the "narrowest of margins."[29] Accordingly, he called on NSS to deal with the issue "much more vigorously and effectively."

NSS officials secured the temporary services of some agricultural employees during April 1944 in Alberta and Ontario. MacNamara decided that the long-term answer for the Alberta plants was to use interned Japanese men. On 15 April MacNamara approached C.H. Millard, the National Director of the Packinghouse Workers of America, concerning the use of 400 Japanese workers.[30] This was badly received by both union and management. Owners and managers feared sabotage, union strife, and conflict with American soldiers stationed in Alberta. Municipal officials in Calgary and Edmonton were likewise "unalterably opposed,"[31] though the *Calgary Albertan* observed that it was "surely better to have a hundred Japs in town for a few weeks than to risk a breakdown of one of our chief industries."[32] Opposition voices were also heard from St. Boniface and Prince Albert.[33] MacNamara abandoned his proposal only three days after he had put it forward.[34]

Meanwhile, the industry campaign against government policy continued full blast. In a letter dated 13 April, E.S. Manning, Secretary of the IDCCMP, claimed that provincial agriculture departments had done more for the meatpacking business than had NSS. The removal of hundreds of agricultural workers from the packing workforce, the continued increase in livestock slaughters, and a new federal regulation that required the export of beef carcasses with the bone removed, had produced an "extremely critical" situation in the packing plants.[35] This was a situation, moreover, which the government had so far failed almost entirely to address. Despite the statutory provisions governing separations from employment, the turnover rate in packing plants was "very disconcerting." What was needed from Ottawa was a coordinated policy rather than the piecemeal response of the past: "The packing industry is charged with the responsibility of processing the livestock which the government has asked and encouraged producers to raise. The onus for providing manpower rests with the government as the industry can only carry out the policies which have been laid down for them by the Dominion Department of Agriculture, the Meat

Board, and the WPTB."[36] To date, Manning charged, the attitude of NSS officials had been "none too encouraging."

The criticism crested in late April when several companies across the country placed embargoes on the shipment of livestock.[37] On 22 April, representatives from provincial farm labour committees in Manitoba, Saskatchewan, and Alberta met in Regina to discuss the problems of the meatpackers, but no concrete solutions were forthcoming.[38] Earlier in April, a survey of agricultural labourers in these provinces had failed to identify significant numbers of men willing to remain in packing jobs, and NSS, of course, possessed no power to make them do so. R.M. Putnam, Director of the Alberta Agricultural Extension Service, noted that only fifteen Indians were available for packing employment, that "no further developments" with respect to the use of Army labour could be expected, and that workers displayed a "distinct apathy" towards the industry because of its poor wages and working conditions.[39] At the same time, mobilization officials were challenging the efficiency of NSS civilian operations. Justice J.E. Adamson, Chairman of the Winnipeg Mobilization Board, noted that 841 men had been rejected for military service in his division between 1 October 1943 and 31 March 1944, but that NSS officials had allowed the vast majority of these rejects to "get away into work of their own choosing."[40] At a meeting held in Edmonton on 26 April that brought together farm, packing, Chamber of Commerce, union, and NSS officials, it was agreed that 400 workers were needed immediately in Alberta to avoid a production disaster.[41]

In an effort to supply these workers, MacNamara intervened personally. On 1 May 1944, he decreed that finding the workers required for meatpacking would be placed "before all other essential civilian manpower needs."[42] An intensive recruiting campaign was immediately started among farm labourers, who were engaged in seeding. A farm worker was guaranteed payment of all transportation costs if he stayed in packing employment for two months before returning to agriculture. In the same spirit, Canadian Vocational Training schemes were launched in the Prairie provinces to train meatpacking workers.[43] A big publicity campaign was started to advertise the urgent needs of the meatpacking industry. Finally, all available unskilled labour, including rejects from Army depots, was funnelled to Prairie packing operations.

Arthur MacNamara targeted workers in British Columbia as the prime source of labour to meet the needs of the Alberta packing houses. In April he had ordered NSS Pacific Regional Superintendent William McKinstry to send 400 workers to the neighbouring province.[44] McKinstry initially refused, but MacNamara threatened to remove him from his job if he did not cooperate.[45] On the other hand,

McKinstry could not control what the workers shipped from BC to Alberta actually did when they got there. A.O. MacLachlin, the Acting Manager of the NSS office in Edmonton, chronicled the activities of 140 men who arrived from British Columbia and were issued permits to work in the city's packing plants. Within two weeks of their arrival, only fifty-five of these men remained in packing employment. The remainder had either left without notifying NSS officials or secured separation permits. MacLachlin complained that many of the men had arrived by train in Edmonton at NSS expense, taken the cash advance offered by NSS or company officials, and then returned immediately to BC[46] NSS Chief Enforcement Officer T.R. Walsh confirmed MacLachlin's observations concerning separations; he noted that a background check was rarely done in the case of a separation request because of the administrative difficulty this involved.[47] After only 125 men were secured from British Columbia, MacNamara cancelled the plan on 23 May.[48]

The appeal to farm workers remained the most successful NSS response to the problems of meatpackers. Agricultural officials in the Prairie provinces were now expressing concern that scarce farm labour was being drained from essential employment on the land. The Alberta Federation of Agriculture expressed regret that "the only plan advanced by the authorities" for the meatpacking industry was to drain a supply of farm labour that was "already sorely reduced."[49] Agricultural officials in Manitoba, who had found 100 men on farms to help in the Winnipeg plants, cautioned that NSS officials must be prepared to solve pressing employment shortfalls in August and September when few men could be spared from harvest activities.[50] Moreover, military officials continued to rebuff attempts to secure six month releases for skilled butchers, on the grounds that the drain in packing employment had been "caused as much or more" by workers leaving the industry as by their being recruited from it.[51] On the bright side for NSS, however, industry spokespersons were now praising its efforts in relation to labour supply. In May 1944, IDCCMP Managing Director Todd expressed his satisfaction that the former NSS policy of providing only temporary relief had been abandoned, and that experience had taught the government the necessity of providing a stable workforce for the meat plants.[52]

The meatpacking employment picture on 1 June 1944 revealed the relative success of the NSS efforts during the previous month. Employment had increased to 17,037 from 16,551 workers on 30 April, while unfilled vacancies had decreased over the same period from 1,570 to 1,226. Unfilled vacancies in Prairie plants had declined by almost 50 per cent, but the labour turnover rate continued to be a problem; 1,774 men and women had left packing employment during the month of May.[53] Presented with this evidence of an improving work situation in the industry, ILPC Chairman Sheldon Ross sought to reduce the labour priority rating for packing labour from A to B. This was effected for thirty-six meatpacking plants at an ILPC meeting on 8 June.[54] Department of Agriculture officials were shocked by the ILPC decision. G.S.H. Barton complained that the change would "probably reproduce in more acute form" the shortages of the previous year.[55] After Ross refused to reconsider, he was overruled by MacNamara. Although he was "sorry to take this rather definite position," the deputy minister emphasized his "constant personal attention" to the situation in meatpacking and the "extreme lengths" of NSS involvement to alleviate the labour shortage facing the industry.[56] As a result of his intervention, the priority rating for packinghouse labour was indefinitely restored to A on 22 June 1944.[57]

Prior to 1 August 1944, NSS officials remained reasonably optimistic about the future of labour supply to the meatpackers. Between 1 January and 1 August 1944, the number of men and women employed in the industry had grown from 15,957 to 17,409. In those same seven months, however, there were more than 9,500 separations from employment.[58] J.H. Stewart, the Regional Employment Officer in Montreal, argued that NSS efforts were "rather nullified" in view of the high separation rate, and that regulations should be "rigidly enforced to kill this annoying situation."[59] A spot survey of packing plants showed that while the bulk of separations were granted to men returning to agriculture, many were granted for unconfirmed medical reasons or for no reason whatsoever. NSS officials realized that this "excessive turnover" was inexcusable and that "vigorous enforcement of the regulations" would have to be countenanced in order to maintain the required complement of workers.[60]

Another phase of NSS policy began in August 1944 with the realization that employment requirements would be higher in the coming autumn than they had been in the autumn of 1943. In Quebec, 40 per cent more hogs and 40 per cent more cattle were expected, while in Ontario abattoirs were preparing for 15 percent more hogs and 20 per cent more cattle. Moreover, Western abattoirs had made plans to send overflow livestock runs to Ontario slaughterhouses. IDCCMP officials estimated that a minimum of 1,000 additional workers would be needed to handle packing requirements in Quebec and Ontario alone.[61] Meanwhile, the employment trend in the industry was the exact opposite. Thus, between 29 July 1944 and 1 September 1944 the number of men and women on the job fell from 17,409 to 16,270. Separations in this period numbered 2,512, and net labour demand at the end of the period was almost 1,700.[62] NSS was faced with another crisis in the making.

The agency responded by again looking to NRMA personnel for help. NRMA recruits with packing experience were encouraged to apply to their commanding officers for industrial leaves, and NSS lobbied military officials to comply with all requests. On 25 September 1944, DND officials agreed to participate in the release of skilled packing workers from NRMA commitments,[63] and, on 4 October, military personnel on active duty were also granted permission to return to essential industries.[64] Active recruitment of farm labour and other seasonal workers was also commenced, and a nationwide advertising campaign was started in the press and on the radio. In Ontario, workers were recruited north of Toronto as far as Manitoulin Island. In the same spirit, farm labour committees across the country sent personal letters to agricultural workers encouraging them to take employment in meatpacking.[65] Despite all these efforts, however, the number of workers employed in the industry continued to decline during September, when there were 1,743 separations. On 1 October 1944, the workforce numbered 16,018 persons.[66]

In these strained circumstances, relations between industry and government officials, at least in certain parts of the country, continued to fester. In October 1944, the Canadian Federation of Agriculture pressed the view that NSS was obligated to provide labour to accommodate increased livestock movements to abattoirs nationwide. While farmers had a "magnificent" record in meeting the wartime demand for greater production, their achievement was being tarnished by labour troubles and shortages elsewhere in the economy.[67] As ever, NSS countered such criticism with the claim that, because of their refusal to improve working conditions, the packing companies bore much of the responsibility for the difficulties they now faced. At a July meeting in Montreal with national representatives of Swift's, Canada Packers, and Wilsils, NSS officials had complained that existing working conditions would not "induce men and women to voluntarily apply" for packing work; hence the continuous referral of "drifter types" to meatpacking firms.[68] Within NSS, the Swift's plant in Moncton was regarded as the worst example of the evils that beset the industry. This particular plant was said to be congested from slaughterhouse to storage sheds, and to have wet and unsanitary floors that were covered with particles of refuse.[69]

Despite everything that was wrong, NSS managed, through the recruitment of agricultural workers and the release of hundreds of men from the military, to meet the needs of the packing plants in the last months of 1944. An emergency appeal to staff the Swift's plant in

Moncton resulted in the addition of sixty-eight men to the payroll by 1 November. In Manitoba, more than 300 farm workers moved to Winnipeg packing plants, and in November about 200 Saskatchewan labourers and conscientious objectors joined them. The Ontario Farm Labour Committee recruited close to 700 men for packinghouse employment in southern Ontario. Nevertheless, Department of Agriculture officials continued to lobby MacNamara to the effect that packing plants should be "absolutely saturated" and that "fine calculations" should not be considered when assigning labour to them. By 1 December, however, it was clear to all that the employment situation in the industry had changed materially. During October and November 2,500 persons took meatpacking jobs and by 1 December the workforce reached 18,777. Although more than 3,000 separations occurred during this same period, close to 6,000 hirings were reported across the country. At the end of November, net labour demand was only 471. Moreover, only 25 per cent of the jobs waiting to be filled were for skilled workers.[70] In December 1944, many packing plants cancelled all orders with NSS for further help.[71]

During the first months of 1945, livestock runs began to decline significantly in Canada. In November 1944, just over 153,000 cattle had been slaughtered; by contrast the March 1945 figure was approximately 126,000. For the same months hog slaughters numbered 828,409 and 599,822 respectively. Indeed, in the first three months of 1945 about 32 per cent fewer hogs were slaughtered than in the same period in 1944.[72] Packing plants began to lay off large numbers of both men and women. At the Canada Packers plant in Winnipeg, for example, 480 men and 265 women were let go in the two months prior to 6 February 1945.[73] Although NSS officials insisted that it was "almost impossible to make any reliable prediction" about the future size of livestock runs,[74] they began discussing measures for the return of large numbers of men to agricultural employment in the spring of 1945.

A meeting of the IDCCMP and Prairie NSS representatives in Winnipeg on 24–25 January revealed just how much the meatpacking industry had come to rely on seasonal workers. On 1 February 1945, 723 Alberta, 460 Saskatchewan, and 447 Manitoba farmers were employed in packing plants. In total they represented close to 16 per cent of all meatpacking workers in the Prairie provinces.[75] Plant representatives identified 750 of these farmers as being essential to the successful working of their operations. As NSS braced for the exodus of the farmers from the industry, its sole initiative was to maintain the A-A labour priority rating for the majority of the plants. This was done over the opposition of Sheldon Ross, who argued that the time had come to downgrade the packing houses to B-B.[76]

By 14 April 1945, only 167 farmers remained in packing houses in the Prairie provinces. Likewise, in Ontario the numbers of farmers working in slaughterhouses declined from 675 on 3 February to eleven in the second week of April. By 28 April 1945, only 14,044 men and women were working in the meatpacking sector, and net labour demand was again above 1,000.[77] Department of Agriculture officials warned MacNamara that the liberation of Europe might lead to a big new export demand for Canadian meat.[78] Uncertainty was also evident in Ontario where a renewed labour shortage had led to seven packing plants being given the coveted A(E) priority category for male labour in March 1945. This, however, had not met the need. During the first week of June 228 experienced men were needed by the Swift plant in Toronto alone and another 300 men were urgently needed by other Toronto plants and in Kitchener.[79]

During the summer months of 1945, the general labour situation in meatpacking employment remained relatively unstable. Eventually, eleven firms in Quebec, Manitoba, and Alberta were added to the list of Ontario firms possessing the A(E) priority rating.[80] NSS also continued to struggle with the old problem of separations from meatpacking employment. During June, 393 placements were made in Ontario meatpacking firms, but there were 280 separations. This led Ontario NSS Regional Superintendent B.G. Sullivan to lament that "employees are leaving by the back door almost as fast as we put them in the front door." In response, Sullivan ordered exit interviews of packing workers seeking separation notices. Beyond this, NSS did not attempt any new solutions, although it was realized in the agency that the labour problem in meatpacking was once more "quite serious." On 31 August 1945, at the end of a week in which there were 433 separations from packing employment, net labour demand in the industry reached 1,466 men and women.[81]

In the autumn of 1945 Army men were again brought in to help. Four plants received priority in the use of military personnel: the Canada Packers plants in Toronto, St. Boniface, and Winnipeg, and the Swift Canadian plant in Toronto. Altogether more than 500 Army labourers were employed in these plants,[82] and meatpacking detail ranked second only to construction work in terms of employment priority for Army workers.[83] Another important source of labour for packing operations in this period was found through the Industrial Selection and Release Plan. Employers were encouraged to petition Selection and Release Committees for the early discharge of essential workers and to ask former employees to petition their commanding officers for quick demobilization. Eventually, more than 450 skilled butchers became available for work through the ISRP scheme.[84]

As the country adjusted to peacetime conditions, meatpacking labour relations as well as labour supply became an issue for Ottawa. When strike action was threatened at Burns, Swift's, and Canada Packers, in the autumn of 1945, the federal government took control of the packing plants by naming a Controller for each company. These officials were given full authority to arbitrate labour disputes. Claiming that the disruption of meat shipments to Europe "would be considered by Canadians as little less than criminal," Humphrey Mitchell called on both company and union officials to negotiate in good faith to reach a mutually satisfactory contract arrangement,[85] a call that eventually was heeded by packing and union negotiators.[86] There was good news for the government also in the growing availability of workers for the industry. At the end of September, only 845 vacancies in packing employment were reported, and by the end of November the workforce had jumped to 18,000 men and women.[87] The next month, NSS instructed local offices to no longer submit monthly reports on employment in the meatpacking industry since "the emergency [had] been met."[88]

8 Female Primary Textile Workers and Nurses

Canada relied on the influx of women into the labour force to meet war production requirements as hundreds of thousands of men went into the armed forces. As early as 1941, the Labour Supply Investigation Committee had warned that tapping the vast supply of female labour was perhaps the only way out of a looming human resource crisis. Women responded to the call to duty in overwhelming numbers. By the end of 1944, more than one million women were employed full time in non-agricultural employment, a figure double that of 1939 female employment levels. Hundreds of thousands of women also worked on a part-time basis or shouldered a large portion of the burden in the agricultural sector. For the first time in Canadian history, women also streamed into the armed forces, with almost 50,000 women entering the military during the war.

While NSS officials possessed a measure of legislative control over men, however haphazardly it may have been used, they possessed no powers to compel women to enter specific occupations or to freeze women in essential jobs. Canadian women were, therefore, the beneficiaries of a seller's market for labour in which they could accept employment in any economic sector. War industries that could offer artificially inflated wages and excellent working conditions attracted all the workers they needed; traditional industries with a spotty record of treating women in a fair or progressive manner struggled to maintain their staffing levels. Two sectors of the workforce were dominated by women, the primary textile industry and general duty hospital nursing. Both sectors had chronic problems which NSS addressed, however ineffectively.

Female workers in aircraft plants were the highest paid women during the war, earning an average of 83 cents per hour in 1944, while women in the iron and steel industry earned almost 70 cents per hour. In the same year, by contrast, female primary textile workers in the wool cloth sector of the primary textile industry stood twenty-third on the manufacturing remuneration scale and earned a paltry wage of less than 39 cents per hour, while women in the wool yarn sector ranked thirty-fourth on the pay scale with a rate of less than 37 cents per hour. While virtually every manufacturing and industrial sector experienced significant growth in the number of female employees during the war, the number of women employed in the primary textile industry declined slightly, from 48,221 in 1942 to 47,460 in 1944 for example. Women constantly migrated from the textile industry, and labour turnover combined with the loss of 8,000 male primary textile workers during the war meant that the industry failed to meet its production goals. Primary textile output declined across the board between 1941 and 1945. During this period, for example, cotton yarn output declined from 212 million pounds to 163 million pounds, and cotton broadwoven fabric output declined from 366,000 yards to 277,000 yards.

The record of NSS in relation to women in the primary textile industry provides a telling illustration of its general failure to achieve its regulatory objectives.[1] There are several reasons for this. First, there were underlying weaknesses as in the labour priorities system, the mechanism that anchored the NSS effort to supply labour to essential industries. Despite its seemingly comprehensive nature, the priority classification system proved to be largely ineffective in meeting the needs of the primary textile industry for female workers. Second, these was poor coordination among the government departments responsible for the production of essential civilian goods, most notably the WPTB and NSS. Third, NSS had little control over the movement of women in the Canadian workforce. Since women were not obliged to remain in textile employment, large numbers of experienced female textile workers abandoned the industry for higher pay and better conditions elsewhere. Similarly, many women who had been directed to textile employment, based on the essential nature of the industry, either refused to work for textile firms or else soon separated from them to seek more lucrative employment opportunities elsewhere. Finally, there was great political resistance within the King government and among Canadian employers to boost poor wages and improve working conditions.

In the first sixteen months of its existence, NSS found itself swamped with complaints from primary textile firms about absenteeism, separations from employment, and competition for scarce labour from other industries.[2] As early as May 1942, W.N. Hancock, Managing Director of the Narrow Fabric Weaving and Dyeing Company in Galt, informed DMS officials that 35 per cent of his female employees had left to work in other local firms. In February 1943, A.K.A. Ziz, Manager of the Brampton Knitting Mills plant, protested that many of his employees, both male and female, were leaving his employ to work at the Victory Aircraft plant in nearby Milton, despite the fact that Brampton Knitting Mills had an A rating for female labour. In April, Ziz reported that all five of his experienced male knitters had either quit or handed in seven-day separation notices. This action had created a production bottleneck that had forced the company to cancel its war order with the DMS. In the same vein, officials of Penman's Ltd. of Paris, Ontario, reported in April 1943 that their outerwear department had been reduced from 120 to 44 employees. At the same time, the Penman's plant in Brantford had been reduced to a staff of 210 from a normal complement of 375.[3]

As NSS consolidated its authority after the passage of PC 246 early in 1943, it recognized the problem in textile manufacturing, but declined to take the drastic action advocated by lobbyists for the industry. Some NSS officials welcomed the outflow of textile workers into industries thought to be more essential to the war effort while they blamed employment shortfalls on parsimonious textile firm owners who underpaid their employees.[4] By August of 1943, however, the rising tide of complaints from the industry prompted specific action. In the final five months of 1943 three steps were taken. Blanket increases in priority ratings were granted to all primary textile firms. An attempt was made to get the textile firms themselves to address known problems in relation to working conditions and benefits. Finally, a massive publicity campaign was started in Ontario and Quebec to recruit new female workers for the textile industry.

The campaign for increased priority ratings for textile plants originated in August 1943 with the Wartime Prices and Trade Board and its representative on the Inter-departmental Labour Priorities Committee, G.G.E. Raley. Raley used the example of the Patons and Baldwins worsted spinning mill in Toronto to galvanize support for his cause. Average weekly production of cotton goods in this plant had declined from 32,705 pounds in 1941 to 23,955 pounds during the first six months of 1943, and to only 20,000 pounds during July.[5] Raley insisted that this plant must return to a weekly cotton output of more than 30,000 pounds – an objective that would require the addition of eighty-two women and five men to the existing staff of 344 persons. Under intense pressure from the WPTB, the ILPC agreed on 12 August to grant a blanket priority of B-A to all fourteen primary textile industry subdivisions, ratings that were to be reviewed on 31 December 1943.[6] Raley insisted that there was a shortage of 1,500 female workers in the primary textile industry in Ontario and Quebec and that this problem could only be solved through priority referrals from local NSS offices. Some 400 textile firms stood to benefit from the change in priority ratings made at Raley's insistence.[7]

NSS went along with this, but its officials were still inclined to blame the manufacturers for the crisis. During the summer of 1943, H.F. Irwin, the NSS Regional Employment Advisor for Ontario, was assigned to Ottawa to liaise with the Primary Textiles Institute (PTI), an umbrella organization consisting of members of the Canadian Woollen and Knit Goods Manufacturers' Association, the Cotton Institute of Canada, and the Silk Association of Canada.[8] Irwin's first step was to meet with textile officials in Montreal and Toronto in August and place before them a comprehensive questionnaire aimed at standardizing and improving conditions in the industry.[9] While recognizing that the industry's problems could not be solved immediately, Irwin maintained that standardizing conditions and reforming employment practices would "give prestige to an industry which has long been associated in the public mind with low pay and poor working conditions." Irwin forwarded the questionnaire to primary textile mills in September and the results were distributed in February 1944.[10] A total of 166 firms with a total workforce of 45,715 persons responded. Only 59 per cent of the firms had a systematic training program for employees; fewer than half had rest periods twice per day; only a third had rotating night shifts; only 10 per cent provided medical examinations; only 21 per cent employed a company doctor; fewer than 20 per cent employed an on-duty registered nurse, and fewer than 30 per cent provided any form of sickness insurance. There were six industry subdivisions – Knitting, Woollen, Cotton, Rayon, Worsted, and Miscellaneous. The thirty-eight woollen mills, employing close to 6,000 workers, reported results below the industry average in all fifteen report categories. These results proved that conditions in many textile factories were only tolerable at best and certainly inferior to conditions in many of the new war industries that were springing up. Irwin used these results to lobby the industry to improve working conditions.[11]

A publicity campaign was launched to recruit more female textile workers in Hamilton and in Montreal. Responding to a shortage of 1,000 women workers in the Hamilton area, Fraudena Eaton, Associate Director of the NSS Women's Division, supervised a well-orchestrated campaign that commenced on 3 November. It featured radio and newspaper appeals, the display of promotional material in movie theatres and local businesses, exhortations by clergymen from the pulpit, and the mobilization of local women's groups. The media campaign appealed directly to the perceived role of women in domestic life: "since time immemorial" women had made clothing for "their children, their menfolk, and themselves," and the call to service in textile factories was simply an extension of this cherished legacy of care.[12] The enthusiastic support of community groups for the public relations campaign in Hamilton was not matched in Montreal.[13] Several factors explain this. First, Quebec had a lower rate of female participation in the workforce than was the case elsewhere.[14] Second, vociferous opposition arose to the policy of targeting women workers. Early in 1942, the National Catholic Unions of Trois Rivières had warned Prime Minister King of the "ill-fated consequences" of female participation in war employment.[15] NSS officials also visited ninety-eight Montreal area parishes to drum up support for their plan, and although several priests indicated a keen interest in visiting plants to view conditions for themselves, a number condemned the recruitment of female labour as destructive of family life and "contrary to the principles of the Church."[16]

In Hamilton, the publicity campaign resulted in 420 referrals to primary textile employment; of this group 217 women actually accepted full-time or part-time employment in these plants. While NSS officials were generally satisfied with this result, many industry officials questioned the value of what had been achieved. In Montreal, NSS public relations efforts in the autumn of 1943 produced only 142 referrals and sixty-nine hirings, an outcome that the agency itself described as "mediocre."[17]

Despite all that was done in the second half of 1943 to get more women workers into textile manufacturing, the employment situation in the industry continued to deteriorate. Experienced female employees continued to leave for better jobs elsewhere, and many women who joined the textile workforce quit their new jobs in short order. Labour turnover in two large Toronto firms typified the situation in Ontario.[18] In the Joseph Simpson Knitting Mills, 148 women were hired between 1 July and 30 November 1943, but 136 women separated from employment during the same period. Over the same five months, 176 women were hired by Patons and Baldwins, and 222 women left. In Montreal, 661 women had been referred to the massive Dominion Textile operations during 1943; 291 of these had been hired, but only 197 women had actually reported for work.[19]

The criticism directed at NSS measures, the generally poor results of the publicity campaigns in Montreal and Hamilton, and the slow pace of reform in the primary textile firms convinced ILPC Chairman Sheldon Ross, despite the best efforts of Raley and the WPTB to the contrary, to abandon the blanket priority system for the industry. At the ILPC meeting of 11 November 1943, Ross asked Raley to provide the committee with a list of the primary textile firms deemed essential by the WPTB.[20] Remarkably, Raley submitted a list of 419 firms. Convinced that WPTB demands were unrealistic, Ross moved to prune this list. Over Raley's protestations, the ILPC decided in January 1944 that only sixty-three firms would be given the highest priority rating of A-A. All other firms reverted to schedules B-B, C-B, or C-C.[21] With this decision, the first phase of concerted and well-defined NSS policy ended. While WPTB officials railed against the ILPC decision, some NSS officials wished to set off in a new direction.

In the first five months of 1944, the stream of industry complaints against NSS with respect to female labour continued to flow. The ILPC continued to tinker with the female priority rating for specific firms, but PTI and WPTB officials demanded more concerted and decisive action. Leaders of the PTI insisted that the decision to grant many war plants concessions in wage and price ceilings had drawn large numbers of women away from their industry. According to the PTI, while some textile firms were beginning to take advantage of War Emergency Training programs, the industry as a whole remained particularly susceptible to external market forces because of its unusual mix of male and female workers. While 23 per cent of non-ferrous metal workers, 17 per cent of iron workers, and 9 per cent of non-metallic mineral workers were female, fully 60 per cent of textile workers were female as of 1 October 1943. This made the industry especially vulnerable to shifts in labour demand.[22]

NSS data continued to validate PTI concerns. The Hochelaga Mill of the Dominion Textile Company reported in April 1944 that it needed to add more than 400 workers to its existing complement of 1,084 in order to meet its production requirements. From Valleyfield, the Montreal Cottons plant reported a shortfall of more than 500 workers, more than 15 per cent of its total workforce.[23] In May 1944, H.D. Ovendon, Manager of the Welland, Ontario NSS office, told Fraudena Eaton that it was "not so very difficult to explain" why women continued to stream out of textile employment in his area. Ammunition plants operated by the United Steel Corporation and Atlas Steels Limited had opened locally, and there was a "great difference" between their wages and those of the textile manufacturers.[24]

In May and June 1944, NSS again recast its policy. Convinced that another massive advertising campaign would be futile, Mary Eadie, Supervisor of the Toronto Women's Division, called for a "new approach." This would involve working with the PTI to identify specific emergency situations in a limited number of plants.[25] Eaton joined Ross in criticizing WPTB officials, and Raley in particular, for advancing so many priority rating requests.[26] Since the textile industry was marked by low wages and long hours, Eaton noted the futility of promising the WPTB large numbers of new recruits. If the WPTB could be more discriminating, perhaps a way forward could be found by modifying the priority ratings for the most essential primary textile firms.[27] Raley defended his department, but, after being condemned by Ross for his actions on the priority front,[28] agreed to meet with NSS officials on 6 June 1944 to devise a new strategy along the lines favoured by Eadie and Eaton.

Prior to this meeting, the WPTB and the PTI were each asked to submit a list of primary textile firms in the Toronto area to be identified as essential. Raley submitted the names of seventeen firms on behalf of the WPTB while H.F. Irwin put forward the names of fourteen firms on behalf of the PTI. A comparison of the two lists provided Ross with all the ammunition he needed to shred the credibility of the WPTB, since only a single firm was named on both lists. Ross lashed out at Raley and other WPTB representatives, insisting that the ILPC would no longer delay lowering priority ratings unless Raley admitted his duplicity in encouraging production in less-essential textile plants.[29]

NSS officials proceeded to act on their own current thinking about female employment in primary textile firms. The new measures were tested by Mary Eadie on a trial basis in the Toronto area. Under this scheme, the fourteen Toronto firms Irwin identified as most essential were studied carefully to ascertain the minimum number of women required to fill essential production. Irwin reported that 146 women were needed immediately in these plants. Eadie was instructed to submit weekly reports on the employment situation in the Toronto mills, and on the progress of the training and referral programs and on the results of an effort to recruit women workers in Manitoba and Nova Scotia. During the summer of 1944, the new initiative seemed to alleviate the shortage in Toronto to some degree, a fact acknowledged by all parties involved, including the WPTB. By 1 October, eighty-nine women had taken full-time employment in the fourteen designated Toronto firms. Similar initiatives in Hamilton showed a measure of success; in September 1944 almost half the workers needed by five key Hamilton textile plants were found. Many NSS officials, however, remained sceptical. Fraudena Eaton had stated in August 1944 that NSS had "about exhausted its possibilities" in augmenting textile payrolls. NSS bureaucrats in Hamilton believed in weathering "critical shortages" by relying on the inevitable cancellation of munitions contracts. Whenever this happened, women went "scampering to textile mills in search of permanent employment."[30]

In Welland, NSS efforts met with much less success. In August, Empire Cottons reported a desperate need for 100 women to reverse a production trend that had seen output decline by 50 per cent during the previous year.[31] Working conditions had been markedly improved at this plant, but wages and hours continued to hamstring recruitment efforts. Thus while the starting wage at Empire Cottons was 30.2 cents per hour for the day shift, the starting wage at munitions plants in the area was 46 cents per hour. In these circumstances, women brought in from distant areas to work in the local textile firms almost immediately left their jobs for better ones. Moreover, the standard working week at Empire Cottons was a demanding fifty-four hours per week: five ten-hour shifts Monday to Friday and a four-hour stint on Saturday. Even bleaker was the situation in Montreal, where the new NSS approach made very little difference.[32] With NSS thus floundering once more by the winter of 1944–45, the WPTB, led by G.G.E. Raley, returned to the offensive.

In March 1945, bypassing the ILPC, Raley produced a detailed report that chronicled the depressed labour situation of the primary textile industry in general while concentrating on two of its sub-groups: Industry 2211, Cotton Yarn and Broad Woven Goods, and Industry 2231, Woollen and Worsted Woven Goods.[33] According to Raley, in Industry 2211, the number of employees had fallen from 25,817 in October 1942 to 22,183 in January 1945; in Industry 2231 the decline over the same period had been from 10,371 to 9,904. Cotton firms based primarily in Quebec had lost close to 24 per cent of their workforces in the two years before October 1944, despite the fact that ten of the firms in question had operated under priority ratings above the industry average. A second WPTB report by Raley, submitted in April 1945, placed the textile labour situation in a context of severe production shortfalls that necessitated direct WPTB control.[34] In late 1943, the WPTB had launched a production directive program that required manufacturers to fill essential civilian and military requirements before devoting material to non-essential orders.[35] By 1 April 1945, five primary textile divisions had been placed under directive control, forcing firms to adjust their production. Raley also produced payroll figures that showed a 7 per cent drop in expenditure in seven key primary textile groups between October 1942 and October 1944. Nor did this figure tell the full story, which would have to take account of the greatly increased use of part-time labour, heavy turnover and absenteeism, loss of skilled workers to the armed forces, and their replacement with unskilled labour. Raley called for "immediate and more strenuous efforts" by all concerned. High labour turnover continued to plague the primary textile industry; thus, in the thirty days preceding 7 April 1945, 332 women had been placed in jobs in woollen plants but 337 women had quit the same operations.[36]

The renewed WPTB campaign moved NSS to try new and more comprehensive measures. The ILPC agreed to re-institute the industry-wide priority ratings abandoned fifteen months earlier. In April 1945, a priority rating of A-A was granted to all establishments in four key textile industry sub-groups whose production fell entirely under WPTB directive; at the same time, an increased priority rating of B-B was granted to knit outerwear plants under WPTB directive. The ILPC agreed to extend the A-A designation to three additional primary textile industry groups if and when they were placed under directive. Clearly, Sheldon Ross conceded much before the WPTB onslaught, though he remained unconvinced that tinkering with the priority system would "be of very much help."[37]

In concert with the priority revisions, various NSS officials met in March and April 1945 to re-examine the conundrum of female textile employment. One of the most ambitious proposals to emerge from these meetings targeted the textile mills in the Hamilton area for special attention. On 20 March, thirteen representatives of the leading textile firms in this region met with NSS officials to discuss the feasibility of recruiting several hundred women workers in Nova Scotia.[38] The mill representatives offered to send recruiting agents to Sydney on condition that the women hired remain in textile employment for a minimum of six months and that NSS pay the cost of selection, transportation, and room and board. Although they had originated the proposal, NSS leaders ultimately proved wary of it on the grounds that there was "no purpose in bringing people 1,000 miles to have them unemployed in Hamilton instead of Sydney."[39] Local NSS officials also identified another potential drawbook to the scheme. Since the Sydney workers would be "mingling at their work with other employees of foreign extraction and possibly quite a low social standing," Hamilton residents would possibly object to billeting the Sydney women in their homes.[40] In the circumstances, NSS decided to let the whole proposal die.[41]

A more constructive NSS plan was devised after Arthur MacNamara, under pressure from the WPTB and the PTI,[42] created a Special Committee on Textiles, which was chaired by Fraudena Eaton. The purpose of this committee, which met for the first time on 18 April 1945, was to work out a comprehensive, though non-legislative, response to WPTB demands for concerted action in relation to the textile industry.[43] As a result of the committee's deliberations, a big radio and newspaper publicity campaign was launched in May by NSS and the PTI. It was now decided to extend to the whole of Ontario a procedure that had been introduced by the Toronto NSS office. Since February 1945 all women seeking employment spoke with a counsellor versed in textile operations before being considered for general employment. In addition, all women separating from textile employment were required to meet with this special textiles officer for an exit interview to determine why a woman was leaving her job and to persuade her to stay in the textile industry. This was a highly successful initiative, though it came almost two years too late. In Hamilton, 402 women were interviewed by the special textile officer between 10 May and 24 May and 178 referrals were made to textile employment. In Toronto, exit interviews persuaded close to 50 per cent of women separating from employment in textile plants to return to their old jobs.[44]

Many wartime restrictions were being lifted. In November 1944, all restrictions on women seeking permits to move from one NSS geographic jurisdiction to another had been rescinded.[45] After 15 May 1945, women were no longer required to obtain permits to secure employment, although many still used NSS offices to search for work.[46] Advertising restrictions were likewise lifted and Labour Minister Humphrey Mitchell announced in August that the employment freeze on male workers would be cancelled on 17 September 1945. From that date all compulsory directives regarding male employees would be abandoned.[47] However, times remained tough for the textile industry. An attempt to transplant procedures established in Ontario offices to Montreal failed,[48] and labour turnover rates remained high. In Ontario, 436 workers were placed in primary textile plants between 21 June and 15 August 1945, while 1,073 separations occurred in the same period. Of these, 854 were women.[49] In the final months of 1945 and the first months of 1946, NSS officials admitted that little had been accomplished during the three-year effort to alleviate the shortage of female labour in primary textile mills. The Special Committee on Textiles continued to note that low wages and poor working conditions were the primary cause of declining payrolls.[50] The Special Committee itself remained in operation until early 1946, and Eaton strongly supported Arthur MacNamara's "quite revolutionary" proposal for a minimum wage for women in the textile industry. However, this badly needed reform was not made.

Hospital nursing staffs in Canada were strained to the limit during the war for a variety of reasons. First, almost 4,500 civilian nurses entered the military during the war and served as nursing sisters in one of the three service branches. Second, thousands of hospital nurses left their employment to enter more lucrative positions in industrial and public health nursing. Hospital wages in many cities were notoriously low, and working weeks of sixty hours were not uncommon. In 1942, the average monthly wage for nurses in large hospitals with more than 200 beds was a paltry $59.35 plus maintenance. As hospital sub-staffs were depleted during the war and nurses took on more non-nursing responsibilities, thousands of nurses opted to leave hospitals for industrial nursing positions. Third, defections to military and industrial nursing could not be readily offset with new student nurses. Since it took a minimum of two years to train a nurse – even taking accelerated training courses into account – hospitals could not count on a stable supply of newly minted nurses until the final two years of the war. Fourth, shortfalls in nursing supply were exacerbated by a significant increase in hospital admissions during the war. The number of patient-days in public and private hospitals (excluding mental hospitals and tuberculosis sanatoria) increased by more than 22 per cent between 1940 and 1945, while the number of individual patient discharges from these hospitals increased almost 35 percent during the same period from less than 874,000 persons to more than 1,178,295 persons.[51] Finally, thousands of trained nurses remained at home during the war while their husbands served in the armed forces, and NSS initiatives were ineffective in channelling these women into hospitals on a full- or part-time basis.

The relationship between NSS and the CNA resembles that between NSS and the universities. Arthur MacNamara willingly allowed the Canadian Nurses Association (CNA), an autonomous professional organization, to direct the scope of mobilization efforts affecting its membership. By failing to be more interventionist, however, he tolerated a situation in which hospitals across the country faced severe nursing shortages. The cornerstone of NSS policy was a 1942 decision to exempt nurses from all mobilization provisions affecting women. In a concession to private interests, the CNA was left to regulate itself through local nursing registries, provincial nursing associations, and its own administrative structure. Faced with continued nursing shortages in 1943 and 1944, NSS engineered a series of surveys and publicity campaigns designed to persuade inactive nurses – the only untapped source of nursing labour – to enter hospital employment. Many idle nurses, particularly those who were married, resisted these calls to return to a workplace dominated by low wages and poor working conditions.

While women in the primary textile industry were poorly organized and mounted few campaigns to improve their lot during the war, the Canadian Nurses Association (CNA) provided its members with a strong and effective lobby to guarantee that NSS would not infringe upon the independence of nurses. At the heart of the CNA desire to protect its autonomy lay the issue of safeguarding the recognition of nursing as a profession. In the decades before World War II, the CNA had waged a battle to ensure that the provision of nursing care would not be balkanized among a disparate group of qualified and unqualified practitioners. In the 1920s, Ontario nurses had fought for licensing and the recognition of professional qualifications. During the Great Depression, however, there had been a setback in the struggle, as many untrained nursing practitioners found work in hospitals.[52] Furthermore, the majority of practising nurses were employed as private duty nurses, with hospital administrators relying mainly on overworked student nurses to staff their wards.[53] CNA officials clearly viewed the onset of war in 1939 as an opportunity to improve nurses' economic status, to elevate their professional status, and to increase their employment opportunities in hospitals. To these ends, the organization launched an aggressive campaign soon after the war started.

First and foremost, CNA leaders steadfastly opposed any government regulation of nurses. Their strategy received the formal endorsement of the entire CNA in late 1941,[54] and representatives of the organization thereafter submitted a request to the Dominion government for a sum of $125,000. The government was asked to provide financial support to encourage the enrolment of more student nurses, to publicize the need for married nurses and nurses not employed in hospital settings to take institutional work, and to augment the teaching staffs of nursing schools. The Department of Pensions and National Health allotted $115,000 to the CNA for the 1942–43 fiscal year for student recruitment, publicity, and augmentation of teaching staffs.[55] In 1943–44, this grant was increased to $250,000 per annum for the duration of the war.[56] The effect of this grant was positive but hardly dramatic. Student nurse numbers rose from 8,500 in the 1939–40 academic year to 11,163 in 1941–42, but in 1942–43 there was only a small increase in registrants, which brought the total to 11,266. Enrolments in 1943–44 and 1944–45 were 11,359 and 12,254, respectively.[57] On the other hand, 7,216 nurses left the civilian nursing force during the war.

As might be expected, the CNA also lobbied hard to increase the salaries and improve the working conditions of nurses. In this regard, the efforts of the organization were directed at the Canadian Hospital Council (CHC), the national umbrella organization of provincial hospital bodies. The case put forward by the CNA was simple and direct. Spiralling hospital admissions and the depletion of hospital sub-staffs were placing an enormous strain on nurses in Canadian hospitals, who were now being forced to add non-nursing responsibilities such as domestic duties to their normal responsibilities. A National Health Survey conducted in 1943 revealed that 15 per cent of all general duty nurses in hospitals worked an average of more than 121 hours per fortnight.[58] On top of this, the salaries of nurses were notoriously unstable and inconsistent. Because of poor pay and difficult working conditions, the CNA refused to accept any measure of blame for the wartime nursing shortages. At the same time, the CHC demanded that the problem be solved by strictly regulating the economic and occupational freedom of nurses. Caught in the middle was NSS.

During the first eight months of 1942, the dimensions of the problem became apparent to all concerned. A steady stream of nurses was entering the armed forces, and many other nurses and essential hospital employees were leaving their jobs to take advantage of more lucrative opportunities in industry. During this period, for example, almost 40 per cent of nurses resigning from the Victorian Order of Nurses migrated to positions in industry or the public health field.[59] To monitor this situation, early in 1942 the CNA appointed Kathleen W. Ellis as Emergency Nursing Advisor. She was to travel across the country to gauge the extent of the difficulties which had arisen and to recommend remedial measures.[60] Ellis proved to be a formidable and energetic advocate of CNA autonomy. Educated at Johns Hopkins and Columbia Universities, she had been Director of Nursing at the Vancouver General Hospital and a nursing professor at the University of Saskatchewan.[61] In the first seven months after her appointment, Ellis spent 157 days in various provinces tirelessly promoting the advantages of a nursing career to students, directing provincial advertising campaigns, and fiercely asserting the need for nurses to have professional autonomy and be free of government regulation.[62] Despite Ellis's work, she admitted in November 1942 that there was a "startling degree of inadequacy" in the supply of nurses, although she refused to countenance direct government intervention to solve the problem.[63]

Not surprisingly, her efforts encountered stiff resistance from the CHC. Through its Secretary, Dr. Harvey Agnew, the CHC called on the government to limit the migration of both nurses and other skilled hospital employees from health care employment. In particular, the CHC insisted that hospital work be given a higher labour priority rating by the ILPC so as to guarantee the supply of hospital sub-staff workers. This, in turn, would avoid further demands being placed on already overworked nursing personnel. If immediate legislation or regulation was not possible, Agnew wanted large sums of money spent on advertising to persuade hospital workers to remain in their employment. J.A. MacMillan, President of the Maritime Hospital Association, called on NSS to freeze all hospital workers in their positions and exempt them from military service. Many provincial health officials supported the CHC call for strict regulation of health care workers, although the Ontario Minister of Health noted that any government initiatives should include wage and working condition improvements to make hospital employment competitive with industrial occupations.[64] Other medical officials lashed out at the weakness and arbitrariness of NSS regulations as the source of the nursing shortage. For example, Margaret Jamieson, Superintendent of the Restigouche and Bay of Chaleur Memorial Hospital in New Brunswick, complained bitterly about NSS restrictions on advertising; these made a bad situation "infinitely worse." Jamieson felt betrayed, and claimed that she had been foolish to believe that the introduction of civilian mobilization measures would help the hospitals in any meaningful fashion.[65]

Finally, NSS Associate Director Fraudena Eaton called a conference of NSS, CNA, and CHC representatives in Ottawa on 22 October 1942 to discuss hospital conditions. Prior to this meeting, K.W. Ellis set the limits of discussion: only cooperation with, and not the coercion of, the CNA would be considered, and debate must centre on the establishment of "minimum requirements" of living, salary, and working conditions. Ellis asked all provincial nursing groups to bring forward their ideas at the conference, but in fact little that was new was discussed there. The CNA delegation reiterated that only better wages and working conditions for nurses could begin to alleviate the crisis and that voluntary workers or hospital aides could not substitute for trained nursing professionals. The only CNA concession was an expression of willingness to endorse a professional permit system which would document the availability of nurses. The CHC brief to the conference called for the freezing of all hospital staff members in their existing employment, the placing of all hospital personnel at the highest level of essentiality, and the granting of primacy to hospital employment in the allocation of workers by NSS officers. Both the CHC and the CNA called for a massive publicity campaign, to be funded by the government, to highlight the benefits and essentiality of hospital employment.[66]

Beyond this, the October conference failed to produce any plan of action. The proposal for the registration of nurses quickly died, and a litany of complaints about nursing shortages continued to be heard at NSS headquarters in Ottawa. The unanimous opinion of key officials there was that further surveys of the nursing situation should be undertaken to give the CNA – this was revealing – "a much better idea of how they can recommend solving their own problems."[67] The CHC continued to press for more regulation of hospital employees but the CNA continued to lobby for the unrestricted management of its own affairs.

Although plans to register nurses through the WBTP were abandoned in late 1942, the idea of a registration drive to determine the number of nurses in Canada, regardless of current occupation, gained momentum early in 1943.[68] On 12 February, it was decided to have a three-day registration in late March, and a proclamation to this effect was issued on 15 February. While the majority of nurses were required to register at hospitals or local Employment Offices, arrangements were made for nurses living more than five miles from an NSS office to register through the post office. Large advertisements about the registration were placed in every daily newspaper in Canada on 15 March, and information was also circulated to every hospital and post office across the country. The registration was compulsory for all nurses under sixty-five years of age who were not enlisted in the armed forces, regardless of marital status or existing employment.

The final tally of the national registration drive occurred in June 1943, although the returns were not widely circulated for four more months because of CNA objections. The registration proved that there was a large number of nurses who were not practising. Table 8 summarizes the results of the registration by region and employment status. The nationwide ratio of practising nurses to total population was 1:520. Ontario had the most favourable ratio (1:381) and Saskatchewan the most unfavourable (1:897). The registration revealed that most nurses who were not practising their profession were married housewives and that 50 per cent of all practising nurses were not employed in general duty in hospital wards. More than 1,000 individuals indicated a willingness to resume nursing on a full-time basis, although 484 of these insisted on remaining in their own locality.

With the registration results in hand, Eaton and other NSS officials launched a series of consultations across the country. In Montreal, meetings were held with local hospital and nursing officials on 28 and 29 June. The business discussed included the feasibility of grants from the Dominion government to local hospitals, the granting to hospitals of further exemption from NSS regulations, and the sponsorship by the

Table 8
Results of the March 1943 Nursing Registration

Occupation	Maritimes	Quebec	Ontario	Prairies	BC	Canada
Private Duty	717	1,126	3,397	703	384	6,327
General Duty	899	2,002	4,342	2,030	1,432	10,705
Industrial Nursing	28	425	658	180	65	1,356
Other Nursing	268	922	1,542	662	386	3,780
Housewives	2,922	2,424	11,457	5,306	3,173	25,282
Industry, Business	71	121	487	94	166	939
Other Non-Nursing	80	94	511	95	50	830
All Occupations	4,985	7,114	22,394	9,070	5,656	49,219

Source: NA, RG 27, Volume 1522, File XI–2–12 pt. 2

Dominion government of more recruitment drives for nurses. Eaton recognized that the decision to allow the CNA to regulate the flow of nurses through local nursing registries had not worked. The Manitoba registration system, for example, had failed to produce nurses for rural areas or tuberculosis sanatoria. In July 1943, NSS officials reported that the Winnipeg Nursing Registry was "practically begging" for nurses to alleviate acute shortages in hospitals outside the city. Moreover, despite threats from Manitoba nursing officials to deny them private duty referrals, members of the Winnipeg registry had refused even to attend meetings to discuss the situation and to vote on possible improvements in the registry system.[69]

Yet, while she recognized the increasing shortage of professional help in Canadian hospitals, Eaton steadfastly resisted direct NSS control of the placement of nurses. In a July 1943 letter to the CNA, she summed up her position as follows: "I have not yet lost faith in my original belief that the CNA and the individuals of the nursing profession will find ways and means to arrive at a solution through self-regulation when the situation is placed fairly before them."[70] Eaton assured Marion Lindeburgh that NSS plans centred on the CNA and provincial nursing associations assuming "more responsibility for the adjustment of their situation"; cooperation, not compulsion, would continue to guide government policy.[71] On their side, CNA officials remained adamant in the view that they were not to blame for the shortage of nurses. Responding to Harvey Agnew's complaint about the high rate of separations among nurses and his corresponding call for an employment freeze on nurses, Jean Wilson noted that the root of the problem lay in the parsimonious salaries and poor working conditions defended by the CHC:

While it is imperative that all nurses co-operate in meeting the needs of nursing services in this crisis, it would seem that before any regulations [advocated by Agnew] are affected they should be very carefully considered by representatives of all groups immediately concerned. Whatever might be done through regulations, we do want to be certain that it will be done in the best interests of the nursing service ... While the present may not seem the time to advocate more favourable working conditions and uniformity of salaries on various levels, we are of the opinion that hospital authorities can afford no longer to avoid their responsibilities in these matters. Until nurses receive the same consideration as the majority of other workers, who have much less preparation and carry less responsibility, the situation will remain a serious problem, and it is particularly accentuated in wartime.[72]

CNA and various provincial nursing representatives attempted to find solutions within the established framework of practice. One of the most ambitious efforts was made in Manitoba. At a conference in August 1943, the Manitoba Association of Registered Nurses passed two helpful resolution: that a committee be struck to interview all members of the provincial nursing directory in order to direct nurses where they were most needed, and that this committee make a special effort to mobilize physically fit women with no dependents to work in hard-pressed rural areas,[73] especially in the tuberculosis sanatorium at Ninette and the various psychiatric hospitals scattered about the province. The committee contacted 300 nurses but with decidedly mixed results. Of the ninety-five single nurses interviewed in person, forty-three refused assignment in tuberculosis or psychiatric wards while thirty-three said that health problems or domestic duties made work in rural areas impossible for them. Of the sixty-six married nurses interviewed, forty-six refused to consider posts in psychiatric or tuberculosis institutions. Of 153 nurses reporting by telephone, only fifty-three were able to serve even in a limited capacity to alleviate the nursing shortage in the province.[74]

A second important CNA initiative was launched in June 1943 at a meeting of the executive of the Association. A Joint Committee on Nursing was formed to meet with representatives of the CHC. Nine prominent CNA officials, including K.W. Ellis, were named to the committee, which was to consider all problems relating to the supply and distribution of qualified nurses in Canada. While the CNA proclaimed proudly that it would handle the professional aspects of the shortage of nurses, its officials also made plain that they could not "assume the responsibility for rectifying or improving the economic factors involved in this problem."[75] The CHC agreed to participate in the work of the Joint Committee and appointed a four-member group to represent its interests. At a meeting of the fully constituted Joint Committee on 31 August 1943, the CNA members endorsed the following: (1) a minimum payment to general duty nurses of $100 per month plus maintenance; (2) an eight-hour day and a six-day week for this same group; (3) a salary of four dollars per day plus maintenance for general duty work of more than one week but less than one month; (4) the payment of the prevailing private duty nursing rate for all general nursing work of less than a week; (5) the elimination of non-nursing duties from the workload of general duty nurses; (6) the limiting of private duty nursing to necessary cases only; (7) the increased use of subsidiary nursing groups; and (8) no freezing of nurses in their existing employment through government regulation.[76]

In response, the CHC members present invited the CNA to raise these concerns at the CHC annual meeting to be held on 8 September. At this gathering both the CNA and NSS were officially represented. A variety of topics were discussed, including the need for more money to be found for student nurses. NSS officials suggested that the CNA approach the Department of Labour about the availability of scholarship money under the Canadian Vocational Training Act to supplement the block grant the CNA received from the Department of Pensions and National Health.[77] An NSS proposal that the CHC employ interned Japanese women in hospital work was quickly squelched; CHC representatives from British Columbia pronounced that the "rest of the country could do as they liked" but that BC hospitals had no interest in these women "except to have them removed as far as possible" from the province.[78] The CNA-CHC Joint Committee list of remedies for the nursing crisis received an indifferent response from the CHC executive. The CNA demands were placed far down on the agenda of the annual meeting on the grounds that the CHC had not met specifically to discuss the recommendations. Not until January 1944 did the CHC endorse in general terms the submission put forward by the Joint Committee. However, its recommendations were simply passed along to the provincial hospital councils for study, without any firm guidelines for action to improve the wages and working conditions of women attached.[79] In a 1946 document, the CNA summarized the tepid response of the CHC to the wartime proposals of the Joint Committee as follows: "The recommendations of the CNA, formulated in 1943, although generally agreed to in principle by the provincial hospital associations, actually were not strongly supported by the latter or generally implemented. Very little, in fact, was done during the war years to hold nurses in the hospital field."[80]

By the beginning of 1944, therefore, the pattern of interest-group response to the problem of meeting the demand for nurses was well established. Central to this was the refusal of NSS to tell nurses where and when to work. Eaton had welcomed the establishment of the Joint Committee in the hope that it would "overcome the need for directive control of nurses,"[81] although she admitted that it was evident that inactive nurses were not responding to calls to accept employment "on the basis of duty rather than privilege."[82] The CNA remained opposed to NSS interference and continued to seek a solution to the problem by increasing the supply of nurses through recruitment and training. At every opportunity, the CNA pressed its case that the root cause of all that had gone wrong was to be found in the realm of salaries and working conditions. The CHC, of course, rejected this analysis and looked to legislative remedies to solve the crisis.

By February 1944 it was clear that the Joint Committee had failed. Nevertheless, K.W. Ellis told Eaton that even so innocuous an idea as an NSS proposal to provide local employment offices and provincial nursing registries with the lists from the March 1943 registration was opposed by the CNA. Eaton maintained her conciliatory approach and answered that the registration results would only be distributed "during any emergency which might arise" and that NSS would not act without the approval of the CNA and the provincial nursing agencies.[83] In April, NSS and CNA officials met again. Remarkably, the only measures they adopted had already been tried: there would be another national publicity campaign; Arthur MacNamara and Fraudena Eaton would write to all non-practising nurses in the country, and there would be another national survey of hospital requirements. CNA leaders resolutely maintained that the situation "did not warrant the placing of controls over the employment of nurses," and Eaton wholeheartedly supported their request for the publicity campaign.[84] It featured newspaper and radio advertisements and a National Film Board short film, which was released in theatres on 25 May.[85] The personal letter jointly signed by MacNamara and Eaton in June 1944 urged nurses to examine the relative importance of the work they were performing and emphasized that nurses had not been subject to any form of regulation. Nurses were asked to register at a local employment office or put their names on the local nursing registry to express their willingness to fill hospital nursing vacancies.[86]

NSS officials in Ottawa received scores of letters from nurses explaining why they could not respond to MacNamara and Eaton's appeal. While the majority of the letter writers cited health and home concerns,[87] a vocal minority targeted bureaucratic regulations within both government and the nursing profession itself. Mrs. F.E. Clark of Sidney, British Columbia, had trained as a nurse in England and had served in the Royal Infirmary in Scotland during World War 1. After her husband had died in 1940, her application to enlist as a nurse in the Royal Canadian Navy had been declined on account of her age. Next, her application for an exit permit to return to England to accept a nursing post had been refused. Finally, she had moved to Saskatchewan and responded to an "outcry about the shortage of private nurses" in Saskatoon, but she was denied employment by the local nursing registry because she lacked a midwifery certificate, which would have involved separate training in England. Clark wondered if the nursing shortage was really as severe as NSS officials claimed it was.[88] Poor wages and working conditions in hospitals were also singled out for complaint. H.R.M. McDougall of Toronto berated hospital officials for paying nurses lower wages than they paid to charwomen. She challenged MacNamara to send a circular letter to hospital administrators asking them to improve voluntarily the working conditions of nurses. Responses to MacNamara and Eaton's letter made it clear, once again that, given the historical pattern of low wages, a patriotic appeal to nurses would not solve the problem; it was like trying to solve the military manpower problem by shaming "the zombies into active service."[89] Muriel Locke of Toronto castigated MacNamara for "threatening" nurses into cooperating in order to avoid regulation; a better approach would be to provide government funds to augment nursing incomes.[90]

The results of the national hospital survey were published in June 1944. A total of 694 hospitals were surveyed; these employed 8,655 full-time and 805 part-time nurses. The report showed that 2,135 additional nurses were needed immediately by these institutions, with Ontario alone requiring 935 full-time and seventy-three part-time nurses. It also highlighted the disturbing fact that more than 10 per cent of all nurses employed in hospitals had separated from employment in at least one hospital during the month of April 1944.[91] The average monthly wage in most areas of the country was between $70 and $90 per month; the lowest wage was $50 per month at the Hotel Dieu Hospital in Bathurst and the highest wage was $115 per month at the Belcher Hospital in Calgary. Above all, the survey showed that nurses were expressing their discontent over salaries and working conditions by voting with their feet. High-wage hospitals across the country usually had full staff complements while low-wage hospitals were short of nurses. In Ontario, for example, the Nicholl's Hospital in Peterborough paid salaries of $110 per month and reported no nursing shortages; by contrast, St. Joseph's Hospital in the same city paid only $70 per month and had a 25 per cent staff shortage. In Calgary, the Belcher Hospital reported no shortage, while the Calgary General Hospital needed thirteen nurses to supplement the work of the thirty-five nurses on staff who were being paid $83 per month.[92]

The results of the hospital survey reinforced a rising tide of criticism directed at both nursing and government officials during the summer of 1944. Harvey Agnew of the CHC was quick to point out that tuberculosis sanatoria and psychiatric hospitals were not the only institutions suffering acute staff shortages. Agnew complained that war industry manufacturing plants with unlimited budgets were hoarding nurses whose chief concerns were to "inquire about headaches and bandage cut fingers" while hospital patients "hovering near death" were being denied proper nursing care.[93] Horace Atkin, Superintendent of the Metropolitan Hospital in Windsor, Ontario, complained that the lack of regulation of nurses enabled many of them to "enjoy a tourist excursion across Canada." Not surprisingly, he wanted strict controls put on the profession to alleviate shortages.[94] In Welland, Ontario, thanks to a grant of $165,000 from wartime construction funds, the County Hospital had been able to add a fifty-bed wing to the original 100-bed facility. A shortage of twenty-six nurses, however, meant that only fifty of the 150 beds were in use.[95]

Continuing shortages and a poor response to the advertising campaign forced NSS and CNA representatives to meet again to discuss a more comprehensive response to the nursing crisis, although Fraudena Eaton reiterated that NSS did not want to countenance any coercive control of nurses "until all other means [had] been exhausted."[96] At this meeting, which was held in Ottawa in August, the two parties agreed that (1) financial inducements in the form of supplementary allowances under NSS jurisdiction should be extended to nurses; (2) a plan should be devised to bar any nurse who had graduated since 1942 from accepting private duty work; (3) hospitals should be encouraged to make better use of auxiliary medical organizations such as the Red Cross Society and the St. John's Ambulance Society; (4) local community resources should be more fully utilized by hospitals; (5) student nurses should be eligible for a $200 grant from the Student Aid Schedule of the War Emergency Training Plan; and (6) concessions on NSS advertising and recruiting rules should be made to allow hospitals greater freedom in obtaining hospital sub-staff.[97] These were comprehensive recommendations indeed, but no concrete action was forthcoming from the meeting. The proposal to use autonomous auxiliary hospital organizations fell flat.[98] It was clear that government subsidies and the restriction of private duty nursing had the greatest potential to ease the shortage of nurses. Neither measure, however, was administered with any degree of conviction.

Section 213 of Order-in-Council PC 246, the NSS Civilian Regulations, authorized NSS officials to pay transportation costs and separation allowances to workers who transferred to essential jobs away from their current employment. On 11 August 1944, NSS officials issued Circular 356 allowing local NSS officers to pay separation allowances to all trained nurses not currently employed in their profession who were willing to accept general-duty hospital positions for a minimum period of six months. Nurses accepting transfer would be guaranteed reinstatement in their former employment upon the completion of their nursing duties and NSS would pay all transportation costs, a payment in lieu of wages lost during travel to a nursing position, a separation allowance if a nurse was required to live apart from dependents, and an advance for living expenses and uniforms.[99] But even this approach proved ineffective. Almost three months after they were introduced, Eaton announced that the allowances were "not proving to be of value" and that only a single nurse in Canada had received a separation allowance to 2 November 1944.[100]

Attention shifted to the clause in Circular 356 stating that only nurses not currently employed in their profession were eligible for separation allowances. Eaton took the position that this clause should be interpreted to mean any nurse not employed in a hospital, since

NSS officials had turned down applications for the allowance from several private-duty nurses seeking full-time positions in hospitals. The CNA, however, immediately condemned any offer of funds to private duty nurses that was not also available to general duty nurses. This could only have the effect of creating friction among hospital nurses.[101] In December, Eaton issued a second circular reducing the minimum employment period from six months to two months for any nurse seeking to claim the allowance. Despite this measure, however, she was eventually forced to concede that the worth of the entire supplementary allowance scheme had been "extremely limited," because it had not been possible to target a large number of nurses.[102]

The August 1944 proposal to regulate private-duty nurses also failed. CNA officials demanded that the need for such a restrictive regime be "thoroughly demonstrated" before regulations were put into effect.[103] A draft of the rules called for the amendment of Section 207 of PC 246 in six key respects, affecting all nurses who had completed their training since 31 August 1942. Henceforth, it was proposed, no nurse could engage in private-duty nursing without a permit; no one could employ a nurse in a private-duty position without seeing the permit; an NSS officer could set conditions regarding the place and duration of private-duty employment; an NSS officer could cancel or extend the permit of a nurse at any time; no person could employ a private-duty nurse after the expiration of the permit; and no private-duty nurse could continue private-duty nursing once the permit expired. These were stiff proposals, but, faced with the usual pressure from the CNA, NSS did not enact them. In March 1945, Eaton had admitted that NSS had a failed record with respect to the regulation of nurses. Arthur MacNamara offered this remarkable response in denying her request that NSS reconsider imposing the restrictions on private-duty nursing: "I think we should try to avoid justification for criticism [for not imposing private duty restrictions] on the ground that we knew of the shortage and knew that it was going to get worse *yet we did nothing about it.*"[104]

For the remainder of the war, the positions of the CNA, the CHC, and NSS remained true to form. Nurses continued to vehemently oppose any proposal to centralize control of nurses in the hands of NSS. M.A. Gibson of Regina informed Eaton that the "severe condemnation" of nurses in many publications was completely unwarranted and that the failure of the Dominion government to improve funding to hospitals was the primary reason for the nursing crisis.[105] Even after being informed that there was a surplus of nurses in some Ontario cities, such as Windsor, Eaton steadfastly refused to countenance NSS involvement in the situation; "no consideration" was being given to the compulsory transfer of nurses from a surplus area to a shortage area and NSS took "no responsibility" for stemming the flow of nurses into industrial nursing.[106] The CHC continued to show lukewarm support for the cherished NSS idea of increasing the number of nursing aides. Provincial hospital councils were canvassed to see how many aides could be profitably employed, but Harvey Agnew noted in March 1945 that early replies "cast some doubt on the desirability of putting too much effort on this proposed development."[107]

In May 1945, Eaton reported to MacNamara that the CNA was "no longer reluctant" to co-operate with NSS. While admitting that the nursing situation still had the "emergency quality which is disappearing from other employment situations affecting women,"[108] she claimed in July 1945 that her office had done a "good deal" to improve matters. The government should "get out of the picture fairly soon" and leave all re-adjustment problems to the CNA.[109] This position belied the evidence flooding into NSS offices of a continuing crisis, with Toronto hospitals alone needing 204 nurses.[110] As it became clear that the war was ending, moreover, a new problem arose when many married nurses left hospital employment in anticipation of the discharge of their spouses from the armed forces. In a November 1945 comment on this particular situation, Eaton claimed that NSS had "exhausted all means" to address nursing shortages during the war but the agency no longer had any role to play in the post-war era.[111]

9 A Recapitulation

In January 1944, Gordon Graydon, the Leader of the Opposition gave the House of Commons an assessment of the government's effort to mobilize troops and workers for essential industries and services. Graydon claimed that National Selective Service had justly earned for itself the title of "Canada's greatest wartime muddle".

Despite the optimism of the Minister of Labour, the operation and administration of National Selective Service has been a bitter and disillusioning experience for the Canadian people. The government sought and was accorded unlimited powers for the full mobilization of our manpower; they obtained all the necessary – and perhaps some unnecessary – machinery. But they lacked the will and the courage to put it into effective operation at the proper stage of our manpower difficulties.[1]

The case studies examined in Chapters 2 through 8 support Graydon's observations. Broad statutory powers were granted to NSS officials, but a hallmark of the mobilization effort in Canada between 1939 and 1945 was the lack of coordination among government departments involved in the prosecution of the war. NSS, a branch of the Department of Labour, proved to be a convenient, and often justified, target for other departments and agencies with more clout in Cabinet circles.

NSS and the Wartime Prices and Trade Board were the agencies primarily responsible for Canada's domestic war effort. Donald Gordon and other WPTB officials within the Department of Finance clearly towered over NSS administrators. For example, Gordon led the charge in the autumn of 1942 against NSS director Elliot Little's plan for a comprehensive armed forces mobilization strategy. Moreover, WPTB opposition to the limited curtailment options proposed by NSS officials effectively crippled NSS civilian labour force policies. Between the two agencies responsible, in theory, for the maintenance of essential civilian production and the provision of labour to the same vital industries, the only effective link was through the Inter-departmental Labour Priorities Committee, but this link was not very strong. G.G.E. Raley's attempt to guarantee a constant supply of women workers to textile plants, for example, was ineffective because of the determined opposition he faced from ILPC Chairman Sheldon Ross.

Strong regional control of the mobilization process also character-ized NSS supervision of the war effort. By January 1944, much of the civilian mobilization effort was statutorily devolved to Regional Advisory Boards; this complemented the dominance of Registrars and Mobilization Boards within the National Resources Mobilization Act conscription scheme. It remains the most compelling example of the de-centralized execution of mobilization policy in Canada. Registrars and Mobilization Board chairmen were responsible for the patchwork of policies affecting the call-up of Natives. Vancouver Mobilization Board chair Justice A.M. Manson's opposed virtually every NSS initiative to maintain viable university enrolment totals in essential disciplines or to staff essential industries. Manson and his colleagues on Mobilization Boards across the country destroyed any goodwill existing between NSS and industrial officials involved with the Industrial Mobilization Survey Plan and played a key role in its failure. Repeated government studies illustrated that Divisional Registrars were not capable of handling the enormous logistical task involved in processing men for NRMA service.

A lax regulatory approach is a third striking feature of the history of NSS. The withdrawal of hundreds of thousands of men and women from the workforce for military service created acute labour supply shortages across the country. Since NSS officials were either unable or unwilling to curtail non-essential industry, chaos existed in many critical sectors of the Canadian economy. In the case of meatpacking, no concerted or forward-looking plans were formulated. Instead, a series of frantic and often unsuccessful initiatives was augmented with a dependence on seasonal agricultural workers and military personnel. The problem of separations bedevilled NSS attempts to bring a semblance of order to the civilian labour force. Although Little's successor as NSS director, Arthur MacNamara, and other NSS administrators recognized this problem, few measures were enacted to enforce existing

NSS regulations to combat labour turnover. Even when NSS statutory authority was strong, as in the case of coal miners and longshoremen, day-to-day administration tended to be half-hearted. Because NSS control did not extend to the distribution of men within each coal company, its recruitment effort did not increase bituminous coal production. Only the provision of a paid reserve pool of labour and the relatively limited size of the longshore labour force allowed NSS officials to be successful in increasing the cargo capacity of Halifax.

A fourth, and final, challenge to the implementation of NSS goals relates to NSS collaboration with non-government structures. The National Conference of Canadian Universities and the Canadian Nurses Association provided autonomous administrative structures that NSS could use as quasi-mobilization agencies. Armed with sanctioned government demands, MacNamara went to the critical NCCU conference in August 1943 – and promptly capitulated to NCCU proposals sharply different from the original NSS proposal for a comprehensive re-structuring of student deferment schemes. Similarly, NSS acquiesced to the CNA demands for professional autonomy and allowed nursing representatives to dictate the pace of domestic nursing mobilization. NSS was reduced to an advertising and survey body trying to cajole women with nursing credentials to alleviate pressing shortfalls in Canadian hospital staffs.

At the same time, NSS had a great capacity for gathering information. One is struck in examining the NSS archival collection by the enormous effort expended to study a sweeping range of mobilization problems. Strenuous efforts to consult a wide range of government and non-government agencies and organizations were undertaken. These extraordinarily revealing statistical compilations and comprehensive consultation efforts were rarely incorporated into strategies designed to mobilize the Canadian population in an effective manner. The Industrial Mobilization Survey Plan is a striking illustration. NSS officials completely ignored six months of effort expended tabulating the Coal Labour Survey. Statistical surveys of the nursing profession were not followed by measures to mobilize inactive nurses to alleviate general-duty nursing shortages.

It must be remembered that there was extraordinary opposition to even limited mobilization from many sectors of the Canadian population. The absence of a nationwide surge of unselfish patriotism among all sectors affected by NSS operations partly explains the limited achievements of the agency. Sectors of the Native community drew on centuries of resentment to non-Native authority and actively opposed the compulsory mobilization of Canadian Indians. Although the NCCU established an amicable relationship with government authorities, five years of the war had expired before comprehensive measures to limit enrolment in non-essential academic disciplines were proposed. Strident union opposition to labour controls was evident in the coal and longshore labour sectors. Thousands of women took advantage of lucrative employment options in non-traditional employment sectors to separate from textile employment, a movement that involved NSS administrators in a three-year, unsuccessful, struggle to augment payrolls in the primary textile field. The nursing profession waged a strong campaign against government intringement upon the autonomy of the CNA. Owners and managers of manufacturing plants jealously guarded their payroll complements and fought to limit the impact of the IMSP, which was designed to withdraw medically fit men from the civilian workforce and conscript them for military service.

The study of archival documents relating to NSS and human resource mobilization policy offers a new perspective on Canada's role in World War II. It challenges the dominant view that extols the virtues of Mackenzie King's handling of the manpower question. Indeed, conventional viewpoints that praise King as the "master chemist" in relation to the manpower problem must be reconsidered.[2] The crucial Cabinet decisions to dramatically expand Canada's overseas army in January 1942 and, paradoxically, to emasculate NSS Director Elliot Little's plans for a national curtailment and labour mobilization strategy were made when the ultimate Allied victory was but a distant speck on the horizon. Although his political instincts were unmatched, King took a calculated gamble in 1942 that Canada would indeed be able to muddle through the human resource dilemmas facing the country without resorting to comprehensive mobilization strategies. The margin for error was razor-thin, however, and any significant Allied setback in the Mediterranean or European theatres in 1943 or 1944 could have precipitated a political crisis in Canada matching the tumultuous events of 1917 and 1918.

Furthermore, historians of the 1944 manpower crisis have pointed to external shocks such as wastage rates and replacement shortfalls as the factors behind the derailment of an otherwise comprehensive and well-orchestrated mobilization program. The 1944 manpower situation and King's ultimate reversal on conscription, however, were the direct results of domestic mobilization policies that were rooted in the concepts of gradualism and voluntarism. In the autumn of 1942, King chose to emulate Pilate and washed his hands of any responsibility to enact thorough manpower strategies. This decision effectively crippled Arthur MacNamara and NSS, who could not possibly respond to the manpower demands of the NRMA and surging war industries in a coordinated or effective fashion while the civilian economy remained virtually unaffected by the war. This study, therefore, complements a growing body of scholarship that highlights a decidedly mediocre record of military and civilian endeavours during World War II.[3]

The appraisal of NSS mobilization policy offered here also complements micro-studies of Canada's war effort that focus on the sensitive issues of race, gender, and ethnicity. In particular, it allows further light to be shed on the wartime experience of women. It is a telling sign of the embryonic nature of Canadian social history that Ruth Roach Pierson's pioneering study, published in 1986, remains the principal account of the role of women in society between 1939 and 1945. Only Diane Forestell has stepped forward to question some of Pierson's conclusions.[4] The case studies dealing with primary textile workers and nurses are significant additions to Pierson's narrative since she devotes only marginal portions of her work to these topics. The range of case studies presented here broadens our understanding of the interaction of the government with the Canadian population.

The wartime record of NSS sheds light on the development of the Canadian state during the war and in the postwar era. NSS mobilization policies dominated by Mackenzie King's philosophies of gradualism and compromise aptly characterize Canada's postwar development. In the first two decades following 1945, Canada developed neither a comprehensive and centralized government administrative system nor a prominent alliance among government, business, and military interests. A series of judicious social initiatives such as family allowances allowed a succession of Liberal and Conservative governments to cautiously support a limited but visible role for the federal state before 1970. The Department of Labour itself emerged from the war as a superministry. But its function, building on its wartime heritage, was largely as a monitoring agency in the fields of labour relations and industrial standards rather than as an activist regulatory agency seeking to develop a national manpower policy. Indeed, when the federal government actively intervened in the labour market again during the 1960s, control of human resource policy was stripped from the Department of Labour and vested in new administrative bodies.

Finally, a history of NSS offers insights into the nature of leadership in the Canadian government during the war years and in the postwar era. In contrast to nationally prominent centralizers and planners in such agencies as the Departments of Finance and Reconstruction, Arthur MacNamara is perhaps a more appropriate person to highlight as the quintessential government planner shaping wartime and postwar policy in Canada.[5] While there can be no doubt that the war allowed a group of skilled intellectuals to achieve prominence in the administration of government affairs, the commitment of most "Ottawa men" to a planned and centralized national government was not unequivocal. Cautious, deliberate, flexible, and often ineffective initiatives such as those endorsed and adopted by NSS officials were the rule and not the exception in government circles during World War II and the years following 1945.

Obviously, therefore, there is much that is questionable in previous assumptions about mobilization policy in Canada during the Second World War. But Michael Bliss is also incorrect when he asserts that the war effort was "not a triumph of organization and intelligence, but rather a riot of irrationality and mismanagement, waste, and savagery."[6] Doug Owram offers a more balanced analysis when he notes that government bureaucrats like MacNamara "may have been good managers, but they were not magicians and their theories were not the key to the promised land."[7] In the end, MacNamara's fundamental belief in conciliation, voluntarism, and compromise combined with an inherent weakness in the administrative capacity of the Canadian state to allow opponents of a radical and coercive mobilization agenda to carry the day in wartime Canada.

Notes

INTRODUCTION

1 See Granatstein and Hitsman, *Broken Promises*, 188–204, and Stacey, *Arms, Men, and Governments*, 409–12, for the best account to date of NSS. The information used by these historians was culled mainly from the records of the Department of National Defence and from Orders-in-Council. The main body of information on NSS activities, however, is to be found in the records of the Department of Labour. Works by scholars such as Pierson and Socknat deal with specific issues under the jurisdiction of NSS and make only limited use of the available archival material. See Pierson, *"They're Still Women After All"* and Socknat, *Witness Against War*. Books dealing with the conscription issue – and usually emphasizing Mackenzie King's brilliant handling of the crisis – include Granatstein's magisterial account, *Canada's War*, Burns, *Manpower in the Canadian Army, 1939–45*, Dawson, *The Conscription Crisis of 1944*, Hutchison, *The Incredible Canadian*, and Nolan, *King's War*.
2 See Granatstein and Hitsman, *Broken Promises*, 192–3; Granatstein and Neary, *The Good Fight*, 10.
3 Excellent accounts of the Cabinet manpower debates concerning the size of the Canadian Army can be found in Stacey, *Arms, Men, and Governments*, Part I; Stacey, *Six Years of War*, Chapter III, and Wilson, "Close and Continuous Attention."
4 A copy of this report and correspondence relating to it can be found in NA, RG 27, Records of the Department of Labour, Volume 987: files 8–9–74 pts. 1–3.

5   NA, MG 27 III B11, Ralston Papers, Volume 113, file "Military Manpower vs. Manpower for War Production" – Howe to Ralston, 11 July 1942.

6   NA, MG 27 III B11, Volume 112, file "Army Program, 1942–1943" – Appendix D of Memorandum on Manpower Requirements, 2 July 1942.

7   It is a telling sign of Mitchell's standing in the government that his department, which was in theory responsible for the equitable distribution of human resources between Howe and Ralston, was never included in the membership of the Cabinet War Committee. Mackenzie King welcomed Mitchell into the Cabinet in 1941 with high hopes that he would buttress Liberal support among trade unionists, especially those affiliated with the Trades and Labour Congress, which he had led for many years. By the end of 1942, however, his habit of equivocation meant that Mitchell had expended his political capital with King and he remained an ineffectual member of Cabinet for the duration of the war. See Pickersgill, *The Mackenzie King Record Volume 1*, 310–11.

8   Little was the president of Anglo-Canadian Pulp and Paper Mills Ltd. in Quebec, a university educated electrical engineer, and a veteran of the Royal Air Force in World War I. Little's penchant for confrontation when combined with his no-nonsense manner quickly earned him the animosity of most members of the Cabinet. Grant Dexter of the *Winnipeg Free Press* noted that Little knew nothing about how to work in Ottawa, while Mackenzie King regarded Little as "something of a blatherskite." See Gibson and Robertson, eds., *Ottawa at War*, 369, 378.

9   NA, RG 2, Records of the Cabinet, Series 7c, Volume 10, Cabinet War Committee Minutes, 17 September 1942.

10 NA, MG 27 III B11, Volume 113, file "Manpower, volume 1" – Cabinet War Committee document 34, 26 November 1941.

11 *Toronto Globe and Mail*, 20 August 1942, 1.

12 NA, MG 27 III B11, Volume 114, file "Manpower, volume 2" – Undated Memorandum on Manpower Submitted by Director of National Selective Service.

13 Ibid.

14 NA, RG 2, Series 7c, Volume 10 – Cabinet War Committee Minutes, 23 September 1942, and Cabinet War Committee Document 291, 22 September 1942.

15 Pickersgill, *The Mackenzie King Record*, 446.

16 The best account of the curtailment debate between the WPTB and NSS can be found in Waddell, "The Wartime Prices and Trade Board," chapter 5.

17 See Gibson and Robertson, *Ottawa at War*, 384–5.

18 NA, RG 27, Volume 974, file 2 NSS Curtailment of Industry, Heeney to Ilsley, 29 September 1942.

19 Ibid., NSS Statement of Civilian Curtailment Policy.

20 Gibson and Robertson, *Ottawa at War*, 369.

21 *Winnipeg Free Press*, 8 August 1950.

22 Gibson and Robertson, *Ottawa at War*, 411–12.

23 NA, RG 27, Volume 1518, file R8 part 2 – Labour Supply and Curtailment in the Pulp and Paper Industry, Mitchell to MacNamara, 31 May 1943.

24 *Canadian Unionist* 17, no. 10 (March 1944), 250.

25 See *Labour Gazette* (April 1942), 402–3.

26 The best account of the poor record of government intervention in the labour market is Struthers' *No Fault of Their Own*. For a good account of the Dominion-Provincial Youth Training Program, see Pierson, *"They're Still Women After All"*, Chapter 2.

27 When selecting the case studies for inclusion in this study, no attempt has been made to cull a limited number of failed NSS initiatives to bolster a pre-conceived notion of the effectiveness of NSS efforts. NSS records themselves are organized on a case-study basis and there are roughly fifteen case studies for which a complete run of records exist. Several case studies also highlight NSS mobilization successes. Finally, most case studies deal with large sectors of the workforce or highlight specific features or characteristics of the NSS regulatory effort.

CHAPTER ONE

1 NA, RG 27, Volume 3003, file A – MacNamara, Deputy Minister of Labour, 1943–45, McLaren to MacNamara, 14 September 1943.

2 Granatstein and Hitsman, *Broken Promises*, 142–3.

3 NA, RG 35(7), Volume 19, file Report on Operations of National Registration and Military Mobilization During World War II – "Report on the Operations of National Registration and Military Mobilization in Canada During World War II," 9–23.

4 Ibid., 51. Men aged thirty-eight and over, in fact, were never called.

5 NA, RG 27, Volume 3018, file Orders-in-Council, National War Service Regulations, 1940 (Recruits).

6 "Report on the Operations of National Registration and Military Mobilization in Canada During World War II," 33–7.

7 Stacey, *Arms, Men, and Governments*, 406.

8 "Report on the Operation of National Registration and Military Mobilization in Canada During World War II," 101–9.

9 NA, RG 27, Volume 1493, file 2–270–3 pt. 1; file 2–270 pt. 2 – Circular Memorandum 897, 11 August 1943, and Circular Memorandum 901, 20 August 1943; Circular Memorandum 907, 3 September 1943.

10 W.R. Feasby, *The Official History of the Canadian Medical Services, 1939–1945, Volume I: Organization and Campaigns* (Ottawa: Queen's Printer, 1956), 498–507.

11 NA, RG 27, Volume 2350, file 94 – Circular Memorandum 986, 23 February 1944.

12 "Report on the Operations of National Registration and Military Mobilization in Canada During World War II," 111–19. Less than 30 per cent of Canada's population lived in Quebec in 1945. See *Canada Yearbook, 1950* (Ottawa: King's Printer, 1950), xvii.

13 Ibid., 84–85, 90.

14 The Hooper Holmes Bureau was authorized through Order-in-Council PC 2238 of 22 March 1943 to attempt to find and report on draft evaders. Of 92,774 cases referred to all civilian reporting agencies between 13 September 1943 and 3 June 1944, information was received on 46,022 individuals. The total number of cases reported on by police during this period was 52,066. See NA, RG 27, Volume 1479, file 2–117–10 pt. 3–Hooper Holmes Bureau, "Tracing."

15 *Montreal Gazette*, 21 April 1941, 1, 6.

16 *Montreal Star*, 6 May 1941, 3, 12.

17 NA, RG 27, Volume 1497, file 2-E-50-D-1 pt. 3 – LaFlèche to Thorson, 25 June 1941.

18 See *Montreal Journal*, 12 June 1941; *Montreal Star*, 12 June 1941, 3, 32; *Montreal Star*, 13 June 1941, 3, 6; *Montreal Gazette*, 14 June 1941, 17, 23, and *Montreal Gazette*, 10 December 1941, 8. Tarte eventually volunteered for active service in lieu of jail time, while all the Syrian-Canadians charged in the case pleaded guilty.

19 *Halifax Chronicle*, 9 February 1943, 8.

20 NA, MG 27 III B11, Volume 116, file "Manpower Shortages in the Armed Forces," – Riley to MacNamara, 5 July 1943.

21 NA, RG 27, Volume 3003, file unlabelled, Unsigned, undated memo – "National Registration Activities in Relation to Mobilization."

22 NA, RG 27, Volume 1485, file 2–146–10 – NSS Examination of Mobilization Records, Ballantyne to McLaren, 31 March 1945, and MacNamara to Ranger, 23 June 1945, 8.

23 *Halifax Chronicle*, 30 December 1942, 8.

24 An excellent, brief account of Embury and his actions can be found in Stan Hanson and Don Kerr, "Pacifism, Dissent, and the University of Saskatchewan, 1938–1944," *Saskatchewan History* 45, no. 2 (Fall, 1993), 3–14.

25 *Regina Leader-Post*, 26 November 1943, 1.

26 *Ottawa Journal*, 14 December 1943, 7.

27 *Regina Leader-Post*, 2 December 1943, 1, 19.

28 NA, RG 27, Volume 3003, file Statistics and Reports on National Registration – "The Canadian Manpower Situation."

29 NA, RG 35(7), Volume 19, file National Employment Service – "History of the National Employment Service, 1939 to December 1945," 2–3.

30 NA, RG 35(7), Volume 19, file Development of NSS During World War II, "The Development of the National Selective Service Civilian Organization in World War II to December 31, 1945," 3–4.

31 NA, RG 27, Volume 1484, file 2–141 pt. 3 – NWS National Labour Supply Council, Circular Memorandum 826, 28 March 1943.

32 NA, RG 35(7), Volume 19, file Development of NSS During World War II – "The Development of the National Selective Service Civilian Organization in World War II to December 31, 1945," 6.

33 NA, RG 27, Volume 968, file 4 – NSS Field Organization and Activities of Employment Service Division, "Field Organization – Employment Service."

34 An excellent and detailed analysis of the labour priority system can be found in NA, RG 35(7), Volume 19, file Labour Priority System, "Labour Priorities."

35 NA, RG 27, Volume 1514, file O-11 – NSS Inter-Departmental Priority Committee, Ross to Phelan, 16 March 1946.

36 The nine major divisions were: Division A – Agriculture; Division B – Fishing, Forestry, and Trapping; Division C – Mining; Division D – Manufacturing; Division E – Construction; Division F – Public Utilities Operation; Division G – Retail and Wholesale Trade; Division H – Finance, Industry, and Real Estate; and Division I – Service.

37 Granatstein and Hitsman, *Broken Promises*, 202.

38 Correspondence concerning the administration of the seven Compulsory Transfer Orders can be found in NA, RG 27, Volume 988, files 1–11–12–1, 1–11–12–2, 1–11–12–3, 1–11–12–4, 1–11–12–5, 1–11–12–6, and 1–11–12–7.

39 NA, RG 27, Volume 3003, file Statistics and Reports on National Registration – "Report on Transfer of Labour Under Compulsory Employment Orders 1–7 Inclusive to February 15, 1945."

40 NA, RG 27, Volume 988, file 1–11–12–8 – NSS Compulsory Employment Order No. 8, Ross to Hereford, 12 September 1944.

41 NA, RG 27, Volume 968, file 2 – NSS Statistics, "Statistics."

42 NA, RG 27, Volume 988, file 1–11–8 – NSS Circular 282, 16 September 1943.

43 While NSS officials acknowledged the severity of labour turnover, they refused to commission comprehensive studies to examine the causes of separations. See NA, RG 27, Volume 982, file 13 – NSS Labour Turnover, "Labour Turnover"; NA, RG 27, Volume 1514, file O-8 – NSS Labour Turnover in Canada, "The Problem of Labour Turnover from the Point of View of the War Effort."

44 The labour demand figures in this table should be viewed with caution. Women were not included in the August and September 1943 figures. Moreover, the totals for the period November 1944 to the end of the

war include skilled and semi-skilled loggers, a category separated from the male labour demand totals. It is unclear if the demand statistics before this date include loggers in the male totals. Finally, and most importantly, the labour demand totals do not include those men and women referred to employment who had not secured employment. A rough calculation shows that approximately 20 per cent of the labour vacancies had potential employees referred to them.

45 NA, RG 27, Volume 971, file 4 – NSS Administration Board, Minutes of the NSS Administration Board, 16 May 1944.

46 NA, RG 27, Volume 974, file 2 – NSS Curtailment of Industry, Ross to Hereford, 9 June 1944.

47 NA, RG 27, Volume 3005, file Miscellaneous – Saunders to MacNamara, 24 November 1944.

48 NA, RG 35(7), Volume 19, file History of the National Employment Service to December, 1950 – "History of the National Employment Service to December, 1945," 26–7.

49 NA, RG 27, Volume 605, file 6–24–1 pt. 3 – Employment of Women, NSS Circular 379, 11 May 1945.

50 NA, RG 27, Volume 988, file 1–11–12 – Department of Labour News Release, 17 August 1945.

51 NA, RG 27, Volume 984, file 2 – NSS Manpower, General, Undated, undirected memo of Arthur MacNamara.

52 *Vancouver Province*, 20 March 1945, 1–2. The War Industries Coordination Committee in British Columbia, a coalition of personnel directors and business executives, insisted that "the natural laws of supply and demand" would govern the labour force in the postwar era. Business groups in Montreal and Toronto also rejected any comprehensive federal control of the labour market once the war ended.

53 NA, RG 35(7), Volume 19, file Labour Priority System – "Labour Priorities," 39.

CHAPTER TWO

1 *Winnipeg Free Press*, 3 August 1943, 11.

2 See Titley, *A Narrow Vision* for a good discussion of Indian policy in Canada between 1913 and 1932. A harsher evaluation of government policy towards Native Canadians can be found in Shewell, "Origins of Contemporary Indian Social Welfare in the Canadian Liberal State." General scholarly accounts of the history of Native Canadians tend to ignore the issue of conscription. Olive Dickason's and J.R. Miller's excellent surveys each devote a single sentence to Canadian Indian military participation in the Second World War. More specialised narratives dealing with the experience of Native Canadians between

1939 and 1945 have been written by Fred Gaffen, Janet Frances
Davison, and Janice Summerby. See Dickason, *Canada's First Nations:
A History of Founding People's From Earliest Times* (Norman: Univer-
sity of Oklahoma Press, 1992), 328–9; Miller, *Skyscrapers Hide the
Heavens* (Toronto: University of Toronto Press, 1989), 220–1; Gaffen,
Forgotten Soldiers (Penticton: Theytus Books, 1985); Davison, "'We
Shall Remember': Canadian Indians and World War II," (M.A. Thesis,
Trent University, 1992); and Summerby, *Native Soldiers, Foreign Bat-
tlefields* (Ottawa, 1993). See also *Report of the Royal Commission on
Aboriginal Peoples, volume 1: Looking Forward Looking Back*
(Ottawa, 1996), Chapter 12.

3 This is the official recorded estimate of Indian participation in the war
effort. Unofficial estimates of Native participation reach as high as
6,000. See *Report of the Department of Mines and Resources, 1946*
(Ottawa, 1946), 195; Dickason, *Canada's First Nations*, 329.

4 The accounts by Gaffen, Davison, and Summerby are limited in scope
and focus on the heroism and bravery of a small number of overseas
volunteers who served in the military during the war. These three individuals did not consult the records of the DNWS and NSS contained in
the Dominion Department of Labour archival collection. Their use of
Indian Affairs Branch records within the Department of Mines and
Resources archival collection is, in my opinion, selective and not
representative of the general thrust of these documents.

5 A dispute arose immediately concerning the registration of Natives.
T.R.L. MacInness originally informed all Indian Agents on 6 August
1940 that Natives were not required to register, but this decision was
reversed when it was discovered that many Indians were being denied
employment because they did not carry a registration card. A circular
letter addressed to all Indian Agents was distributed on 4 September 1940
asking all Agents to supervise the registration on reserves. NA, RG 10,
Records of the Department of Mines and Resources, Volume 6770, file
War 1939, Correspondence Regarding National Registration of Indians,
1941–1945, part 2, MacInness to Agents, 4 September 1940.

6 NA, RG 27, Volume 1485, file 2–15–3, part 1, McDonell to LaFlèche,
30 September 1940.

7 Ibid., LaFlèche to McDonell, 2 October 1940.

8 Ibid., Picard and Vincent to Gardiner, 14 October 1940.

9 Ibid., Indian Affairs Branch to Bastien, 25 October 1940. This reminder
reinforced a circular letter from MacInness to all Agents that Natives
were subject to DNWS regulations. See NA, RG 10, Volume 6768,
file 452–20, part 4, MacInness to Agents, 28 September 1940.

10 NA, RG 27, Volume 1485, file 2–15–3, part 1, Gros-Louis to Department
of National Defence, 4 November 1940.

11 Ibid., Picard and Vincent to DND, 12 November 1940.
12 Ibid., Drouin to LaFlèche, 7 December 1940.
13 Ibid., Sioui to Drouin, 30 December 1940.
14 Ibid., Elliot to LaFlèche, 19 October 1940.
15 NA, RG 10, Volume 6768, file 452–20, part 4, Devlin to MacInness, 2 October 1940; Randle to MacInness, 21 November 1940.
16 *Montreal Daily Star*, 17 January 1941, 32.
17 NA, RG 27, Volume 1485, file 2–15–3, part 1, Savard to Davis, 7 January 1941.
18 Ibid., LaFlèche to All Divisional Registrars and Chairmen, 30 January 1941.
19 NA, RG 27, Volume 1485, file 2–15–3, part 1, Benoît to Irwin, 28 March 1941.
20 Ibid., Edwards to King, with copies to Lapointe and Ralston, 26 April 1941.
21 Ibid., LaFlèche to Edwards, 6 May 1941.
22 Ibid., Edwards to Heeney, 16 May 1941.
23 Ibid., Heeney to Thorson, 25 June 1941.
24 Ibid., George to Davis, 7 July 1941.
25 Ibid., Plaxton & Company to Irwin, 7 July 1941.
26 Ibid., Edwards to Benoît, 30 July 1941.
27 Ibid., McIsaac to Whitecourt Postmaster, 24 June 1941; Whitecourt Postmaster to McIsaac, 27 June 1941; McIsaac to LaFlèche, 8 July 1941.
28 NA, RG 10, Volume 6769, file 452–20–4, Garton to District Officer Commanding, 17 February 1943. For an excellent account of the testimony affecting Canada's Native population before the Special Committee, see Shewell, "Origins of Contemporary Indian Social Welfare in the Canadian Liberal State," 372–93.
29 NA, RG 27, Volume 1485, file 2–15–3, part 1, MacInness to Benoît, 20 November 1941.
30 Ibid., Pennock to Benoît, 25 November 1941.
31 As late as December 1941, Dr. J.R. Hurtubise, the M.P. for Nipissing, Ontario, informed DNWS officials that several individuals from the Nipissing Reservation had contacted his office concerning their liability for military service. See ibid., Hurtubise to LaFlèche, 18 December 1941.
32 NA, RG 27, Volume 1485, file 2–15–3, part 1, McIsaac to Benoît, 10 February 1942.
33 NA, RG 10, Volume 6768, file 452–20, part 4, MacKay to MacInness, 24 April 1942.
34 NA, RG 27, Volume 1485, file 2–15–3, part 1, MacInness to Benoît, 1 June 1942.
35 Ibid., Crandall to Recruiting Representatives, 20 February 1942. Kenora was in the Winnipeg district. The refusal of Winnipeg authorities to

enrol many Native recruits remained a source of contention. Enlistment ratios were lower in Manitoba than in any other province. A rough calculation of Indian recruits to provincial Native population in 1942 (both male and female) reveals the following percentages in descending order: P.E.I.: 6.5 per cent; New Brunswick: 5.5 per cent; Nova Scotia: 3.4 per cent; Saskatchewan: 2.2 per cent; Ontario: 1.8 per cent; Quebec: 0.8 per cent; B.C.: 0.7 per cent; Alberta: 0.5 per cent; Manitoba: 0.3 per cent. Manitoba and Alberta remained on the bottom rungs of the participation ladder for the duration of the war. For Native totals in Armed Forces see *Report of the Department of Mines and Resources, 1942* (Ottawa, 1942), 134. For the provincial breakdown of Indian population, see NA, RG 27, Volume 605, file 6–19–1, Johnson to Robinson, 11 May 1943.

36 NA, RG 27, Volume 1485, file 2–15–3 pt. 1, LaFlèche to All Divisional Registrars and Chairmen, 31 March 1942.

37 Ibid., MacInness to Benoît, 30 June 1942. Indian Affairs Branch officials insisted that the proposal should not exempt Indians, but ensure that in the most remote areas Natives who did not respond to calls "would not be followed by prosecution or other drastic action." Although lists of areas deemed remote were submitted to MacInness for approval, the adoption of this policy within NSS circles did not occur for nearly two years. See NA, RG 10, Volume 6768, file 452–20, part 4, MacInness to Superintendents and Inspectors, 17 April 1942.

38 NA, RG 27, Volume 1485, file 2–15–3, part 1, Benoît to English, 25 August 1942.

39 See NA, RG 27, Volume 1485, file 2–15–3, part 2, MacLean to Ralston, 27 August 1942; Sylliboy to King, 15 October 1942.

40 Ibid., Sioui to Taché, 28 January 1943.

41 Ibid., Armitage to Taché, 1 April 1943.

42 See *Calgary Albertan* 22 June 1943, 8, and NA, RG 10, Volume 6769, file 452–20–10, part 1, Written Decision of Lazure, King vs. Harris Smallfence, 21 June 1943.

43 NA, RG 10, Volume 6769, file 452–20–4, Garton to Winnipeg District Officer Commanding, 17 February 1943.

44 NA, RG 27, Volume 1485, file 2–15–3, part 2, Adamson to MacNamara, 25 February 1943.

45 Ibid., Henry to MacNamara, 1 March 1943; MacNamara to Adamson, 1 March 1943.

46 Ibid., Adamson to MacNamara, 4 March 1943.

47 Ibid., Edwards to Taché, 31 March 1943.

48 Ibid., Kay to Taché, 7 February 1943.

49 Ibid., Harris to Taché, 31 May 1943; Taché to Harris, 3 June 1943, McLaren to Jackson, 21 July 1943; and Jackson to McLaren, 31 July 1943.

50 Many Natives did help with timber and agriculture harvests on the
    Prairies. More than 4,000 Indians, for example, were recruited for the
    harvest period in the autumn of 1944. See NA, RG 27, Volume 605,
    file 6–19–1, Morris to Greenwood, 2 December 1944.

51 NA, RG 27, Volume 1485, file 2–15–3, part 3, Henry to All Chairmen
    and Divisional Registrars, 31 August 1943. Much of the material for
    this circular came from a Department of Mines and Resources circular
    that had been sent to all Indian Agents one month earlier. See NA, RG 10,
    Volume 6769, file 452–20–8, MacInness to Indian Agents, 31 July 1943.

52 NA, RG 27, Volume 1485, file 2–15–3, part 3, Harris to Taché,
    13 September 1943.

53 Ibid., Mingo to Henry, 27 September 1943.

54 Ibid., Werry to Camsell, 7 January 1944.

55 *Montreal Standard*, 27 October 1943.

56 NA, RG 10, Volume 6769, file 452–20–10, part 1, Brisebois to McGill,
    2 December 1943.

57 NA, RG 27, Volume 1485, file 2–15–3, part 3, McLaren to Werry,
    14 January 1944.

58 Ibid., Edwards to McLaren, 21 February 1944.

59 Ibid., McLaren to Edwards, 2 February 1944.

60 Ibid., Cummings to Edwards, 28 February 1944.

61 Ibid., Letson to Winnipeg District Officer Commanding, 6 March 1944.

62 The Winnipeg military authorities also refused to enrol Negroes, although
    they, like Indians, were not on a list of racial minorities deemed unac-
    ceptable for military service. Although Arthur MacNamara informed
    Winnipeg Registrar C.D. McPherson, who approved of racial exclusions,
    that this position was "very indefensible," broad discretionary powers
    were given to local military commanders in this area, powers that
    Winnipeg officials chose to exercise. See NA, RG 27, Volume 1486,
    file 2–162–9, McPherson to Henry, 6 December 1943; MacNamara
    to McPherson, 12 January 1944; and HQS 23F.D.3, Enlistments
    and Employment of Aliens and Naturalized Canadian Citizens,
    30 November 1943.

63 NA, RG 27, Volume 1485, file 2–15–3, part 4, Morrison to Officer
    Commanding, Toronto RCMP, 18 November 1943.

64 NA, RG 10, Volume 6769, file 452–20–8, RCMP 'O' Division Circular,
    22 November 1943.

65 NA, RG 27, Volume 1485, file 2–15–3, part 4, Matters to Indian Affairs
    Branch, 15 February 1944.

66 Harold McGill, Deputy Superintendent of the Indian Affairs Branch,
    was shocked at this development. He pointed out that the DMR circu-
    lar of 31 July 1943 and NSS Circular Memorandum 905 urged all
    Indian agents "to take all necessary measures to see that the Indians

complied with the regulations," and demanded to know why the policy had been abandoned. See NA, RG 10, Volume 6769, file 452–20–8, McGill to Ranger, 30 May 1944.

67 Ibid., McLaren to All Chairmen and Registrars, 29 February 1944.

68 NA, RG 27, Volume 1485, file 2–15–3, part 4, Davidson to Ranger, 14 June 1944.

69 Ibid., Wilson to Bjarnason, 24 June 1944.

70 Ibid., McRae to Ranger, 15 August 1944.

71 NA, RG 10, Volume 6769, file 452–20–3, Report from the Kwawkewlth Indian Agency, March 1944.

72 The Indian Affairs Branch and its predecessor before 1936, the Department of Indian Affairs, had a longstanding record of opposition to any attempt by Natives to organize themselves. To stifle opposition to government policy, for example, an amendment to the Indian Act in 1927 forbade Indian bands from employing lawyers or organizations to make claims against the Dominion government. See Titley, *A Narrow Vision*, 59.

73 *Ottawa Journal*, 8 June 1944.

74 For a discussion of the broader political significance of Sioui's efforts, see Shewell, "Origins of Contemporary Indian Social Welfare in the Canadian Liberal State," 394–412.

75 *Le Canada*, 29 September 1944.

76 NA, RG 10, Volume 6769, file 452–20–8, Swartman to MacInness, August 1943.

77 NA, RG 27, Volume 1485, file 2–15–3, part 4, Ranger to Brunet, 19 January 1945.

78 Ibid., J.R. Roy to Brunet, 6 February 1945. It is difficult to document Sioui's activities through all of this. The initial NSS request in April 1943 for Sioui's prosecution to commence appears to have been ignored by officials in Quebec. In August 1943, Harry Hereford, Chief Registrar of Canada, asked the deputy attorney general of Quebec to prosecute Sioui "without delay." It took more than a year. Sioui's case finally went to trial in September 1944. While he appealed his conviction for failing to register, Sioui seemed to remain beyond the reach of the law. Indeed, RCMP officials reported in February 1945 that Sioui helped them locate and serve notice on delinquent Natives at Lorette to avoid being arrested himself. Sioui's appeal of his September 1944 conviction was dismissed on 26 February 1945. At this late stage of the war, prosecution of Native delinquents was being relaxed, and it seems that in the end Sioui never registered with mobilization officials. See NA, RG 27, Volume 1485, file 2–15–3 part 2, Hereford to Desilets, 10 August 1943; NA, RG 27, Volume 1485, file 2–15–3 part 4, Roy to Brunet, 9 February 1945, and Boisvert to Varcoe, 28 February 1945.

79 Ibid., McPherson to McLaren, 21 October 1944.

80 Ibid., Edwards to McLaren, 7 November 1944.

81 Ibid., MacNamara to McLaren, 8 December 1944.

82 NA, RG 10, Volume 6768, file 452–20, part 6, Heeney to Crerar, 26 December 1944.

83 Ibid., Jackson to Hoey, 2 January 1945. The following agencies were affected by the ruling: Treaty 3 – Fort Frances, Kenora, Port Arthur, Sioux Lookout; Treaty 6 – Rocky Mountain House, Saddle Lake, Battleford, Carlton, Duck Lake, Onion Lake, Edmonton, Hobbema; Treaty 8 – Athabaska, Fort St. John, Lesser Slave Lake; Treaty 11 – Fort Norman, Fort Simpson, Fort Resolution. Three hundred and twenty four Natives from these areas had enlisted prior to the Cabinet decision. It does not seem that the actual contents of these treaties formed the basis of the exemption. Instead, "statements made by the Commissioners prior to the making of the treaties" allowed for Indians covered by these treaties to be spared from overseas service, although they did not affect Home Defence call-up provisions. See ibid., Jackson to Heeney, 11 December 1944.

84 NA, RG 27, Volume 1485, file 2–15–3, part 4, McLaren to All Chairmen and Registrars, 1 February 1945.

85 Problems continued on the Caughnawaga Reserve throughout 1944 and well into 1945. On 14 March 1945, Chief Dominic Two Axe informed the Governor General that he would "kill every Mountie that comes on the reservation" in pursuit of draft delinquents, a threat that NSS officials declined to prosecute after considerable discussion. See NA, RG 10, Volume 6769, file 452–20–10, part 1, Two Axe to Governor General, 14 March 1945; Kemp to McGill, 26 May 1945.

86 NA, RG 27, Volume 1485, file 2–15–3, part 4, McLaren to Lyons, 12 February 1945.

87 Ibid., H. Mitchell to Crerar, 24 March 1945.

CHAPTER THREE

1 NA, RG 27, Volume 1482, file 2–133–6 – NSS University Advisory Board, Fennell to MacNamara, 22 July 1944.

2 The literature on universities in Canada during World War II is scant. McKillop, *Matters of Mind: The University in Ontario, 1791–1951* provides a solid chapter on the experience of Ontario universities between 1939 and 1945. Several university histories also deal with student and academic life on campus during wartime, including Gibson *To Serve and Yet Be Free: Queen's University, 1917–1961, vol. 2,* C.M. Johnston and John Weaver, *Student Days: An Illustrated History of Student Life at McMaster University from the 1890s to the 1980s* (Hamilton: McMaster University Alumni Association, 1986), and W.P. Thompson,

Yesteryears at the University of Saskatchewan, 1937–1949 (Saskatoon: University of Saskatchewan, 1969).

3 For an interesting, but limited, study of the NCCU, see Pilkington, "A History of the National Conference of Canadian Universities, 1911–1961," Chapter Five.

4 NA, RG 27, Volume 2–133 pt. 6, University and College Students, Unsigned letter to Maingot, 17 September 1945. There were 8,353 students taking campus military training in 1942, 8,957 in 1943, and 7,183 in 1944.

5 NA, RG 27, Volume 1481, file 2–133 pt. 1 – NWS University and College Students, Magee to LaFlèche, 12 February 1941.

6 Only single men between the ages of 21 and 24 were callable under mobilization regulations at this stage of the war. It was not until March, 1942, that the age liability pool for military service was expanded.

7 *Montreal Gazette*, 4 March 1941, 13–14.

8 NA, RG 27, Volume 1481, file 2–133 pt. 1 – NWS University and College Students, LaFlèche to Gardiner, 7 March 1941.

9 For an account of LaFlèche's undistinguished career during the war, see Granatstein, *The Generals: The Canadian Army's Senior Commanders in the Second World War*, 243–7. For an acerbic critique of LaFlèche from his Cabinet colleagues, see Gibson and Robertson, *Ottawa at War*, 374–5.

10 NA, RG 27, Volume 1481, file 2–133 pt. 1 – NWS University and College Students, LaFlèche to Embury, 29 August 1941.

11 Ibid., Embury to LaFlèche, 23 September 1941.

12 Ibid., Smith Speech Circulated Through NWS Circular Memorandum 339, 30 September 1941.

13 *Toronto Evening Telegram*, 25 September 1941.

14 NA, RG 27, Volume 1498, file 2-E-133 – NWS University and College Students, Division E, LaFlèche to Kay, 24 January 1942.

15 NA, RG 27, Volume 1481, file 2–133 pt. 2 – NWS University and College Students, Read to Ralston, 2 October 1941.

16 Ibid., Ralston to Read, 14 October 1941.

17 NA, RG 27, Volume 1481, file 2–133 pt. 2 – NWS University and College Students, Westman to LaFlèche, 16 December 1941.

18 Ibid., LaFlèche to Westman, 17 December 1941.

19 Ibid., LaFlèche to Kay, 7 January 1942.

20 Ibid., Circular Memorandum 433 – LaFlèche to All Chairmen and Registrars, 20 January 1942; Circular Memorandum 455 – LaFlèche to All Chairmen and Registrars, 12 February 1942.

21 Ibid., Thompson to MacNamara, 10 September 1941.

22 Ontario officials continually thwarted Ottawa's desire for a comprehensive Student Aid Agreement. Ontario did not agree to the schedule to support medical, science, and engineering students until the 1944–5

fiscal year. See NA, RG 27, Volume 701, file Y12–2–6 pt. 8, Marsh to Thompson, 14 April 1942; ibid., Mitchell to MacNamara, 27 April 1942; NA, RG 27, Volume 703, file Y12–2–6 pt. 16, Thompson to Duncan, 15 June 1943; and NA, RG 27, Volume 703, file Y12–2–6 pt. 20, Thompson to MacNamara, 14 March 1944.

23 NA, RG 27, Volume 1481, file 2–133 part 2, Thompson to LaFlèche, 3 February 1942. See also Pilkington, "A History of the National Conference of Canadian Universities, 1911–1961," 321.

24 NA, RG 27, Volume 1482, file 2–133–6 pt. 2 – Conference of Representatives of Universities and Deans of Engineering & Science Faculties, LaFlèche to Benoît, 7 April 1942.

25 Ibid., LaFlèche to Little, 1 May 1942.

26 Ibid., "WBTP Report to the Deputy Minister for the Month of May 1942."

27 Ibid., LaFlèche to Westman, 9 July 1942.

28 *Toronto Star*, 21 July 1942, 1.

29 NA, RG 27, Volume 1481, file 2–133 pt. 2 – NWS University and College Students, LaFlèche to Palmer, 23 July 1942.

30 NA, RG 27, Volume 1482, file 2–133–6 pt. 2 – NWS Conference of Representatives of Universities and Deans of Engineering & Science Faculties, Circular Memorandum 660, LaFlèche to All Chairmen and Divisional Registrars, 12 August 1942.

31 NA, RG 27, Volume 1481, file 2–133 pt. 2 – NWS University and College Students, Benoît to Robertson, 20 August 1942.

32 NA, RG 27, Volume 1482, file 2–134 – NWS Applications for Postponement Orders, Dorey to LaFlèche, 25 March 1941; LaFlèche to Dorey, 28 March 1941.

33 NA, RG 27, Volume 1498: file 2-E-133 – NWS University and College Students, Division E, Benoît to Ranger, 3 June 1941.

34 NA, RG 27, Volume 1481, file 2–133 pt. 2 – NWS University and College Students, Dorey to LaFlèche, 14 November 1942.

35 NA, RG 27, Volume 1496, file 2-B-133 – NWS University and College Students, Division B, Firth to LaFlèche, 29 October 1942.

36 Ibid., LaFlèche to Firth, 3 November 1942.

37 NA, RG 27, Volume 1481, file 2–133 pt. 2 – NWS University and College Students, Taché to Edwards, 20 November 1942.

38 NA, RG 27, Volume 1481, file 2–133 pt. 3 – NWS University and College Students, Circular Memorandum 768, 30 December 1942, MacNamara to All Chairmen and Divisional Registrars.

39 NA, RG 27, Volume 1501, file 2-M-133 – NWS University and College Students, Division M, Embury to LaFlèche, 15 April 1941; LaFlèche to Embury, 18 April 1941.

40 Ibid., Moats to Davis, 4 December 1941.

41 Ibid., Coldwell to Thorson, 5 December 1941.

42 Ibid., Davis to LaFlèche, 9 December 1941.

43 See NA, RG 27, Volume 1501, file 2-M-133 – NWS University and College Students, Division M, Embury to LaFlèche, 18 April 1941; Moats to Davis, 4 December 1941; Coldwell to Thorson, 5 December 1941; Davis to LaFlèche, 9 December 1941; Bickerton to Coldwell, 13 December 1941; Coldwell to Bickerton, 23 December 1941; Embury to LaFlèche, 29 December 1941; LaFlèche to Embury, 5 January 1942; Coldwell to Embury, 20 January 1942; LaFlèche to Embury, 14 March 1942; and Embury to Taché, 4 December 1942.

44 NA, RG 27, Volume 1481, file 2–133 pt. 4 – University and College Students, Fennell to MacNamara, 18 January 1943.

45 An intense debate had been ongoing since the summer of 1942 between government and university officials. Supported by influential press organs such as the *Globe and Mail*, McGill Principal Cyril James and Queen's Principal Robert Wallace proposed that Arts programs at Canadian universities be scaled back. On 9 January 1943, MacNamara addressed a special NCCU meeting and hinted that the time had come for the universities to "ruthlessly weed out the incompetent and mediocre students." He emphasized, however, that any changes in government policy would be made "after full consultation with university authorities." A Wallace motion to force some Arts students into the Armed Forces was defeated. It is interesting to note that academics have emphasized this January 1943 meeting while ignoring the critical August 1943 NCCU convention. See Gibson, *To Serve and Yet Be Free*, 206–12; McKillop, *Matters of Mind*, 531–5, and the *Globe and Mail*, 24 December 1942, 6. Pilkington also devotes 20 pages to the January 1943 NCCU meeting, one of the "most dramatic episodes in the history of Canadian universities," while the critical August 1943 meeting is summarized in a single page. See Pilkington, "A History of the National Conference of Canadian Universities, 1911–1961," pp. 322–343.

46 NA, RG 27, Volume 1481, file 2–133 pt. 3 – NWS University and College Students, Hanson to MacNamara, 16 June 1943.

47 Ibid., Hanson to MacNamara, 22 June 1943.

48 Ibid., Henry to All Divisional Registrars, 23 July 1943. The questionnaire had five categories: 1)Postponement of Students under Section 12 (10) of Mobilization Regulations (five questions); 2)Period of Postponement under Section 12 (7) of Mobilization Regulations (five questions); 3)Prompt Service of Order-Military Training on Students Failing to Pass Term or Yearly Academic Examinations Required under Section 12 (3) (c) of Mobilization Regulations (five questions); 4)Change of Address under Section 6 (12) and Section 6 (14) (six questions); and 5)General Remarks on Administration of Section 12 (one question).

49 Ibid., Responses to 23 July 1943 Questionnaire. All Registrars' responses are contained in this file except for the Toronto Registrar.

50 NA, RG 27, Volume 1482, file 2–133–6 pt 2(a) – NWS Conference of Representatives of Universities and Deans of Engineering & Science Faculties, Henry to All Chairmen, 12 August 1943.

51 See NA, RG 27, Volume 1482, file 2–133–6 pt. 2(a) – NWS Conference of Representatives of Universities and Deans of Engineering & Science Faculties, Henry to All Chairmen, 12 August 1943; Adamson to Henry, 13 August 1943; Manson to Henry, 24 August 1943; Lajoie to Henry, 17 August 1943; and Fortier to Henry, 19 August 1943.

52 Ibid., MacNamara Address to the NCCU, 30 August 1943.

53 NA, RG 27, Volume 1481, file 2–133 pt. 4 – University and College Students, Minutes of a Conference Between Representatives of the Member Institutions of the NCCU and the Director of NSS Held in Ottawa on 30 August 1943. Representatives from the DND, DMS, and WBTP were also present at this conference.

54 See NA, RG 27, Volume 1482, file 2–133–6 pt. 2(a) – NWS Conference of Representatives of Universities and Deans of Engineering & Science Faculties, Brown to MacNamara, 14 September 1943; Riley to MacNamara, 14 September 1943; Sully to MacNamara, 16 September 1943; and MacNamara to Sully, 18 September 1943.

55 Ibid., Smith to MacNamara, 2 September 1943.

56 Ibid., Neville to MacNamara, 25 September 1943.

57 NA, RG 27, Volume 1481, file 2–133 pt. 4 – University and College Students, Secret Circular Memorandum No. 59 Containing Interpretive Letter No. 5, 17 September 1943. Interpretive letters were used to highlight changes in government policy that were not formed on an official statutory basis.

58 NA, RG 27, Volume 1481, file 2–133 pt. 2 – NWS University and College Students, Owens to LaFlèche, 16 November 1942.

59 NA, RG 27, Volume 1481, file 2–133 pt. 5 – University and College Students, Owens to MacNamara, 30 September 1943; MacNamara to Riley, October 5, 1943.

60 Ibid., Owens to King, 18 October 1943.

61 Ibid., MacNamara to Owens, 30 October 1943.

62 NA, RG 27, Volume 1482, file 2–133–6 – NSS University Advisory Board, Minutes of the First Meeting of the University Advisory Board, 6 January 1944. Members of the Board were: 1)Humphrey Mitchell (Minister of Labour); Arthur MacNamara (Director of NSS); Paul Goulet (NSS); S.H. McLaren (NSS); J.C. Fogo (DMS); H.W. Lea (WBTP); Sidney Smith (President, University of Manitoba); H.J. Cody (President, University of Toronto); Monsignor Cyrille Gagnon (Rector, University of Laval); J.S. Thomson (President, University of Saskatchewan); and Paul Beique (Consulting Engineer, Montreal).

63 The eleven disciplines labelled as essential were: Medicine, Dentistry, Engineering or Applied Science, Architecture, Agriculture, Pharmacy, Forestry, Education, Commerce, Veterinary Science, and specialized courses in mathematics, physics, chemistry, biology, and geology.

64 NA, RG 27, Volume 1481, file 2–133 pt. 5 – University and College Students, Secret Circular Memorandum 70 (containing Interpretive Letter No. 7), 10 February 1944.

65 W.P. Thompson, *The University of Saskatchewan: A Personal History* (Toronto: University of Toronto Press, 1970), 129.

66 NA, RG 27, Volume 1481, file 2–133 pt. 6 – University and College Students, Christie to MacNamara, 11 January 1945. All correspondence between Campbell and Manson was included in this letter.

67 Ibid., Manson to Campbell, 25 January 1945.

68 NA, RG 27, Volume 1482, file 2–133–6 – NSS University Advisory Board, Minutes of the 27 November 1944, Meeting of the University Advisory Board.

69 Ibid., Minutes of the 18 January 1945 Meeting of the University Advisory Board. Two other recommendations adopted at this meeting concerned the exclusion of discharged personnel from the proposed stringent regulations concerning students, and the idea that courses which had already been subject to the 50 per cent rule for the 1943–4 session would not be reduced further in numbers.

70 Ibid., Minutes of the 29 May 1945 Meeting of the University Advisory Board. When a proposal to destroy the minutes of the January UAB meeting surfaced, J.S. Thomson of the University of Saskatchewan convinced the Board that "it was certain that a historical record of the part the universities played in the war would be prepared and that all available material would be of value."

71 NA, RG 27, Volume 1481, file 2–133 pt. 6 – University and College Students, MacNamara to Ranger, 12 May 1945.

72 Ibid., Responses from UAB Members to Ranger, May 1945. On 16 May 1945, Ranger had sent these recommendations to UAB members.

73 Ibid., Minutes of the 24 August 1945 Meeting of the University Advisory Board.

CHAPTER FOUR

1 NA, RG 27, Volume 1504, file 10–1–2 pt. 4 – NSS Industrial Mobilization Surveys, Davidson to McLaren, 15 September 1944.

2 NA, RG 27, Volume 974, file 2 – NSS Curtailment of Industry, Adams to Gunn, 14 December 1942.

3 NA, RG 27, Volume 984, file 4 – Manpower Survey Committee, MacNamara to Goldenberg, 11 December 1942; Minutes of Manpower Survey Committee, 21 December 1942; Scott to Goldenberg,

3 February 1943; MacNamara to Scott, 6 February 1943; and Minutes of the Manpower Survey Committee, 20 July 1943.

4 Surveys in the Charlottetown Administrative Division were to be handled by Halifax.

5 An excellent overview of the IMSP is contained in NA, RG 27, Volume 986, file 4 – History of IMS Plans, "History of the Industrial Mobilization Survey Plan."

6 NA, RG 27, Volume 1504, file 10–1–2–2 pt. 2 – NWS MSC Division B, Toronto, Ritchie to MacNamara, 27 September 1943.

7 NA, RG 27, Volume 1503, file 10–1–2 pt. 2 – Industrial Mobilization Survey, Mitchell to Hereford, 18 October 1943.

8 Ibid., Hereford to Mitchell, 27 October 1943.

9 Ibid., Scott to Ambridge, 27 October 1944.

10 Ibid., Nash to MacNamara, 25 October 1943.

11 NA, RG 27, Volume 1504, file 10–1–2–1 pt. 1 – NSS MSC Division A, London, Scott to Sullivan, 28 February 1944; Scott to Thomas, 14 March 1944; Scott to Fogo, 28 February 1944; and Scott to MacNamara, 21 March 1944.

12 NA, RG 27, Volume 1503, file 10–1–2 pt. 2 – Industrial Mobilization Surveys, Nash to MacNamara, 31 August 1943.

13 Ibid., Masson to Scott, 27 August 1943; Westman to MacNamara, 24 September 1943; MacNamara to Nash, 27 September 1943; Westman to MacNamara, 5 October 1943; and Letson to All District Officers Commanding and General Officers in Charge, 15 October 1943.

14 NA, RG 27, Volume 1504, file 10–1–2–2 pt. 1 – NWS MSC Division B, Toronto, Frost to Scott, 10 July 1943.

15 Ibid., Frost to Sullivan, 29 October 1943.

16 NA, RG 27, Volume 984, file 4 – NSS Manpower Survey Committee, Minutes of the Manpower Survey Committee, 20 October 1943.

17 NA, RG 27, Volume 1503, file 10–1–2 pt. 2 – Industrial Mobilization Surveys, MacNamara to Scott, 8 November 1943, and NA, RG 27, Volume 1503, file 10–1–2 pt. 3–Industrial Mobilization Surveys, Scott to Anderson, 5 January 1944.

18 NA, RG 27, Volume 1504, file 10–1–2 pt. 4 – NSS Industrial Mobilization Surveys, Mayall to Gordon, 13 February 1944.

19 Ibid., Fogo to Mitchell, 18 February 1944.

20 NA, RG 27, Volume 1504, file 10–1–2–1 pt. 1 – NSS MSC Division A, London, Thomas to Sharpe, 14 January 1944.

21 NA, RG 27, Volume 1504, file 10–1–2 pt. 4 – NSS Industrial Mobilization Surveys, Thomas to Scott, 14 April 1944.

22 Ibid., Scott to Thomas, 20 April 1944.

23 NA, RG 27, Volume 1505, file 10–1–2–4 pt. 1 – NSS MSC Division E, Montreal, Masson to Scott, 30 July 1943; Prefontaine to Masson, 23 September 1943; and Riley to Ranger, 30 September 1943.

24 NA, RG 27, Volume 1989, file 26–5–2, Ritchie to MacNamara, 31 January 1944.

25 NA, RG 27, Volume 1505, file 10–1–2–7 – NSS MSC Division H, Saint John, Crosbie to Scott, 18 March 1944; Crosbie to Scott, 29 March 1944.

26 Ibid., McIntyre to Roberts, 22 April 1944.

27 NA, RG 27, Volume 1989, file 26–1, George to Scott, 15 April 1944.

28 NA, RG 27, Volume 1503, file 10–1–2 pt. 2 – Industrial Mobilization Surveys, Rutherford to Hereford, 4 October 1943.

29 NA, RG 27, Volume 984, file 4 – NSS Manpower Survey Committee, Minutes of the 4 May 1944 Meeting of the Manpower Survey Committee.

30 NA, RG 27, Volume 1504, file 10–1–2 pt. 4 – NSS Industrial Mobilization Surveys, Scott to MacNamara, 15 May 1944.

31 NA, RG 27, Volume 1989, file 26–5–1, Order No. 19, 8 June 1944; Order No. 20, 8 June 1944.

32 NA, RG 27, Volume 1504, file 10–1–2 pt. 4 – NSS Industrial Mobilization Surveys, Humphrey Mitchell Radio Address, 8 June 1944. Labour unions expressed few reservations about the expansion of the IMSP into civilian plants. Canadian Congress of Labour President A.R. Mosher promised to "cooperate in every way possible and participate to the fullest extent." Trades and Labour Congress President Percy Bengough, however, was less supportive and asked that the government demonstrate the need of the plan before seeking his cooperation. See NA, RG 27, Volume 1504, file 10–1–2 pt. 5 – NSS Industrial Mobilization Surveys, Mosher to MacNamara, 14 July 1944; Bengough to MacNamara, 16 July 1944.

33 See NA, RG 27, Volume 3003 – file Statistics & Reports on National Registration, Manpower, & Employment, "Report on Transfer of Labour Under Compulsory Employment Orders 1–7 Inclusive, Reports to 15 February 1945." The majority of the transfers made under these seven CTOS came in 1943 and early 1944, before the decision to expand the IMSP process.

34 NA, RG 27, Volume 1505, file 10–1–2–6 – NSS MSC Division G, Halifax, Mingo to McLaren, 3 July 1944.

35 Ibid., Mingo to MacNamara, 3 July 1944.

36 Ibid., Scott to MacNamara, 7 July 1944. NSS officials reported repeated problems in their dealings with Mingo. T.C. McIntyre, NSS Regional Employment Officer, reported to Scott on 8 May 1944 that the feeling between Mingo and Army officials was "very bitter" and McLaren reported to MacNamara in December 1944, that NSS "would be better off without this man." See NA, RG 27, Volume 3003, file A. MacNamara, 1943–1945, McIntyre to Scott, 8 May 1944; McLaren to MacNamara, 1 December 1944.

37 NA, RG 27, Volume 1505, file 10–1–2–6 – NSS MSC Division G, Halifax, Saunders to Mingo, 30 June 1944.

38 Ibid., George to Scott, 12 August 1944.
39 Ibid., George to Scott, 23 September 1944. In September 1944, Arnold
    Frame replaced Nicholson as the IMSC Chair in Halifax
40 NA, RG 27, Volume 1504, file 10–1–2–1 pt. 1 – NSS MSC Division A,
    London, Thomas to McFarquar, 7 August 1944.
41 NA, RG 27, Volume 1504, file 10–1–2–2 pt. 3 – NWS MSC Division B,
    Toronto, McDermott to Scott, 27 September 1944.
42 NA, RG 27, Volume 1504, file 10–1–2 pt. 5 – NSS Industrial Mobiliza-
    tion Surveys, MacNamara to Anderson, 7 October 1944.
43 See ibid., Cochrane to MacNamara, 16 October 1944; Kelly to
    MacNamara, [?] October 1944; Harvey to MacNamara, 16 October
    1944, and de Lalanne to MacNamara, 19 October 1944.
44 NA, RG 27, Volume 984, file 4 – NSS Manpower Survey Committee,
    Minutes of the Manpower Survey Committee, 2 November 1944.
45 NA, RG 27, Volume 986, file 4 – History of IMS Plans, "History of
    Industrial Mobilization Survey Plans."
46 NA, RG 27, Volume 1504, file 10–1–2 pt. 6 – NSS Industrial Mobiliza-
    tion Surveys, Scott to Roberts, 6 December 1944.
47 Ibid., Scott to MacNamara, 14 December 1944.
48 NA, RG 27, Volume 1505, file 10–1–2–7 – NSS MSC Division H,
    Saint John, Crosbie to Mooney, 3 November 1944.
49 Ibid., O'Brien to MacNamara, 18 January 1945.
50 It is difficult to gauge the support for the IMSP within the business
    community. On 3 November 1944, Willard Scott told Arthur MacNamara
    that he was sending him more than 200 letters from business owners
    concerning the IMSP. These letters, unfortunately, have been purged
    from NSS files. NA, RG 27, Volume 1504, file 10–1–2 pt. 6 – NSS Indus-
    trial Mobilization Surveys, Scott to MacNamara, 3 November 1944.
51 NA, RG 27, Volume 1504, file 10–1–2–4 pt. 2 – NSS MSC Division E,
    Montreal, Scott to Masson, 12 February 1945; Masson to Scott,
    16 February 1945.
52 NA, RG 27, Volume 1505, file 10–1–2–5 pt. 2 – NSS MSC Division F,
    Quebec City, Masson to Scott, 7 March 1945.
53 Ibid., Scott to Masson, 24 April 1945.
54 Ibid., Masson to Scott, 25 August 1944.
55 Charlottetown affairs were handled by the ISRC in Halifax and the
    Winnipeg ISRC handled Port Arthur cases.
56 Soldiers released from military commitments through ISRP procedures
    were not always given full discharges. Army personnel in Home Defence
    units could be given leave without pay to attend to industrial duty. Air
    Force, Navy, and all overseas personnel were always discharged under
    ISRP provisions. NA, RG 27, Volume 1506, File 10–1–4 pt. 2, Ruther-
    ford to MacNamara, 5 July 1945; Tosland to Ranger, 24 July 1945.

57 NA, RG 27, Volume 1506, File 10–1–4 pt. 2, Baxter to MacNamara, 13 July 1945.

58 NA, RG 27, Volume 1507, File 10–1–4–1, Carter to Tosland, 29 June 1945.

59 NA, RG 28, Volume 105, File 2-I-11, Flahiff to Henry, 13 July 1945.

60 NA, RG 27, Volume 3018, File Report on the Operations of the ISRP, "Report on the Operations of the Industrial Selection and Release Plan, May 24, 1945 to May 31, 1946."

61 NA, RG 27, Volume 1506, File 10–1–4 pt. 2, MacKinnon to Mitchell, 3 July 1945.

62 Ibid., Crosbie to Ranger, 13 July 1945.

63 NA, RG 27, Volume 1507, File 10–1–4–2 pt. 1, Halls to Ilsley, 12 July 1945.

64 Ibid., Ellis to Ilsley, 13 July 1945.

65 Ibid., Cochrane to MacNamara, 18 July 1945.

66 NA, RG 27, Volume 1506, File 10–1–4 pt. 2, Pickersgill to MacNamara, 23 July 1945.

67 Ibid., McNaughton to Mitchell, 7 August 1945.

68 NA, RG 27, Volume 1506, File 10–1–4 pt. 3, MacNamara to Ranger, 11 August 1945.

69 NA, RG 27, Volume 1506, File 10–1–4 pt. 1, Administrative Bulletin No. 22, 14 August 1945.

70 Ibid., MacNamara to all ISRC chairmen, 14 August 1945.

71 NA, RG 27, Volume 27, File Report of the Operations of the ISRP, "Report on the Operations of the Industrial Selection and Release Plan, May 24, 1945 to May 31, 1946.

72 NA, RG 27, Volume 1506, file 10–1–4 pt. 3, Gibson to Mitchell, 5 September 1945.

73 Ibid., Ranger to MacNamara, 19 September 1945.

74 NA, RG 27, Volume 1506, File 10–1–4 pt. 4, Mackenzie to Ranger, 9 October 1945.

75 NA, RG 28, Volume 105, File 2-I-11, Scully to MacNamara, 15 October 1945.

76 NA, RG 27, Volume 1506, File 10–1–4 pt. 4, Gordon to MacNamara, 15 October 1945.

77 Ibid., Reynolds to MacNamara, 13 November 1945; Henderson to MacNamara, 13 November 1945. See also NA, RG 27, Volume 1507, File 10–1–4–7, Baxter to MacNamara, 23 November 1945.

78 NA, RG 27, Volume 1506, File 10–1–4 pt. 4, Ranger to McLaren, 5 November 1945.

79 NA, RG 27, Volume 1507, File 10–1–4–4, MacDonald to DND Secretary (Air), 5 December 1945.

80 NA, RG 27, Volume 1506, File 10–1–4 pt. 4, Ferguson to Ranger, 27 November 1945.

81 Ibid., McPherson to Ranger, 23 January 1946.
82 Ibid., Ranger to MacNamara, 24 January 1946.
83 Administrative Bulletin 61 of 26 February 1946 streamlined each ISRC to consist of only three members, one each from the Department of Labour, the Employment Service, and the Department of National Defence. See NA, RG 27, Volume 983, File "NSS ISRB Bulletins," Administrative Bulletin 69, 26 February 1946.
84 NA, RG 27, Volume 1506, File 10–1–4 pt. 4, Ranger to MacNamara, 20 April 1946.
85 Ibid., MacNamara to Mitchell, 23 April 1946.
86 NA, RG 27, Volume 664, file 6–5–2–1 vol. 2 – Packing Industry, Adamson to MacNamara, 29 April 1944.
87 Department of National Defence, Directorate of History, file 325.009 (D468), McLaren to DND Headquarters, 16 January 1945. In four firms in the Kingston military district, eleven men called for induction into the NRMA under the terms of the IMSP had enlisted in the Navy, were attested, and were promptly returned to civilian employment to await a future call to duty.
88 The "Miscellaneous" category encompassed an offshoot of the ISRP, the Government Service Selection and Release Plan, established under authority of Order-in-Council PC 4644 of 28 June 1945. This Committee made recommendations to the ISRB for the release of civil servants from the armed forces. A total of 865 applications were submitted and 861 were approved – an ISRB acceptance rate of 99.5 per cent. The ISRB also dealt with a number of group applications and individual applications after August 1945.

CHAPTER FIVE

1 All statistical material is derived from the annual *Coal Statistics for Canada, 1942–46.*
2 Labour problems and production shortfalls occurred in the coal industry in Western Canada as well. Labour strife, absenteeism, and declining productivity elicited the same response from NSS officials there as they did in Nova Scotia. A Royal Commission to address the concerns of UMWA District 18 workers in Alberta and British Columbia was organized. Wage concessions were offered to miners in an attempt to boost productivity, and compulsory registration and freezing provisions applied equally to coal miners in all areas of the country. Many of the coal labour problems in the lignite and bituminous mines of western Canada were resolved through the use of agricultural workers in the fall and winter months. (NSS policies affecting a seasonal industry are discussed in the chapter on meatpacking labour.)

3 This examination of NSS policy towards the coal labour force in Nova
   Scotia allows important additions to be made to the historiography of
   the coal industry in Nova Scotia and of Canada's war effort. While the
   impact of the war on other primary industries has been well-documented,
   scholars of the Maritime coal industry have focussed almost exclusively
   on the period prior to 1939, particularly emphasizing the inter-war
   period and the bitter relations between coal companies and miners and
   the widening gap between militant rank-and-file coal workers and their
   increasingly conservative and bureaucratic UMWA leaders. Michael Earle
   has provided an important account of the 1941 slowdown strikes in
   Cape Breton but ignores the critical period from 1942 to 1945, the
   years of heightened government involvement in the coal industry. Other
   accounts of the war, both popular and scholarly, overlook the response
   of District 26 miners to government mobilization initiatives. See David
   Frank, "The Cape Breton Coal Miners, 1917–1926," (Dalhousie University Ph.D. Thesis, 1979); Frank, "The Cape Breton Coal Industry and
   the Rise and Fall of the British Empire Steel Corporation," *Acadiensis*
   7 no. 1 (1977), 3–34; Donald MacGillivray, "Military Aid to the Civil
   Power: The Cape Breton Experience in the 1920s," *Acadiensis* 3 no. 2
   (1974), 45–64; John Manley, "Preaching the Red Stuff: J.B. McLachlan,
   Communism, and the Cape Breton Miners, 1922–1935," *Labour/Le
   Travail* 30 (Fall 1992), 65–114; Michael Earle and H. Gamberg, "The
   United Mine Workers and the Coming of the CCF to Cape Breton,"
   Acadiensis 19 no. 1 (1989), 3–26; John Mellor, *The Company Store:
   J.B. McLachlan and the Cape Breton Coal Miners, 1900–1925* (Halifax:
   Doubleday, 1984); Michael Earle, "'Down With Hitler and Silby Barrett':
   The Cape Breton Miners' Slowdown Strike of 1941," *Acadiensis* 18
   no. 1 (1988), 57–90, and Paul MacEwan, *Miners and Steelworkers:
   Labour in Cape Breton* (Toronto: Hekkert, 1976), 265–70.
4 For an overview of the regulation of the Canadian coal industry during
   World War II, see J. de N. Kennedy, *History of the Department of
   Munitions and Supply* (Ottawa: King's Printer, 1950), chapter 4, and
   Report of the Royal Commission on Coal (Ottawa: King's Printer,
   1946), 532–63.
5 For an overview of industrial relations policies adopted during the war,
   see Laurel Sefton MacDowell, "The Formation of the Canadian Industrial Relations System During World War II," in MacDowell and Ian
   Radforth, eds., *Canadian Working Class History, Selected Readings*
   (Toronto: Canadian Scholar's Press, 1992), 575–94; Bob Russell, *Back
   to Work? Labour, State, and Industrial Relations in Canada* (Scarborough: Nelson, 1990), chapter 6, and Jeremy Webber, "The Malaise of
   Compulsory Conciliation: Strike Prevention in Canada During World
   War II," *Labour/Le Travail* 15 no. 2 (1985), 57–88.

6 See *Labour Gazette* (October 1946), 9, "Wage Rates and Hours of Labour in Canada, 1944," and *Labour Gazette* (March 1940), 131, "Numbers and Earnings of Coal Miners in Canada, 1921-1938."

7 For a compelling account of the lives of coal miners in Nova Scotia, see Ian McKay, "The Realm of Uncertainty: The Experience of Work in the Cumberland Coal Mines, 1873-1927," *Acadiensis* 16 no. 1 (Autumn 1986), 3-57.

8 The most obvious threat to the employment of coal miners was the mechanization of the coal industry, a company strategy that was strenuously resisted in the decades following World War I. See Earle, "'Down With Hitler and Silby Barrett,'" 62; and Del Muise, "Debating Technology's Impact on Coal-Mining Before the Duncan Royal Commission of 1925," (Paper presented to the Canadian Historical Association, June 1997). The coal industry was rationalized and mechanized following the 1947 strike wave, leading to massive job losses in Cape Breton.

9 See MacEwan, *Miners and Steelworkers*, 72-8.

10 For an excellent account of Lewis' life and career as the leader of the UMWA, see Melvin Dubofsky and Warren Van Tine, *John L. Lewis: A Biography* (New York: Quadrangle, 1977).

11 See Michael Earle, "The Coalminers and the 'Red' Union: The Amalgamated Mine Workers of Nova Scotia, 1932-1936," *Labour/Le Travail* 22 (Fall 1988), 99-137.

12 See Earle, "'Down With Hitler and Silby Barrett,'" notes 17-19.

13 DOSCO had allowed the Old Sydney and Acadia companies to go into receivership to exact wage concessions from the employees of these two firms. DOSCO regained control of these two companies in 1938 and refused to offer wage parity among coal miners in all of the mines under its control.

14 Jenkins would eventually follow in the footsteps of John McLeod and become an exceptionally conservative and bureaucratic unionist who was virulently anti-communist. See Earle and Gamberg, "The United Mine Workers and the Coming of the CCF to Cape Breton," 23-4.

15 See "Report, Finding, and Direction of the NWLB in the Matter of an Application of UMWA District 26, 23 March 1942." NA, MG 28 I 103, Volume 33, file 7 – UMWA District 26 Glace Bay, 1940-42, part 1. The NWLB terms for a general contract were eventually agreed to in July 1942. See *Canadian Unionist* 16 no. 2 (July 1942), 43, and *Halifax Chronicle*, 15 July 1942, 3.

16 Many coal miners probably left the strife of the Cape Breton coal fields for the stability and financial security of the Army. In 1942, the average annual wage of a coal miner in Canada was $1,573. Skilled contract miners in Nova Scotia working a maximum number of shifts could approach the $2,000 level in annual earnings, but, by the same token,

large numbers of provincial coal workers earned less than the national average wage. In 1940, wage rates for non-commissioned officers in the Canadian Active Service Army ranged from $1.30 per diem for a private to $4.20 per diem for a warrant officer. Wage rates for skilled tradesmen in the Army ranged from a minimum of $1.50 per diem for a private to a maximum of $4.95 per diem for a warrant officer. Dependents' allowances could also be paid to married soldiers in addition to the per diem rates. By the end of the war, a married soldier with children could receive a dependents' allowance of $57 per month for a private and $85 per month for a warrant officer. After serving a minimum period of time in the Army, therefore, it was possible for a former coal miner to approach or exceed his former annual earnings in civilian life. See *Report of the Royal Commission on Coal*, 309–10; *Financial Regulations and Instructions for the Canadian Active Service Force* (Ottawa: King's Printer, 1940), 65–7; *Pay and Allowance Regulations for the Canadian Army* (Ottawa: King's Printer, 1946), mimeograph chart insert.

17 NA, RG 27, Volume 666, file 6-5-23-1 pt. 1 – Coal Mining, General Correspondence, LaFlèche to Westman, 18 July 1942.
18 Ibid., Report of J.R. Hill on the Coal Situation, 11 August 1942.
19 The number of producers declined from a monthly average of 3,878 in 1940 to only 2,754 in 1944, while the number of underground datal men increased from 7,004 to 7,582. The total number of coal miners, including surface workers, declined slightly from 12,949 in 1940 to 12,469 in 1944. See NA, RG 27, Volume 975, file NSS Submission to Royal Commission on Coal, Coal Labour Survey – "Coal Labour Survey."
20 NA, RG 27, Volume 667, file 6-5-23-11 pt. 1 – Coal Mine Production Problems, Nova Scotia, Minutes of UMWA Meeting to Establish Production Committees, 19 April 1942.
21 Ibid., Unsigned Memorandum to Humphrey Mitchell, 14 May 1942.
22 Ibid., McLeod to Robinson, 21 December 1942.
23 Ibid., Neilson to McCall, 26 September 1942.
24 Ibid., Barrett to Mitchell, 30 November 1942.
25 Ibid., Mitchell to Ling, Barrett, Scott, and Jenkins, 22 December 1942.
26 Ibid., Barrett to Mitchell, 31 December 1942.
27 Ibid., Cross to Mitchell, 5 January 1943.
28 It took almost six months before all details in the levelling up scheme were worked out. The original $500,000 was to be split four ways: $285,000 to adjust general wage rates at DCC and ACC operations; $68,000 to adjust rates paid to machinists in the Dominion Steel and Coal Company to the rates paid in railroad shops of Dominion Steel and Coal; $70,000 to DSCC mechanics who did not receive a 10 per cent wage increase in 1940; and the balance to bring up rates of mine

maintenance employees. In July 1943, $470,000 of the levelling-up money had been distributed, but $34,000 of this sum had been paid to clerical workers in the employ of the Acadia Coal Company. The Department of Labour eventually paid an additional $34,000 to be distributed to non-clerical employees.

29 NA, RG 27, Volume 154, file 611–1–19–8 pt. 1 – Coal Mine Labour Committee, Taché to All Divisional Chairmen and Registrars, 16 October 1942.

30 NA, RG 27, Volume 666, file 6–5–23–2–1 pt. 1 – Coal Mining, Army Men, Letson to GOC Pacific and Prairie DOCs, 24 November 1942, and Letson to Eastern DOCs, 13 January 1943. Soldiers were allowed to be released for a three-month period at the sole discretion of the commanding officer. Soldiers were not paid by the Army during this period.

31 NA, RG 27, Volume 666, file 6–5–23–1 pt. 1 – Coal Mining, General Correspondence.

32 Ibid., Stewart to Gordon,? October 1942.

33 Ibid., Little to Gordon, 4 November 1942.

34 *Vancouver Daily Province*, 29 December 1942, 3.

35 *Montreal Standard*, 26 December 1942.

36 NA, RG 27, Volume 666, file 6–5–23–1 pt. 1 – Coal Mining, General Correspondence, Stewart to MacNamara, 13 January 1943.

37 NA, RG 27, Volume 154, file 611–1–19–8 pt. 1 – Coal Mine Labour Committee, Stewart to MacNamara, 13 January 1943.

38 NA, RG 27, Volume 666, file 6–5–23–1 pt. 1 – Coal Mining, General Correspondence, Roberts to Westman, 12 January 1943, and Stewart to MacNamara, 13 January 1943.

39 Ibid., MacNamara to Needham, 14 January 1943.

40 The original name of this committee was the Coal Mine Labour Committee. The members of the CLSC were C.F. Needham, W.R. Roberts, Allan Mitchell, H.J. Riley, and C.L. O'Brian. All but O'Brian worked within the NSS structure, while O'Brian was a special assistant to the DMS Coal Controller.

41 NA, RG 27, Volume 154, file 611–1–19–8 pt. 1 – Coal Mine Labour Committee, Howe to Mitchell, 27 February 1943.

42 Ibid., Mitchell to Howe, 3 March 1943. Mitchell castigated Howe for telling him how to apportion his staff after Howe called for Needham to be replaced as head of the Coal Labour Survey Committee, and he noted that Howe had no business meddling in the affairs of the Department of Labour.

43 Ibid., Howe to Mitchell, 7 April 1943.

44 Ibid., MacNamara to Mitchell, 16 April 1943.

45 NA, RG 27, Volume 666, file 6–5–23–1 pt. 1 – Coal Mining, General Correspondence, "Industrial Morale Program in the Coal Mining Industry."

46 Ibid., Minutes of the Fifth CLSC Meeting, 21 April 1943.

47 Ibid., Mitchell to MacNamara, 6 April 1943.

48 NA, RG 27, Volume 154, file 611-1-19-8 pt. 1 – Coal Mine Labour Committee, Howe to Heeney, 4 May 1943.

49 NA, RG 27, Volume 666, file 6-5-23-1 pt. 2 – Coal Mining, General Correspondence, Department of Labour Press Release, 11 June 1943.

50 Ibid., Minutes of the Seventh CLSC Meeting, 7 June 1943.

51 Ibid., National CBC Radio Address of Humphrey Mitchell, 14 July 1943.

52 Ibid., "Production Front" CBC Broadcast, 14 July 1943. May interviewed Jim Hayes, a sixty-year-old miner who had been working in the pits since he was eighteen. Hayes claimed he earned $17.55 for five full shifts, but that he earned only an additional $2.90 for a sixth overtime shift once he moved to a higher tax bracket, although he stated to May that he was "not howling or anything."

53 Glace Bay Gazette, 18 May 1943.

54 Toronto Globe and Mail, 24 August 1943, 6.

55 NA, RG 27, Volume 667, file 6-5-23-11 pt. 1 – Coal Mine Production Problems, Nova Scotia, Jenkins to Mitchell, 11 August 1943.

56 NA, RG 27, Volume 155, file 611-1-19-8 pt. 3 – Coal Mine Labour Committee, Income Tax Commissioner to All Coal Companies, 16 August 1943.

57 NA, RG 27, Volume 666, file 6-5-23-1 pt. 2 – Coal Mining, General Correspondence, McInness to Phelan, 19 October 1943.

58 NA, RG 27, Volume 155, file 611-1-19-8 pt. 4 – Coal Mine Labour Committee, Report on Registration of Ex-Coal Miners Under PC 4092.

59 NA, RG 27, Volume 155, file 611-1-19-8 pt. 2 – Coal Mine Labour Committee, Mitchell to MacNamara, 30 June 1943.

60 NA, RG 27, Volume 666, file 6-5-23-3-1 pt. 1 – Coal Mining Reports, General Correspondence, Report on Coal Mining Labour Supply in Eastern Canada, 9 September 1945.

61 NA, RG 27, Volume 155, file 611-1-19-8 pt. 4 – Coal Mine Labour Committee, Cross to Brunning, 30 August 1943.

62 NA, RG 27, Volume 666, file 6-5-23-2-1 pt. 1 – Coal Mining, Army Men, Needham to Nash, 30 September 1943.

63 Ibid., Macdonald to Mitchell, 21 October 1943.

64 NA, RG 27, Volume 667, file 6-5-23-11 pt. 1 – Coal Mine Production Problems, Nova Scotia, Scott to Mitchell, 4 November 1943. The three companies targeted were the Indiancove, Joggins, and Minto coal firms.

65 NA, RG 27, Volume 155, file 611-1-19-8 pt. 5 – Coal Mine Labour Committee, Mitchell to MacNamara, 4 October 1943.

66 Ibid., MacNamara to Mitchell, 8 October 1943.

67 See Muise and McIntosh, Coal Mining in Canada, 44-7, for a detailed description of the longwall method.

68 NA, RG 27, Volume 155, file 611–1–19–8 pt. 4 – Coal Mine Labour
    Committee, Thompson to MacNamara, 13 September 1943, and
    Dwyer to MacNamara, 22 September 1943.
69 NA, RG 27, Volume 155, file 611–1–19–8 pt. 5 – Coal Mine Labour
    Committee, Dwyer to MacNamara, 2 October 1943, and Dwyer to
    MacNamara, 4 October 1943. In the light of continued union intransi-
    gence, Dwyer called for "a test of authority" and suggested that datal
    men be compelled to work at the face.
70 Ibid., Sneed to MacNamara, 28 October 1943. The UMWA finally agreed
    to start another training class in one DCC mine in December, 1943,
    although it took more than three months for the class to commence.
71 Report of the Royal Commission on Coal, 550.
72 The compulsory savings portion of the income tax that was to be refunded
    after the war was eliminated in the budget speech of 23 June 1942.
    See NA, RG 27, Volume 667, file 6–5–23–10 pt. 1 – Coal Mining,
    Coal Labour Survey, McCall to Kelley, 10 August 1944. The
    compulsory savings tax had been levied in 1942 and the refund to
    be paid after the war included two per cent interest. See David Slater,
    War Finance and Reconstruction: The Role of Canada's Department
    of Finance, 1939–1946 (Ottawa: Privately published, 1996),
    Chapter Six.
73 NA, RG 27, Volume 666, file 6–5–23–1 pt. 3 – Coal Mining, General
    Correspondence, Needham to MacNamara, 14 June 1944.
74 NA, RG 27, Volume 667, file 6–5–23–10 pt. 1 – Coal Mining, Coal
    Labour Survey, McCall to Brunning, 7 June 1944.
75 NA, RG 27, Volume 155, file 611–1–19–8 pt. 7 – Coal Mine Labour
    Committee, "Registration of Ex-Coal Miners Under PC 4092."
76 NA, RG 27, Volume 666, file 6–5–23–2–Coal Mining, UIC Reports,
    Mitchell to MacNamara, 30 June 1944.
77 NA, RG 27, Volume 667, file 6–5–23–10 pt. 1 – Coal Mining, Coal
    Labour Survey, McCall to Brunning, 7 June 1944.
78 NA, RG 27, Volume 666, file 6–5–23–1 pt. 3 – Coal Mining, General
    Correspondence, Brunning to MacNamara, 5 June 1944.
79 For the general history of Labour-Management Production Commit-
    tees after 1944, see Peter McInnis, "Teamwork for Harmony: Labour-
    Management Production Committees and the Postwar Settlement in
    Canada," Canadian Historical Review 77 no. 3 (September 1996),
    317–52.
80 NA, RG 27, Volume 667, file 6–5–23–11 pt. 1 – Coal Mine Production
    Problems, Nova Scotia, Minutes of Joint Production Committee Meeting,
    12–3 July 1944.
81 Ibid., Report No. 36 – Acadia Coal Company.

82 Ibid., Production Report of Acadia Coal Company, Intercolonial Coal Company, and Greenwood Coal Company.

83 NA, RG 27, Volume 667, file 6–5–23–10 pt. 1 – Coal Mining, Coal Labour Survey, Needham to MacNamara, 5 August 1944.

84 Ibid., Brunning to MacNamara, 11 August 1944.

85 Ibid., Maclean to MacNamara, 12 August 1944.

86 Ibid., MacNamara to Needham, 16 August 1944. Evidence was readily available that a significant wage differential already existed. NWLB Chairman Justice M.B. Archibald wrote to MacNamara on 2 September 1944 with the wage information for DCC workers. In June 1944, 5,097 datal workers earned an average of $6.21 per day, while 1,600 producers earned an average of $9.44 per day. Even Archibald felt that wage increases had only increased absentee rates, with younger datal men taking advantage of high absentee rates among older workers to remain in datal work and receive extended overtime work schedules. See ibid., Archibald to MacNamara, 2 September 1945.

87 NA, RG 27, Volume 667, file 6–5–23–11 pt. 1 – Coal mine Production Problems, Nova Scotia, Dwyer to MacNamara, 24 August 1944.

88 Ibid., Maclean to Brown, 29 August 1944.

89 NA, RG 27, Volume 667, file 6–5–23–10 pt. 1 – Coal Mining, Coal Labour Survey, Brunning to Howe, 11 September 1944.

90 Ibid., Maclean to Brown, 15 September 1944.

91 Ibid., Goldenberg to Brunning, 15 September 1944.

92 Ibid., Brunning to Goldenberg, 16 September 1944.

93 Ibid., Minutes of Meeting to Deal With Coal Mining Situation in Nova Scotia, 25 September 1944.

94 Angus Morrison from the Calgary UMWA and Justice C.C. McLaurin from Calgary rounded out the Commission's membership.

95 NA, RG 27, Volume 667, file 6–5–23–11 pt. 2 – Coal Mining Production Problems, Nova Scotia, Jenkins to Brunning, 5 October 1944.

96 Ibid., Maclean to MacNamara, 23 October 1944.

97 Ibid., MacNamara to Maclean, 1 November 1944.

98 Ibid., MacNamara to Wade, 4 November 1944.

99 NA, RG 27, Volume 667, file 6–5–23–10 pt. 1 – Coal Mining, Coal Labour Survey, Wade to MacNamara, 7 November 1944.

100 H.R. Pettigrove admitted that NSS officials had no authority to compel workers to move from datal to producing positions, but that the Coal Labour Survey might "by inference" indicate to datal men that medically fit men would be called for military service unless they volunteered to work at the face. See ibid., Pettigrove to Maclean, 14 October 1944.

101 NA, RG 27, Volume 666, file 6–5–23–1 pt. 3 – Coal Mining, General Correspondence, Westman to Brunning, 26 October 1944, and Westman to MacNamara, 13 November 1944.

102 Ibid., O'Brian to Westman, 31 October 1944.

103 NA, RG 27, Volume 667, file 6–5–23–10 pt. 1 – Coal Mining, Coal Labour Survey, George to Scott, 1 November 1944.

104 Ibid., George to Scott, 7 November 1944.

105 NA, RG 27, Volume 667, file 6–5–23–10 pt. 2 – Coal Mining, Coal Labour Survey, MacAulay to Scott, 7 December 1944.

106 Ibid., Undirected O'Brian memo, 22 December 1944.

107 Ibid., Reports of Associate Directors for Week Ending 3 February 1945.

108 A full report on the Coal Labour Survey is found in NA, RG 27, Volume 975, file NSS Submission to Royal Commission on Coal, Coal Labour Survey.

109 NA, RG 27, Volume 667, file 6–5–23–10 pt. 2 – Coal Mining, Coal Labour Survey, Connolly to Scott, 28 February 1945, and McLeod to MacNamara, 6 March 1945.

110 Ibid., MacNamara to Brunning, 21 March 1945.

111 Ibid., Burchell to Howland, 5 October 1945.

112 Ibid., Brunning to MacNamara, 22 March 1945.

113 NA, RG 27, Volume 666, file 6–5–23–1 pt. 1 – Coal Mining Reports, General Correspondence, Westman to MacNamara, 14 March 1945.

114 NA, RG 27, Volume 666, file 6–5–23–1 pt. 3 – Coal Mining, General Correspondence, Humphrey Mitchell Radio Address, 19 February 1945.

115 NA, RG 27, Volume 667, file 6–5–23–11 pt. 2 – Coal Mining Production Problems, Nova Scotia, McLeod to Robinson, 30 June 1945.

116 NA, RG 27, Volume 666, file 6–5–23–3–1 pt. 1 – Coal Mining Reports, General Correspondence, Westman to MacNamara, 9 May 1945.

117 NA, RG 27, Volume 666, file 6–5–23–1 pt. 3 – Coal Mining, General Correspondence, Westman to MacNamara, 18 June 1945.

118 Ibid., Mitchell to Jenkins, 19 June 1945.

119 NA, RG 27, Volume 666, file 6–5–23–3–1 pt. 1 – Coal Mining Reports, General Correspondence, Westman to MacNamara, 9 May 1945.

120 NA, RG 27, Volume 984, file 10 – NSS ISRP, "Statistical Report No. 2, Industrial Selection and Release Committee."

121 NA, RG 27, Volume 666, file 6–5–23–1 pt. 3 – Coal Mining, General Correspondence, Brunning to MacNamara, 13 November 1945.

CHAPTER SIX

1 The best description of the Halifax longshore situation can be found in Ian McKay, "Class Struggle and Mercantile Capitalism: Craftsmen and

Labourers on the Halifax Waterfront, 1805–1902," in Rosemary Ommer and Gerald Panting, eds., *Working Men Who Got Wet* (Proceedings of the Fourth Conference of the Atlantic Canada Shipping Project, Memorial University, 1980), 287–319. A good source for descriptions of dock labour in general is Charles Barnes, *The Longshoremen* (Philadelphia; Survey Associates, 1915). See also Robert Babcock, "Saint John Longshoremen During the Rise of Canada's Winter Port, 1895–1922," *Labour/Le Travail* 25 (Spring 1990), 15–46. A good overview of the Halifax labour crisis during World War II can be found in Jay White, "Conscripted City: Halifax and the Second World War," (unpublished Ph.D. Thesis, McMaster University, 1994), chapter 5.

2 A good account of the HLA prior to World War II can be found in Catherine Waite, "The Longshoremen of Halifax, 1900–1930: Their Living and Working Conditions," (unpublished M.A. Thesis, Dalhousie University, 1977), especially chapter 3.

3 NA, RG 27, Volume 3001, file Shiploading Operations – Halifax, 1943–45, Summary of Wartime Regulation of Longshoremen.

4 NA, RG 27, Volume 141, file 611–02–46, Summary of Longshore Meeting in Halifax, 3 August 1941.

5 NA, RG 27, Volume 664, file 6–5–6–3–1 part 1, Working Agreement Between the Halifax Longshoremen's Association and the Steamship Companies of Halifax, 3 December 1941.

6 NA, RG 27, Volume 141, file 611–02–46, Huband to Howe, 24 January 1942.

7 Ibid., Report of Shiploading Operations in the Port of Halifax, 12 February 1942.

8 Ibid., Stewart to MacDonald, 18 April 1942; Stewart to MacDonald, 13 April 1942, and MacNamara to Trottier, 28 April 1942.

9 Ibid., MacDonald to Stewart, 6 May 1942.

10 Ibid., MacNamara to MacDonald, 7 May 1942.

11 Ibid., Hudson to Phelan, 9 May 1942.

12 NA, RG 27, Volume 664, file 6–5–6–3–4, Garnier to Mitchell, 2 May 1942.

13 Ibid., Garnier to MacDonald, 17 June 1942.

14 Ibid., MacDonald to MacNamara, 18 June 1942.

15 Ibid., Garnier to Mitchell, 4 July 1942.

16 NA, RG 27, Volume 664, file 6–5–6–3–1 part 1, MacNamara to MacDonald, 9 July 1942.

17 For a discussion of the duties of the position, see Kennedy, *History of the Department of Munitions and Supply, Volume II*, 288–94.

18 NA, RG 27, Volume 664, file 6–5–6–3–2, Stewart to MacNamara, 9 September 1942. Cousins would eventually come to regret his decision not to take control of the labour situation on the Halifax docks.

19 *Halifax Chronicle*, 7 December 1942, 14.

20 NA, RG 27, Volume 664, file 6–5–6–3–1 part 1, MacDonald to MacNamara, 9 December 1942.

21 Ibid., MacDonald Personal Memo, January 1943.

22 NA, RG 27, Volume 664, file 6–5–6–3–4, Mitchell to Garnier, 4 January 1943.

23 *Halifax Star*, 7 December 1942, 6.

24 *Halifax Chronicle*, 9 February 1943, 12; *Halifax Chronicle*, 23 February 1943, 12.

25 The three HLA representatives in the proposed Central Despatching Agency were John Leahy, John Campbell, and John MacDonald. Leahy was paid $250 per month as Assistant Chief Despatcher, while Leahy and Macdonald received $200 per month as Despatchers. See NA, RG 27, Volume 664, file 6–5–6–3–2, MacNamara to Mitchell, 17 February 1943.

26 NA, RG 66 Volume 5, file H-I-5 part 1, Central Despatching Agency Despatching Regulations.

27 NA, RG 27, Volume 664, file 6–5–6–3–1 part 1, Cousins to Howe, 13 March 1943.

28 After construction began in April 1941, intense opposition came from Halifax residents. F.B. Chilman, Secretary of the Young Avenue Citizen's Committee, expressed his "surprise and indignation" that residents of the area were not consulted. Calls to altering the design of the site went unheeded by government officials. Ottawa promised, however, that the complex would be removed after the war. See NA, RG 27, Volume 664, file 6–5–6–3–4, Chilman to Mitchell, 24 April 1943; *Halifax Chronicle*, 26 April 1943, 16.

29 Ibid., MacDonald to Perchard, 4 May 1943; Jones to MacDonald, 15 May 1943, and McLaren to Aikman, 15 May 1943.

30 NA, RG 27, Volume 664, file 6–5–6–3–1 part 2, MacDonald to Mitchell, 17 May 1943; Barclay to MacNamara, 19 May 1943, and Aikman to MacDonald, 25 May 1943.

31 Ibid., MacDonald to MacNamara, 31 May 1943.

32 Ibid., Perchard to MacDonald, 9 June 1943. Many HLA gangs refused to work evening shifts during the summer months and the HLA asked that all staff of the hiring hall be union members.

33 Humphrey Mitchell submitted an original appropriation for the restaurant of $9,000, but Cousins suggested an expanded facility costing $21,500. The catering contract for the bunkhouse with Crawley & McCracken was signed 1 September 1943, with longshoremen paying $8.75 per week for twenty-one consecutive meals. See NA, RG 27, Volume 664, file 6–5–6–3–5, Mitchell to Council, 21 August 1943; Cousins to MacDonald, September 27, 1943; and Contract Between Dominion Government and Crawley & McCracken, 1 September 1943.

34 NA, RG 27, Volume 664, file 6–5–6–3–1 part 2, MacDonald to Aikman, 5 August 1943.

35 Ibid., Aikman to MacDonald, 5 August 1943.

36 NA, RG 27, Volume 664, file 6–5–6–3–4, Riddell to MacNamara, 9 July 1943.

37 NA, RG 27, Volume 665: file 6–6–6–3–6, Reford to Mitchell, 28 July 1943.

38 NA, RG 27, Volume 6–5–6–3–1 part 2, Unsigned, undated Memo Summarizing September Port Activity.

39 NA, RG 27, Volume 664, file 6–5–6–3–5, Cousins to MacDonald, 27 September 1943.

40 NA, RG 27, Volume 664, file 6–5–6–3–1 part 2, Cousins to Howe, 30 September 1943.

41 For a discussion of wartime housing shortages in Halifax, see Jay White, "The Homes Front: The Accommodation Crisis in Halifax, 1941–1951," *Urban History Review* 20 no. 3 (1992), 117–27.

42 NA, RG 27, Volume 664, file 6–5–6–3–5, MacDonald to Sheils, 29 July 1943; Sheils to MacDonald, 5 August 1943; Sullivan to Perchard, 3 September 1943; Rent to Perchard, 1 September 1943; and Goggin to Fogo, 4 October 1943.

43 NA, RG 27, Volume 665, file 6–5–6–3–11, Perchard to MacDonald, 11 November 1943.

44 NA, RG 27, Volume 664, file 6–5–6–3–1 part 1, Hall to Cousins, 13 May 1943.

45 Ibid., Green to Cousins, 17 May 1943.

46 NA, RG 27, Volume 664, file 6–5–6–3–1 part 3, MacNamara to Currie, 22 December 1943.

47 NA, RG 27, Volume 664, file 6–5–6–3–1 part 2, Cousins to Howe, 20 January 1944.

48 See ibid., MacDonald to Mitchell, 22 January 1944; MacNamara to Mitchell, 22 January 1944; Mitchell to Howe, 24 January 1944; Howe to Mitchell, 27 January 1944; and MacLean to MacNamara, 30 January 1944.

49 *Halifax Chronicle*, 24 March 1944, 3.

50 NA, RG 27, Volume 664, file 6–5–6–3–5, Spring to MacDonald, 18 March 1944.

51 NA, RG 27, Volume 664, file 6–5–6–3–1 part 3, Saunders to MacNamara, 20 June 1944.

52 Ibid., MacDonald to Saunders, 5 August 1942.

53 NA, RG 27, Volume 664, file 6–5–6–3–5, Vassey to MacDonald, 6 March 1944.

54 NA, RG 27, Volume 664, file 6–5–6–3–1 part 3, Spring to MacNamara, 12 January 1945.

55 Ibid., Hartley to Peebles, 13 February 1945.
56 Ibid., Spring to MacNamara, 16 July 1945.
57 Ibid., Spring to MacNamara, 21 July 1945.
58 Ibid., MacNamara to MacDonald, 5 September 1945.
59 NA, RG 27, Volume 664, file 6–5–6–3–5, Dwyer to MacNamara, 31 May 1946.
60 Ibid., MacLennan to MacNamara, 18 July 1946.
61 NA, RG 27, Volume 664, file 6–5–6–3–1 part 3, Spring to MacNamara, 17 May 1946; HLA Secretary to Mitchell, 22 May 1946; Saunders to Spring, 28 May 1946; and MacNamara to Parent, 23 June 1950.
62 NA, RG 27, Volume 665, file 6–5–6–3–6, Black to MacNamara, 28 April 1945.

CHAPTER SEVEN

1 NA, RG 27, Volume 1517, file R1.1 pt. 4 – Labour Situation, Meat Products, Pickersgill to MacNamara, 3 January 1945.
2 This case serves as a useful substitute for a study of the wartime agricultural labour force. Agriculture has proved difficult to study because the archival record pertaining to the Dominion-Provincial Farm Labour Program is scattered and lacks detail in many areas. NSS efforts in the meatpacking sector were similar to those launched to supply seasonal workers to the farms of Canada during seeding and harvest periods.
3 *Weekly Earnings and Hours of Work of Male and Female Wage Earners: Employment in the Manufacturing Industries of Canada, 1943–1944* (Ottawa: King's Printer, 1945–46), 10 (1943), 10 (1944).
4 NA, RG 27, Volume 1517, file R1.1–10 – Postponement of Military Training for Essential Personnel in Meatpacking Industry, Blair to Scott, 6 July 1943.
5 NA, RG 27, Volume 1517, file R1.1 pt. 1 – Labour Situation, Meat Products, Barton to MacNamara, 11 June 1943.
6 Ibid., Needham to MacNamara, 28 June 1943.
7 Ibid., MacNamara to Barton, 12 July 1943.
8 NA, RG 17, Volume 3129, file 66–5 pt. 2, McLean to Barton, 17 August 1943.
9 NA, RG 27, Volume 1515, file O-11–1 pt. 2 – NSS Weekly Meetings Re: Labour Priorities, Minutes of the Inter-departmental Labour Priorities Committee, 19 August 1943.
10 NA, RG 17, Volume 3129: file 66–5 pt. 2, Harris to McLean, 19 August 1943.
11 NA, RG 27, Volume 664, file 6–5–2–1 volume 1 – Packing Industry, MacNamara to Rutherford, 24 September 1943.

12 See chapter 1 for an outline of the freezing regulations.
13 NA, RG 27, Volume 1517, file R1.1–10 – Postponement of Military Training for Essential Personnel in Meatpacking Industry, Circular Memorandum No. 922 to all Mobilization Board Chairmen and Registrars, 23 September 1943.
14 NA, RG 17, Volume 3129, file 66–5 pt. 3, Hinchliffe to Armstrong, 23 September 1943.
15 Ibid., Burns to Maynard, 1 October 1943; Maynard to Pearsall, 2 October 1943.
16 NA, RG 27, Volume 1517, file R1.1 pt. 1 – Labour Situation, Meat Products, Todd to Foster, 7 October 1943.
17 NA, RG 27, Volume 3129, file 66–5 pt. 4, Todd to Barton, 18 November 1943.
18 NA, RG 27, Volume 1517, file R1.1 pt. 1 – Labour Situation, Meat Products, Foster to Todd, 22 November 1943.
19 Ibid., David to Manning, 3 April 1944.
20 NA, RG 17, Volume 3129, file 66–5 pt. 4, MacNamara to Barton, 30 March 1944.
21 NA, RG 27, Volume 1517, file R1.1 pt. 1 – Labour Situation, Meat Products, Ford to Barton, 18 April 1944.
22 Ibid., Foster to MacNamara, 10 March 1944.
23 NA, RG 17, Volume 3129, file 66–5 pt. 4, Memorandum Re Estimate of Livestock Slaughters, March to May 1944.
24 NA, RG 27, Volume 1515, file O-11–1 pt. 3: NSS Weekly Meetings Re Labour Priorities, Minutes of the Inter-departmental Labour Priorities Committee, 25 January 1944.
25 NA, RG 27, Volume 971, file 4 – NSS Minutes of Administration Board, Minutes of the Administration Board Meeting, 14 March 1944.
26 NA, RG 27, Volume 1515, file O-11–1 pt. 3 – NSS Weekly Meetings Re Labour Priorities, Minutes of the Inter-departmental Committee of Labour Priorities, 16 March 1944.
27 NA, RG 27, Volume 1517, file R1.1 pt. 2 – Labour Situation, Meat Products, David to MacNamara, 12 April 1944.
28 NA, RG 27, Volume 664, file 6–5–2–1 volume 1 – Packing Industry, Todd to Barton, 29 March 1944.
29 NA, RG 17, Volume 3129, file 66–5 pt. 4, Barton to MacNamara, 30 March 1944.
30 NA, RG 27, Volume 664, file 6–5–2–1 pt. 1 – Packing Industry, MacNamara to Millard, 15 April 1944.
31 Ibid., Harrison to MacNamara, 17 April 1944.
32 *Calgary Albertan*, 19 April 1944, 1.
33 NA, RG 27, Volume 664, file 6–5–2–1 pt. 2 – Packing Industry, White to MacNamara, 20 April 1944.

34 NA, RG 27, Volume 664, file 6–5–2–1 part 1 – Packing Industry, MacNamara to Carnill, 18 April 1944.

35 NA, RG 27, Volume 1517, file R1.1 pt. 2 – Labour Situation, Meat Products, Manning to David, 13 April 1944.

36 Ibid., Manning to Raley, 20 April 1944.

37 Ibid., Pickersgill to Putnam, 15 April 1944.

38 Ibid., Griggs to White, 26 April 1944.

39 Ibid., Putnam to Pickersgill, 18 April 1944.

40 NA, RG 27, Volume 664, file 6–5–2–1 pt. 2 – Packing Industry, Adamson to MacNamara, 29 April 1944.

41 NA, RG 27, Volume 1517, file R1.1 pt. 2 – Labour Situation, Meat Products, Carnill to MacNamara, 26 April 1944.

42 NA, RG 27, Volume 664, file 6–5–2–1 pt. 2 – Packing Industry, MacNamara to Campbell, 1 May 1944.

43 NA, RG 27, Volume 1517, file R1.1 pt. 2 – Labour Situation, Meat Products, Putnam to All Prairie Agriculturalists, 4 May 1944.

44 Ibid., MacNamara to McKinstry, 28 April 1944.

45 NA, RG 27, Volume 664, file 6–5–2–1 pt. 2 – Packing Industry, MacNamara to Rutherford, 3 May 1944.

46 NA, RG 27, Volume 664, file 6–5–2–1 pt. 3 – Packing Industry, MacLachlin to MacNamara, 27 May 1944.

47 Ibid., Walsh to MacNamara, 2 June 1944.

48 NA, RG 27, Volume 664, file 6–5–2–1 pt. 2 – Packing Industry, MacNamara to Carnill, 23 May 1944. MacNamara blandly described the plan as an "expensive operation" that should not be continued. MacNamara also attempted to funnel Chinese men in military age classes to Alberta. While the federal government refused to allow Chinese men to enlist in the armed forces, they apparently had no qualms about uprooting them and directing them in a compulsory fashion to other employment. See Ibid., MacNamara to Adamson, 6 May 1944.

49 NA, RG 27, Volume 664, file 6–5–2–1 pt. 2 – Packing Industry, Alberta Federation of Agriculture Press Release, 2 May 1944.

50 Ibid., 12 May 1944.

51 NA, RG 27, Volume 1517, file R1.1 pt. 2 – Labour Situation, Meat Products, Ralston to Gardiner, 22 May 1944.

52 Ibid., Todd to David, 15 May 1944.

53 Ibid., Meatpacking Employment Report, May 1944.

54 NA, RG 27, Volume 664, file 6–5–2–1 pt. 3 – Packing Industry, Minutes of the Inter-departmental Labour Priorities Committee Meeting, 8 June 1944.

55 Ibid., Barton to MacNamara, 12 June 1944.

56 Ibid., MacNamara to Hereford, 21 June 1944.

57 NA, RG 27, Volume 1515, file O-11–1 pt. 4 – NSS Weekly Meetings Re: Labour Priorities, Minutes of the Inter-departmental Labour Priorities Committee Meeting, 22 June 1944.

58 NA, RG 27, Volume 1517, file R1.1 pt. 3 – Labour Situation, Meat Products, NSS Report Prepared by H.F. Caloren to Be Given to the NSS Advisory Board, 14 June 1944; Meatpacking Employment Report, July 1944.

59 Ibid., Stewart to Rutherford, 5 July 1944.

60 NA, RG 27, Volume 664, file 6–5–3–1 pt. 3 – Packing Industry, Rutherford to Perry, 17 July 1944.

61 NA, RG 27, Volume 1517, file R1.1 pt. 3 – Labour Situation, Meat Products, Rutherford to Raley, 15 August 1944.

62 Ibid., Meatpacking Employment Report, August 1944.

63 NA, RG 27, Volume 1517, file O-5–9 – NSS Army Labour, Cold Storage, Letson to All DOCs and GOCs, 25 September 1944.

64 Order-in-Council PC 7429 of 4 October 1944 allowed active duty men to be detailed to industrial duty. Only personnel not above the grade of private or trained soldiers could be detailed for industrial leave.

65 NA, RG 27, Volume 1517, file R1.1 pt. 3 – Labour Situation, Meat Products, Haythorne to Wood, 23 September 1944.

66 Ibid., Meatpacking Employment Report, September 1944.

67 NA, RG 17, Volume 3129, file 66–5 pt. 4 – Canadian Federation of Agriculture President to MacNamara, 5 October 1944.

68 NA, RG 27, Volume 1517, file R1.1 pt. 3 – Labour Situation, Meat Products, Stewart to Rutherford, 5 July 1944.

69 Ibid., Roberts to Rutherford, 24 October 1944.

70 See ibid., Rutherford to MacNamara, 28 October 1944; Griggs to MacNamara, 1 November 1944; Minutes of the Ontario Dominion-Provincial Farm Labour Committee Meeting, 3 November 1944; Barton to MacNamara, 6 November 1944; Meatpacking Employment Report, October 1944; and Meatpacking Employment Report, November 1944.

71 NA, RG 27, Volume 664, file 6–5–2–1 pt. 3 – Packing Industry, Crabb to MacNamara, 15 January 1945.

72 *Livestock and Animal Products Statistics, 1946* (Ottawa: King's Printer, 1948), 13, 37.

73 NA, RG 27, Volume 664, file 6–5–2–1 pt. 3 – Packing Industry, Duncan to MacNamara, 12 February 1945.

74 NA, RG 27, Volume 1517, file R1.1 pt. 4 – Labour Situation, Meat Products, Hereford to MacNamara, 18 January 1945.

75 Ibid., Crabb to MacNamara, 29 January 1945.

76 NA, RG 27, Volume 971, file 1 – NSS Minutes of the ILPC, Minutes of the Inter-departmental Labour Priorities Committee Meeting, 28 February 1945.

77 NA, RG 27, Volume 1517, file R1.1 pt. 4 – Labour Situation, Meat Products, Meatpacking Employment Report, 3 February 1945 to 14 April 1945.

78 NA, RG 27, Volume 664, file 6–5–2–1 pt. 3 – Packing Industry, Wood to MacNamara, 14 May 1945.

79 Ibid., Rutherford to MacNamara, 9 June 1945.

80 NA, RG 27, Volume 971: file 1 – NSS Minutes of the ILPC, Minutes of the Inter-departmental Labour Priorities Committee, 15 August 1945; Minutes of the Inter-departmental Labour Priorities Committee, 18 July 1945.

81 NA, RG 27, Volume 664, file 6–5–2–1 pt. 3 – Packing Industry, Wells to MacNamara, 11 July 1945; Sullivan to MacNamara, 11 July 1945; Hereford to MacNamara, 16 August 1945; and MacNamara to Ross, 7 September 1945.

82 NA, RG 27, Volume 1517, file O-5–2 pt. 2 – NSS Army Labour, General, Letson to All DOCs and GOCs, 29 August 1945.

83 NA, RG 27, Volume 664, file 6–5–2–1 pt. 3 – Packing Industry, MacNamara to Ross, 7 September 1945.

84 NA, RG 27, Volume 984, file 10 – NSS ISRP, Industrial Selection and Release Committee, Statistical Report No. 2.

85 NA, MG 28 I 103, Volume 37, file 5 – United Packinghouse Workers of America, General, 1944–1947, pt. III, Department of Labour Press Release, 12 October 1945.

86 *Canadian Unionist* 20, no. 2 (February 1946), 37.

87 NA, RG 27, Volume 664, file 6–5–2–1 pt. 3 – Packing Industry, Hereford to MacNamara, 9 November 1945.

88 Ibid., Rutherford to MacNamara, 27 December 1945.

CHAPTER EIGHT

1 For accounts of the primary textile industry prior to 1945, see Joy Parr, *The Gender of Breadwinners* (Toronto: University of Toronto Press, 1991); Gail Cuthbert Brandt, "'Weaving it Together': Life Cycle and the Industrial Experience of Female Cotton Workers in Quebec, 1910–1950," *Labour/Le Travail* 7 (1981), 29–61, and Ellen Scheinberg, "The Tale of Tessie the Textile Worker: Female Textile Workers in Cornwall During World War II," *Labour/Le Travail* 33 (Spring 1994), 153–86.

2 In November 1942, WPTB officials concluded that the labour force in the primary textile industry was strained to its limit and that neither men nor women could not be spared for other industries. See NA, RG 27, Volume 1524, file Proposals for Standardizing Production and Releasing Manpower in the Textile Industry, "Proposals for

Standardizing Production and Releasing Manpower in the Textile Industry, November 1942."

3 NA, RG 27, Volume 1518, file R3 part 1 – Hancock to DMS, 8 May 1942; Ziz to Goldenberg, 25 February 1943; Daly to Rutherford, 8 April 1943; and Raley to Ross, 29 April 1943.

4 Ibid., Ross to Robinson, 17 April 1943.

5 NA, RG 27, Box 1518, file R3 pt. 2 – Raley to Ross, 4 August 1943.

6 NA, RG 27, Box 1514, file O-11–1 pt. 2 – ILPC Minutes, 12 August 1943.

7 NA, RG 27, Box 1518, file R3 pt. 2 – Ross to Raley, 16 October 1943.

8 NA, RG 27, Box 1518, file R3 pt. 3 – Lawson to Gordon, 21 June 1943.

9 NA, RG 27, Box 1518, file R3 pt. 2 – Irwin Memo, 19 August 1943. This questionnaire covered twenty-one broad topics, including personnel management, health policies, sanitation, accident prevention, employee training, wages, and labour turnover; under each topic there were questions dealing with such matters as the provision of annual medical examinations, the extent of daily rest periods, the provision of canteen facilities, and the extent of links between the textile firms and local NSS offices. Irwin believed strongly that only internal reforms and improved training procedures would alleviate shortfalls in primary textile employment. See NA, RG 27, Box 666, file 6–5–21–1 pt. 1 – Hereford to MacNamara, 26 August 1943.

10 NA, RG 27, Box 1518, file R3 pt. 3 – Undated Memo.

11 Irwin worked tirelessly with Ontario textile firms in the final months of 1943 to improve relations between local NSS offices and primary textile mills. He emphasized training options. See NA, RG 27, Box 666, file 6–5–21–1 pt. 1 – Unsigned, Undated Memo.

12 NA, RG 27, Box 1518, file R3 pt. 2 – Unsigned Memo, 28 October 1943.

13 NA, RG 27, Box 605, file 6–24–1 pt. 2 – Leonard Prefontaine Memo, 26 October 1943. The original campaign in Montreal had sought women for all industries, but it was quickly replaced by a campaign that focussed specifically on textile employment.

14 A report prepared in February 1943, showed that the proportion of unplaced applicants to unfilled vacancies was 49 per cent in Quebec, 138 per cent in Ontario, 257 per cent on the Prairies, 497 per cent in B.C., and 583 per cent in the Maritimes. Allan Mitchell, Director of the Unemployment Insurance Commission, stressed that measures needed to be adopted to increase the female labour pool in Quebec. See NA, RG 27, Box 605, file 6–24–1 pt. 1 – Eaton to Mitchell, 20 February 1943.

15 Ibid., Three Rivers NCU to Mackenzie King, 31 March 1942.

16 NA, RG 27, Box 605, file 6–24–1 pt. 2 – Florence Martel Memo, 14 October 1943.

17 NA, RG 27, Box 1518, file R3 pt. 2 – Eaton to Martel, 19 November 1943; Turner to Ovendon, 23 November 1943; and Martel to Eaton, 22 November 1943.

18 Ibid., Sauriol to Eadie, 30 November 1943.

19 Ibid., Dominion Textile Company to Préfontaine, 3 December 1943.

20 NA, RG 27, Box 1514, file O-11–1 pt. 2 – ILPC Minutes, 11 November 1943.

21 NA, RG 64, Box 1463, file untitled – ILPC Minutes, 25 January 1944. Ross reported that sixty-eight firms were given elevated priorities, but a check of the minutes reveals only sixty-three.

22 NA, RG 27, Box 1518, file R3 pt. 3 – Hallam to Ross, 18 February 1944.

23 Ibid., Raley to Ross, 4 May 1944.

24 Ibid., Ovendon to Eaton, 8 May 1944.

25 Ibid., Eadie to Hudson, 9 May 1944.

26 Ibid., Eaton to MacNamara, 10 May 1944.

27 NA, RG 27, Box 666, file 6–5–21–1 pt. 1 – Eaton to MacNamara, 6 June 1944.

28 NA, RG 27, Box 1518, file R3 pt. 3 – Ross to Raley, 30 May 1944.

29 Ibid., Ross to Hereford, 29 June 1944; Ross to Eaton, 19 July 1944.

30 NA, RG 27, Box 1518, file R3 pt. 4 – Eaton to MacNamara, 14 August 1944; Eaton to Irwin, 22 August 1944; Eaton to Irwin, 6 September 1944; Unsigned Report on Hamilton Situation, September 1944.

31 Ibid., Irwin to Rutherford, 17 August 1944.

32 Ibid., Eaton to MacNamara, 8 November 1944.

33 Ibid., Raley to Wood, 6 March 1945.

34 NA, RG 27, Box 1518, file R3 pt. 5 – "Summary Report on the Textile Supply Situation in Canada and Requirements for Labour," 3 April 1945.

35 NA, RG 64, Box 24, file "Chronological History of the Knitted Goods Administration," – "History of the Knitted Goods Administration."

36 NA, RG 27, Box 1518, file R3 pt. 5 – Eaton to MacNamara, 12 April 1945.

37 Ibid., Ross to MacNamara, 27 April 1945.

38 NA, RG 27, Box 1518, file R3 pt. 4 – Rutherford to Roberts, 23 March 1945.

39 Ibid., Rutherford to Dunham, 15 March 1945.

40 NA, RG 27. Box 666, file 6–5–21–1 pt. 1, Minutes of 29 March meeting with Hamilton textile firms. NSS officials calculated that a gross wage of $15.75 would be reduced to only $3.32 per week after all deductions, transportation, and room and board were calculated. See ibid., Hallawell to Anderson, 29 March 1945.

41 NA, RG 27, Box 1518, file R3 pt. 5 – Eaton to MacNamara, 14 April 1945.

42 An emergency meeting between the NSS Administration Board and PTI officials had been arranged on 17 April "through pressure from the WPTB" to allow textile officials to emphasize the scope of the

problem. See NA, RG 27, Box 666, file 6–5–21–1 pt. 1 – Hallam to MacNamara, 12 April 1945.

43 NA, RG 27, Box 1518, file R3 pt. 5 – Eaton to MacNamara, 26 April 1945.

44 Ibid., Eaton to MacNamara, 29 May 1945.

45 NA, RG 27, Box 605, file 6–24–1 pt. 3 – Maclean to Collings, 1 December 1944.

46 Ibid., MacNamara to all NSS Regional Superintendents, 3 May 1945.

47 Canadian Textile Journal 62 no. 17 (August 24 1945), 19.

48 The exit interview plan, however, was extended to other industries in Ontario in September 1945. See NA, RG 27, Volume 1518, file R6 – NSS Exit Interview Plan, Hereford to MacNamara, 21 August 1945.

49 NA, RG 27, Box 1518, file R3 pt. 5 – Unsigned, undated memo, August 1945.

50 NA, RG 27, Box 666, file 6–5–21–1 pt. 2 – Hereford to MacNamara, 15 February 1946.

51 M.C. Urquart, Historical Statistics of Canada (2nd edition) (Ottawa: Statistics Canada, 1983), Series B189–236 and Series B237–60.

52 For discussions of the professionalization of the nursing profession see E. Friedson, Professional Powers: A Study in the Institutionalization of Formal Knowledge (Chicago: University of Chicago Press, 1986); L. McIntyre, "Towards a Redefinition of Status: Professionalism in Canadian Nursing, 1938–1945," (Unpublished Master's Thesis: University of Western Ontario, 1984); M. Moloney, Professionalization of Nursing (Philadelphia: Lippincott, 1987); David Coburn, "The Professionalization of Canadian Nursing: Professionalization and Proletarianization," International Journal of Health Service 18 no. 3 (1988), 437–56, and Kathryn McPherson, Bedside Matters. McPherson's otherwise superb account virtually ignores the critical events of World War II and their effect on the nursing profession.

53 The greatest transformation of nursing as a result of World War II occurred in this field. In 1930, 60 per cent of practising nurses were private duty and 25 per cent worked in hospitals. By 1950, however, 67 per cent of nurses worked in hospitals and only 15 per cent were in private duty positions. See Coburn, "The Development of Canadian Nursing," 446.

54 Canadian Hospital 21 no. 10 (October 1944), 37.

55 CNA Committee Papers, Box ARC WY1 CE Gov. G., file Government Grant Committee Minutes, 1942–45 – "Minutes – Meeting of the CNA Committee Appointed to Approach the Government Regarding Grant, 25 July 1942." Order-in-Council PC 72/6073 of 14 July 1942, authorized the first grant.

56 The $250,000 for 1944–45 was divided four ways: $20,000 for administration; $75,000 for bursaries for supervisor and teacher preparation;

$125,000 for recruitment of student nurses; and $30,000 to support
university and hospital nursing programs. See CNA Committee Papers,
Box ARC WYI CE Gov. G., file Government Grant Committee Minutes,
1942–1945 – "Minutes – Meeting of the CNA Committee Appointed
to Approach the Government Regarding Grant, 25 July 1942." The
1945–46 grant was conditional. Five-twelfths of the $250,000 total
was granted in the summer of 1945 pending further review after the
results of the 1945 election. The remaining seven-twelfths was not
distributed after a government decision in late 1945.

57 CNA Committee Papers, Box ARC WYI CAI CJL 1944–76, file Joint
Committee on Nursing – Reports and Background, 1941–1950, CNA
Brief to the CHC Annual Meeting, 28 January 1946.

58 *Canadian Hospital* 20 no. 6 (June 1943), 16.

59 NA, RG 27, Volume 1521, file X1–2–12 part 1 – "Report of Personnel
of VON, First Nine Months, 1942." A total of seventy-three nurses
resigned from the VON during this period, with twenty-eight leaving for
other employment, eighteen getting married, and thirteen joining the
armed forces.

60 CNA Committee Papers, Box ARC WYI CAI CE ENA, file Advisory
Committee to the Emergency Nursing Advisor of the CNA, Minutes,
1941–43 – "Memorandum of Meeting, 18 January 1942."

61 CNA Committee Papers, Box ARC WYI CAI CE ENA, file Advisory Committee to the Emergency Nursing Advisor of the CNA, Press Releases,
1942–43 – "Appointment of Miss Kathleen Ellis."

62 *Canadian Nurse* 38 no. 9 (September 1942), 640–5; *Canadian Nurse*
39 no. 1 (January 1943), 25.

63 NA, RG 27, Volume 702, File Y12–2–6 part 12 – Kerr to Thompson,
13 November 1942.

64 NA, RG 27, Volume 1521, file X1–2–12 pt. 1 – "Notes on Labour
Situation in Hospitals and Similar Welfare Institutions, 8 May 1943";
Agnew to Little, 1 September 1942; McMillan to Agnew, 2 September
1942; Agnew to Little, 8 September 1942; Swanson to Little, 7 October 1942; Cross to Eaton, 5 October 1942; Ontario Minister of Health
to Eaton, 8 October 1942; and Cross to Eaton, 15 October 1942.

65 Ibid., Jamieson to Eaton, 12 October 1942.

66 See Ibid., Ellis to Eaton, 30 September 1942; "Personnel Needs of Hospitals" (unsigned, undated memo); CNA Brief to the 22 October Conference; and CHC Brief to the 22 October Conference. In addition to NSS,
CHC, and CNA representatives, other delegates came from the Canadian
Tuberculosis Association, the Catholic Hospital Council of Canada, the
Toronto Hospital Council, the Montreal Hospital Conference, the Victorian Order of Nurses, the Department of Pensions and National Health,
and the Royal Canadian Army Medical Services Nursing Division.

67 NA, RG 27, Volume 1522, file X1–2–12 pt. 2 – Mitchell to Eaton, 15 December 1942.

68 NA, RG 27, Volume 1521, file X1–2–12 pt. 1 – Hereford to Eaton, 3 February 1943.

69 NA, RG 27, Volume 1522, file X1–2–12 pt. 3 – Martel to Eaton, 7 July 1943; Eaton to Agnew, 20 July 1943, and Gerry to Eaton, 20 July 1943.

70 Ibid., Eaton to Hall, 26 July 1943.

71 Ibid., Eaton to Lindeburgh, 13 August 1943.

72 Ibid., Agnew to Eaton, 14 July 1943; Wilson to Eaton, 28 July 1943. Brackets mine.

73 Ibid., Botsford to Eaton, 16 August 1943.

74 Ibid., Botsford to Eaton, 2 October 1943.

75 CNA Committee Papers, Box ARC WY1 CA1 CJL, file Joint Committee on Nursing, Reports and Background Documentation, 1941–50 – "Report of the Committee Appointed to Confer with the CHC." The CNA delegation consisted of Marion Lindeburgh, F. Munroe, K.W. Ellis, Gertrude Hall, M. Baker, E. Flanagan, E. Beith, Mother Allaire, and Sister Allard.

76 CNA Committee Papers, Box ARC WY1 CA1 CJL, file Joint Committee on Nursing, Reports and Background Documentation, 1941–50 – "Report of the Committee Appointed to Confer with the CHC."

77 A total of 344 student nurses eventually took advantage of a special $100 bursary offered under the provisions of the 1942 CVT Act. See *Canadian Vocational Training, Annual Report, 1944–1945* (Ottawa, 1945), 10.

78 NA, RG 27, Volume 1522, file X1–2–12 pt. 3 – Eaton to Pammett, 27 September 1943.

79 *Canadian Hospital* 21 no. 1 (January 1944), 24.

80 CNA Committee Papers, Box ARC WY1 CA1 CJL: file Joint Committee on Nursing, Reports and Background Documentation, 1941–50, CNA Submission to the CHC Conference in Toronto, 28 January 1946.

81 NA, RG 27, Volume 1522, file X1–2–12 pt. 3 – Wilson to CNA Executive Committee, 14 September 1943.

82 Ibid., Eaton to Agnew, 20 July 1943.

83 NA, RG 27, Volume 1522, file X1–2–12 pt. 4 – Eaton to Ellis, 14 February 1944.

84 NA, RG 27, Volume 1522, file X1–2–12 pt. 5 – Eaton to Agnew, 10 May 1944.

85 Ibid., NFB script, "Nurses Needed."

86 Ibid., Eaton to MacNamara, 9 May 1944.

87 A total of ninety-seven individual replies remain in NSS records, with fifty-five respondents citing health or domestic reasons for refusing nursing employment. See NA, RG 27, Volume 1522, file X1–2–12–2 pt. 3 – Summary of Responses, 1 September 1944.

88 NA, RG 27, Volume X1–2–12–2 part 2 – Clark to Eaton, 22 June 1944.

89 Ibid., McDougall to MacNamara, 27 June 1944.

90 Ibid., Locke to MacNamara, 8 July 1944.

91 NA, RG 27, Volume 1521, file XI–2–5 – Summary of Questionnaires Received From Employment and Selective Service Offices re Nursing Personnel in Hospitals as of 31 July 1944.

92 The results for each hospital in Canada can be found in NA, RG 27, Volume 1521: files XI–2–2–1, XI–2–2–2, XI–2–2–3, XI–2–2–4, and XI–2–2–5.

93 NA, RG 27, Volume 1522, file XI–2–12 pt. 6 – Agnew to Eaton, 1 June 1944.

94 Ibid., Atkin to Agnew, 21 April 1944.

95 Ibid., Dunham to Sullivan, June 1944.

96 NA, RG 27, Volume 1521, file XI–2–5 – Eaton to Ward, 29 August 1944.

97 NA, RG 27, Volume 1522, file XI–2–12 pt. 7 – Eaton to Greene, 25 August 1944.

98 Meetings held throughout the final months of 1944 indicated a general unwillingness of hospital, nursing, and auxiliary medical officials to adopt the scheme. The Red Cross worried about the effect increased salary and workloads would have on the voluntary nature of the organization. See NA, RG 27, Volume 1522, file XI–2–12–1A – Eaton to MacNamara, 27 November 1944. The issue dragged on into 1945. In March Agnew indicated that consultations "cast some doubt on the desirability of putting too much effort on this proposed development." See NA, RG 27, Volume 1522, file XI–2–12 pt. 9 – Eaton to MacNamara, 15 March 1945.

99 NA, RG 27, Volume 1521, file XI–2–5 – Circular 356, 11 August 1944.

100 Ibid., Eaton to MacNamara, 2 November 1944.

101 Ibid., Hall to Eaton, 13 November 1944.

102 Ibid., Eaton to Agnew, 16 February 1945. See also NA, RG 27, Volume 1522, file XI–2–12 part 9 – Eaton to Fitzgerald, 2 May 1945.

103 NA, RG 27, Volume 1522, file XI–2–12 pt. 7 – Eaton to Greene, 25 August 1944.

104 NA, RG 27, Volume 1522, file XI–2–12 pt. 9 – MacNamara to Eaton, 26 March 1945. Emphasis and brackets mine.

105 NA, RG 27, Volume 1522, file XI–2–12 part 7 – Gibson to Eaton, 3 October 1944.

106 Ibid., Eaton to Sullivan, 25 October 1944.

107 NA, RG 27, Volume 1522, file XI–2–12 part 9 – Eaton to MacNamara, 15 March 1945. Subsidiary workers played an important role, however, in easing staff shortages in hospitals during the war. In 1943, for example, Red Cross Voluntary Aid Detachment workers performed 25,000 hours of free nursing service in the Winnipeg General Hospital. See McPherson, *Bedside Matters*, 222–3.

108 NA, RG 27, Volume 1522, file XI–2–12 pt. 10 – Eaton to MacNamara,
     20 June 1945.
109 Ibid., Eaton to MacNamara, 23 July 1945.
110 Ibid., Eadie to Eaton, 7 July 1945. The Mountain Sanatorium in
     Hamilton reported that a regular staff complement of 101 full-time
     nurses had been reduced to only twenty-seven full-time positions and
     fifty-eight part-time positions. The Toronto General Hospital had a
     waiting list of 380 patients and had been forced to close 100 beds due
     to nurse shortages. See ibid., Bartholomew to Eaton, 16 July 1945;
     Parker to Eaton, 5 July 1945. On 9 July 1945, Eaton issued an urgent
     appeal to all nurses in Canada asking that any available nurse come to
     Toronto to alleviate these shortages. NSS would pay all costs associ-
     ated with this transfer. Every single provincial nursing council replied,
     noting that not a single nurse could be spared. See, for example, ibid.,
     Ellis to Eaton, 10 July 1945.
111 NA, RG 27, Volume 1522, file XI–2–12 pt. 11 – Eaton to Chisholm,
     14 November 1945.

CHAPTER NINE

1 House of Commons, *Debates*, vol. 1, 1944, 23–4.
2 See Hutchison, *The Incredible Canadian*, 354.
3 See Granatstein, *The Generals*; Terry Copp and Bill McAndrew, *Battle
   Exhaustion: Soldiers and Psychiatrists in the Canadian Army, 1939–
   1945* (Montreal and Kingston: McGill-Queen's University Press, 1990);
   and David Zimmerman, *The Great Naval Battle of Ottawa: How
   Admirals, Scientists, and Politicians Impeded the Development of
   High Technology in Canada's Wartime Navy* (Toronto: University of
   Toronto Press, 1989).
4 See Diane Forestell, "The Necessity of Sacrifice for a Nation at War:
   Women's Labour Force Participation, 1939–1946," *Histoire Sociale/
   Social History* 22 no. 4 (1989), 333–47.
5 See J.L. Granatstein, *The Ottawa Men*; Owram, *The Government
   Generation*; Barry Ferguson, *Remaking Liberalism: The Intellectual
   Legacy of Adam Shortt, O.D. Skelton, W.C. Clark, and W.A. Mackin-
   tosh, 1890–1925* (Montreal and Kingston: McGill-Queen's University
   Press, 1994); and Robert Campbell, *Grand Illusions*.
6 Michael Bliss, "Canada's Swell War," *Saturday Night* 18 no. 4
   (May 1995), 42.
7 Owram, *The Government Generation*, 334.

Select Bibliography

PRIMARY SOURCES

National Archives of Canada

RG 27	Records of the Department of Labour
RG 2	Records of the Cabinet
RG 10	Records of the Department of Mines and Resources
RG 17	Records of the Department of Agriculture
RG 28	Records of the Department of Munitions and Supply
RG 35 Series 7	Inter-departmental Committees–Public Records Committee
RG 64	Records of the Wartime Prices and Trade Board
RG 66	Records of the National Harbours Board
MG 27 III B11	J.L. Ralston Papers
MG 28 I 103	Records of the Canadian Labour Congress

Canadian Nurses Association Archives

CNA Committee Papers

University of Western Ontario Regional Room

Records of the C.S. Hyman Leather Company

Department of National Defence, Directorate of History

Files 325.009 (D468), 171.009 (D182), 168.009 (D75), 112.21009 (D195), 324.009 (D274), 326.009 (D5), 111.41 (D1), 112.352009 (D118) vols. 1–3, and 325.009 (D468)

Newspapers and Journals

Calgary Albertan
Canadian Hospital
Canadian Nurse
Canadian Textile Journal
Canadian Unionist
Financial Post
Glace Bay Gazette
Halifax Chronicle
Montreal Daily Star
Montreal Gazette
Montreal Journal
Montreal Standard
New York Times
Regina Leader-Post
Sydney Post-Record
Toronto Globe and Mail
Toronto Star
Toronto Evening Telegram
Vancouver Daily Province
Winnipeg Free Press

SECONDARY SOURCES

Bliss, Michael. "Canada's Swell War," *Saturday Night* 18:4 (May 1995), 39–43.
Burns, E.L.M. *Manpower in the Canadian Army, 1939–1945.* Toronto: Clarke, Irwin, 1956.
Campbell, Robert. *Grand Illusions: The Politics of the Keynesian Experience in Canada, 1945–1975.* Peterborough: Broadview Press, 1987.
Davis, Janet Frances. "'We Shall Remember': Canadian Indians and World War II." Trent University M.A. Thesis, 1992.
Dawson, R. MacGregor. *The Conscription Crisis of 1944.* Toronto: University of Toronto Press, 1961.
Donaghy, Greg, ed. *Uncertain Horizons: Canadians and Their World in 1945.* Ottawa: Canadian Committee for the History of the Second World War, 1997.

Dreisziger, N.F., ed. *Mobilization for Total War: The Canadian, American, and British Experience, 1914–1918, 1939–1945*. Waterloo: Wilfrid Laurier University Press, 1981.

Earle, Michael. "'Down With Hitler and Silby Barrett': The Cape Breton Miners' Slowdown Strike of 1941," *Acadiensis* 18:1 (1988), 56–90.

Feasby, W.R. *The Official History of the Canadian Medical Services, 1939–1945, Volume I: Organization and Campaigns*. Ottawa: Queen's Printer, 1956.

Forbes, Ernest. "Consolidating Disparity: The Maritimes and the Industrialization of Canada During the Second World War," *Acadiensis* 15:2 (1986), 3–27.

Gaffen, Fred. *Forgotten Soldiers*. Penticton: Theytus Books, 1985.

Gibson, Frederick. *To Serve and Yet Be Free: Queen's University, 1917–1961, Volume II*. Montreal and Kingston: McGill-Queen's University Press, 1983.

Gibson, Frederick, and Robertson, Barbara, eds. *Ottawa at War: The Grant Dexter Memoranda, 1939–1945*. Winnipeg: Manitoba Record Society, 1994.

Granatstein, J.L. *Canada's War: The Politics of the Mackenzie King Government, 1939–1945*. Toronto: Oxford University Press, 1990.

– *The Generals: The Canadian Army's Senior Commanders in the Second World War*. Toronto: Stoddart, 1993.

– *Conscription in the Second World War: A Study in Political Management*. Toronto: Ryerson Press, 1969.

– *The Ottawa Men: The Civil Service Mandarins, 1935–1957*. Toronto: Oxford University Press, 1982.

Granatstein, J.L., and Hitsman, J.M. *Broken Promises: A History of Conscription in Canada*. Toronto: Oxford University Press, 1977.

Granatstein, J.L., and Neary, Peter, eds. *The Good Fight: Canadians and World War II*. Toronto: Copp Clark, 1995.

Hart, Douglas. "State Economic Management in Wartime: A Study of the 'Regimentation' of Industry in the Canadian Industrial Mobilization, 1939–1945." York University Ph.D. Thesis, 1980.

Hutchison, Bruce. *The Incredible Canadian: A Candid Portrait of Mackenzie King, His Works, His Times, and His Nation*. Toronto: Longmans, 1952.

Kennedy, J. de N. *History of the Department of Munitions and Supply*. Ottawa: King's Printer, 1950.

Logan, H.A. *Trade Unions in Canada: Their Development and Functioning*. Toronto: Macmillan, 1948.

McIntyre, Linda. "Towards a Redefinition of Status: Professionalism in Canadian Nursing, 1938–1945." University of Western Ontario M.A. Thesis, 1984.

McKillop, A.B. *Matters of Mind: The University in Ontario, 1791–1951*. Toronto: University of Toronto Press, 1994.

McPherson, Kathryn. *Bedside Matters: The Transformation of Canadian Nursing*. Toronto: Oxford University Press, 1996.

Muise, Del, and McIntosh, Robert. *Coal Mining in Canada: A Historical and Comparative Overview.* Ottawa: National Museum of Science and Technology, 1996.

Nolan, Brian. *King's War: Mackenzie King and the Politics of War, 1939–1945.* Toronto: Random House, 1988.

Owram, Doug. *The Government Generation: Canadian Intellectuals and the State, 1900–1945.* Toronto: University of Toronto Press, 1986.

Pickersgill, J.W. *The Mackenzie King Record, 1939–1945.* Toronto: University of Toronto Press, 1960.

Pierson, Ruth Roach. *"They're Still Women After All": The Second World War and Canadian Womanhood.* Toronto: McClelland and Stewart, 1986.

Pilkington, Gwendoline Evans. "A History of the National Conference of Canadian Universities, 1911–1961." University of Toronto Ph.D. Thesis, 1974.

Rankin, Diana. "The Mobilization and Demobilization of Canadian Women in the Workforce During the Second World War." University of Western Ontario M.A. Thesis, 1986.

Russell, Bob. *Back to Work? Labour, State, and Industrial Relations in Canada.* Scarborough: Nelson, 1990.

Shewell, Hugh Edward Quixano. "Origins of Contemporary Indian Social Welfare in the Canadian Liberal State: An Historical Case Study in Social Policy, 1873–1965." University of Toronto Ph.D. Thesis, 1995.

Slater, David. *War Finance and Reconstruction: The Role of Canada's Department of Finance, 1939–1946.* Ottawa: Privately published, 1996.

Stacey, C.P. *Six Years of War: The Army in Canada, Britain, and the Pacific.* Ottawa: Queen's Printer, 1955.

– *Arms, Men, and Governments: The War Policies of Canada, 1939–1945.* Ottawa: Queen's Printer, 1970.

Struthers, James. *No Fault of Their Own: Unemployment and the Canadian Welfare State.* Toronto: University of Toronto Press, 1983.

Summerby, Janice. *Native Soldiers, Foreign Battlefields.* Ottawa, 1993.

Titley, E. Brian. *A Narrow Vision: Duncan Campbell Scott and the Administration of Indian Affairs in Canada.* Vancouver: University of British Columbia Press, 1986.

Waddell, Christopher. "The Wartime Prices and Trade Board: Price Control in Canada During World War II." York University Ph.D. Thesis, 1981.

Waite, Catherine. "The Longshoremen of Halifax, 1900–1930: Their Living and Working Conditions." Dalhousie University M.A. Thesis, 1977.

White, Jay. "'Sleepless and Veiled Am I': An East Coast Canadian Port Revisited," *Nova Scotia Historical Review* 5:1 (1985), 15–29.

– "The Homes Front: The Accommodation Crisis in Halifax, 1941–1951," *Urban History Review* 20:3 (1992): 117–127.

– "Conscripted City: Halifax and the Second World War." McMaster University Ph.D. Thesis, 1994.

Wilson, David A. "Close and Continuous Attention: Human Resources Management in Canada During the Second World War." University of New
Brunswick Ph.D. Thesis, 1997.

Zimmerman, David. *The Great Naval Battle of Ottawa: How Admirals, Scientists, and Politicians Impeded the Development of High Technology in
Canada's Wartime Navy.* Toronto: University of Toronto Press, 1989.

Index